TO DEFEND YOUR EMPIRE
AND THE FAITH

TO DEFEND YOUR EMPIRE AND THE FAITH

Advice on a global strategy offered c.1590
to Philip, King of Spain and Portugal,
by Manoel de Andrada Castel Blanco

Translated from the Spanish and edited by
P.E.H. HAIR

with an account of Spanish material
in Dr Williams's Library, London, by
A.M. Garcia

published for the
DEPARTMENT OF HISTORY
UNIVERSITY OF LIVERPOOL

LIVERPOOL UNIVERSITY PRESS
1990

In acknowledgement of the past close relationship between the Department of History and the Institute of Latin American Studies, this book is dedicated to those scholars who in recent decades believed that the study of the history of continents other than Europe was appropriate for Liverpool, 'town and gown'.

Liverpool Historical Studies, no. 5
General Editor: P.E.H. Hair

Published in Great Britain, 1990
by the Liverpool University Press,
Senate House, PO Box 147, Liverpool, L69 3BX

Copyright © 1990 by P.E.H. Hair

British Library Cataloguing in Publication Data are available

ISBN 0 85323 037 4

Printed in Great Britain by
Antony Rowe Limited, Chippenham

CONTENTS

THE HISTORICAL CONTEXT AND SIGNIFICANCE
OF ANDRADA'S TRACT

Global empire, global strategy

The fifteenth Christian century saw the peoples and polities of Iberia setting in motion a process which led to the creation of the first empire genuinely worldwide - a preliminary step, brash, bloody and faltering, yet effective, towards our twentieth century 'One World'.

The Portuguese sailed southwards, to exploit the empty islands of the Atlantic and to explore the coasts and rivers of western Africa: the Castilians conquered and colonized the Canaries. Then, during the last decade of the century, Christopher Columbus and Vasco da Gama made their way respectively West and East, so that within a generation the flags of the Iberian monarchs met on the other side of the globe. By the final decades of the sixteenth century, the Portuguese possessed an empire of islands, fortified ports, and occasional wider settlements, located in maritime Africa, Brazil, and southern and eastern Asia - an attenuated chain of commerce and influence stretching from Morocco to Macau. And by the same period the Spaniards were ruling vast tracts of America between Florida and River Plate, as well as an outlier across the Pacific, the newly-named Philippine Islands. In 1580 the two empires came under the control of a single monarch, Philip, the First of Portugal, the Second of Spain. Henceforward Philip ruled the first domain in the history of the world for which the claim might justly have been made that, over its constituent territories - 'the sun never sets'.

Global empire calls for global strategy. The Spanish

tract of c.1590 here presented in translation, a tract of advice (**aviso**) addressed by an obscure individual to King Philip, evidences the first world empire and its strategic problems, in the course of suggesting how some of the latter might be met. In its rambling discourse, the tract refers to both hemispheres and to all known continents. With his gratuitous advice extending to Brazil and Siam, Magellan Strait and Aden, Sierra Leone and Peru, its author must be counted among the very earliest of global strategists.

The sea-ways of empire: marine disaster and enemy action

Modern historians stress that King Philip's domain remained, in administrative terms, two empires, the regulation of the Portuguese empire being little affected by the linkage through the monarch with the Spanish empire. Yet the tract treats the two empires as one. This may indeed be because the author is directing his words hopefully towards King Philip. But it also represents an imperial perception widely held in Iberia in the immediate decades after 1580. And since the tract concentrates on the strategic and military situation rather than on the administrative position, the treatment of King Philip's empires as a unity makes much sense. Except when there is specific need to differentiate, we shall hereafter follow the author and speak of a single empire.

The form of composition as well as the content of the tract reflect the situation of King Philip's empire in the final decade of the sixteenth century. The author is alarmed at the empire's fragility, at its openness to military and naval attack by two sets of ideological enemies, in the East the hordes of Islam, in the West the heretics of Northern Europe. Contemplating the immensity of the empire the tract leaps breathlessly from continent to continent, while it piles up exemplary warning instances from the recent past of Portugal and Spain, deployed in no chronological order. The degree of sheer confusion in the style and construction of the tract provides an unwitting parallel to the degree of confusion in the contemporary management of the empire.

Like all human enterprises, the empire was a product of both intention and contingency - that is, of planning and design but equally of unforeseen concatenations of known forces, and of sheer accident. King Philip laboured night and day on imperial correspondence. Indeed, he was such a workaholic that he may even have glanced at the tract (although we have no evidence either way). Moreover, the administration of the empire was subtle, complex and bureaucratically planned. But the processes of history are larger than human endeavour and imagination; and the crises of the period overwhelmed the current technology of management. Nevertheless, to the surprise of many, the global empire sailed through the local difficulties of the 1590s, probably despite King Philip and certainly despite our tractarian; but only to crumble to dust slowly, relentlessly, and not very gracefully, over the next four centuries. Yet not, of course, without leaving an indelible mark on language, society and culture in very many parts of the Outer Continents.

The author's belief that things were falling apart, the centre not holding, was exaggerated and premature. But it sprang from his involvement in the maritime aspect of the joint empire. Himself a Portuguese with considerable overseas experience but now living and working in Spain, he saw the sinews of empire as the sea-routes between the metropolitan countries and their respective imperial possessions overseas. His advice was therefore twofold - how to sustain the imperial traffic of the ocean seaways in the face of the savage forces of nature, but also how to defend that traffic against the bitter human enemies of Iberian empire and Catholic culture.

Maritime disaster had begun to loom large in the thinking of the Portuguese of the time, as is evident in the appearance from the 1550s of the first popular accounts of shipwrecks, later gathered into the series termed the Tragic History of the Sea (**História Trágico-Marítima**).[1] But the Spaniards had their disasters too, and the 1580s and 1590s almost certainly represented a peak in the century's mounting scale of ship losses along the routes both to the East and to America. That the Iberian concern about the crescendo of marine disaster was not mere hyperbolic rhetoric but was based on solid factual considerations is perhaps best shown by noting the raised expectations of the European enemies of the empire. The Dutchman, Jan Huyghen van Linschoten, recorded, at length and with mixed feelings, those disasters to Spanish and Portuguese fleets, partly from storm and tempest, partly from English assaults, he had himself witnessed while living during the 1580s in the Azores - the meeting-place of the East and West ocean routes. This section of Linschoten's writings was promptly extracted by the Englishman, Richard Hakluyt, and, in translation, included in 1598 in the second edition of Hakluyt's **Principal Navigations**, together with several exciting - and inciting - native accounts of English assaults on

---

[1]   Shipwreck episodes from the História Trágico-Marítima are available in English in C.R. Boxer, ed., **The Tragic History of the Sea 1589-1622**, Hakluyt Society, London, 1959, and C.R. Boxer, ed., **Further selections from the Tragic History of the Sea 1559-1565**, Hakluyt Society, London, 1968. The standard modern edition of the whole series in the original Portuguese is António Sergio, ed., **História Trágico-Marítima**, 3 vols., Lisbon, 1955-1957.

Iberian fleets.[2]

It is appropriate that the tract should now appear in
English translation, since the author presents the
English as the chief villains of the marine drama. The
Dutch are not mentioned at all in this context, which
conclusively dates the pamphlet to the early 1590s.[3] The
French are cited mainly for nefarious acts occurring in
decades much earlier than the 1580s. But the English,
named more frequently than either the French or the evil
Moors of the East, are accused in respect of events of
the immediately previous fifteen years. The tract was
correct in supposing that the pace of English irruption
into the Portugese-Spanish sphere was hectically
increasing. By the later 1580s and early 1590s, the
number of English privateers sailing towards the
Caribbean and the South Atlantic was not far short of the
'100 and more [leaving] several times in the year'
asserted by the tract. The leading historian of English
privateering states that between 1589 and 1591 at least
235 English vessels made privateering voyages, and his
considered judgement on the English assault is this.

---

[2] Richard Hakluyt, **The Principal Navigations ... of the English Nation**, 3
vols., London, 1598-1600, the extract from Linschoten in vol. 2, pp.178-187.

[3] The only mention of the Dutch is a reference to 'the ships of Holland and
Zeeland' (f.31), for whose construction the pine trees of southern Brazil would
be suitable. This appears to be a traditional comment on Dutch ship-building,
rather than an indication of awareness of a Dutch challenge overseas, potential
or actual, not least since up to this date the Dutch had shown almost no interest
in Brazil. Therefore what Andrada is recommending is the use of this timber for
the construction of Iberian vessels on the Dutch model. However, addressing his
tract to King Philip, Andrada must also have been concerned not to give the
impression that he treated Holland and Zeeland other than as rebel provinces soon
to be returned to Spanish rule, and this no doubt inhibited him from
contemplating a possible Dutch challenge overseas.

"The contribution of the corsairs to the decline of Spain
was of course one factor among many, but in the
decimation of Iberian Atlantic commerce they played a
decisive part."[4] The privateering war had probably not
quite reached its height when the tract was written but
its author's alarm was justified.

Although he wrote in Spanish, apparently from a base in
Spain, the tract writer was more knowledgeable about the
Portuguese empire than about the Spanish empire, and more
concerned about the former than about the latter. The
Portuguese base in South-East Asia, Malacca, is
mentioned; the corresponding Spanish base, Manila, not
mentioned. More attention is paid to Brazil than to the
Caribbean. Portuguese campaigns in Asia are noted,
Spanish campaigns in America are not. The writer's
personal experience overseas appears to have been almost
wholly within the imperial sphere of Portugal, as shown
in the detailed biography below.

The significance of the tract

Andrada's purpose in writing the tract was exactly what
he stated - to alert the monarchy to the dire state of
maritime affairs, and to suggest measures to remedy
matters, notably by establishing fortified positions at
strategic points on both sides of the South Atlantic, and
by improving the quality of Iberian pilots.[5] His

---

[4]   K.R.Andrews, ed., **English privateering voyages to the West Indies
1588-95**, Hakluyt Society, London, 1959, p.16; K.R.Andrews, **Trade, plunder and
settlement: maritime enterprise and the genesis of the British Empire 1480-1630**,
Cambridge, 1984, p.249.

[5]   Ursula Lamb in 1983 categorised the tract as follows. "The piece is one
of special pleading for a course of action to be taken by the crown, and so comes
under the rubric of the **arbitrista** literature which is characteristic of the

suggestions were individually not novel, and although certain developments subsequently occurred in some of the directions he indicated these were not due to his influence.

One reason why his tract was ineffective was its appalling style. It must be said that it is ill-organised, rambling, and very difficult to follow. Containing little original information on historical events, far from increasing the stock of detailed factual knowledge regarding those events the tract often requires some general knowledge of the events before the reader can understand what exactly Andrada is getting at. The tract does not represent the best information available, either to the crown and its ministers, or to most of the very many other individuals who in this period prepared **avisos** and hopefully inserted them into official

---

later Hapsburg period. It is a sample of information from private sources routed through personal contact to the responsible agency or person in charge of the matter addressed, in hopes that it might reach the crown, most probably through one of the councils. Such advice was offered frequently 'for the sake of my conscience', as Andrada himself states, by public-spirited men or by those in search of recognition of their service. If it reached someone who thought it useful, there might result a request to present the material more formally, and this seems to have been the case with Andrada's presentation, since he says at one point that he gives the information as 'I have been commanded to do'. It is this feature which gives me hope to find another trace of the matter somewhere. It would then fit the pattern of such texts as those of other cosmographers, of Escalante de Mendoza on the **Carrera de Indias**, of Juan Bautista Gesio and Hernando de los Rios Coronel concerning the Pacific." (Lacking both opportunity and competence, I have been unable to follow up Professor Lamb's hint and search Iberian archives for any references to the reception of the tract - or, with one exception, otherwise to Andrada.) Professor J.S.Cummins has commented (in a p.c.) that the **aviso** might additionally be considered as part of the genre known as **preocupación de España**, the almost obsessive and fairly pessimistic concern in contemporary and later Spanish writings for the state of the country and its future.

channels.   Nor was the advice offered by Andrada
especially sound or perceptive.

Nevertheless, the tract is of distinct significance as
historical evidence.   First, because Andrada's advice
covered a wider geographical range than most other
advisors would have dared contemplate, in part because
they were more modest but also in part because Andrada's
claim to wide overseas experience, albeit exaggerated,
was to some extent genuine.   And secondly, because the
tract did not issue from the best persons, from the true
experts, or from the men at the top of the imperial
process.   This instead is 'history from below' - or at
least an approximation to this valuable viewpoint.   Of
course Andrada was not at the very bottom of the Iberian
pile because the lowest ranks, the masses, were not
literate; but as a commoner, a churchman and a non-
official, he was in the lower rank of the literate class.
Despite his repeated claim to have important official
contacts, he was largely an outsider - but an opiniated
outsider.   He can therefore be taken to represent what
there was, in that age and society, of 'public opinion',
that is, specifically, of concern among literate
citizens, based on limited and sometimes confused
information, regarding national and even international
affairs.

Andrada's tract demonstrates how a comparatively humble
Iberian, educated and vocal but of no outstanding
intelligence or scholarship, observed contemporary events
affecting the whole of the Iberian empire - and hence the
world at large.   And how he was thus led to form and
express an imperial strategy of no less than global
proportions.   Andrada's tract thus gives the student of
early modern European and world history something of the
'feel' of the period, as it was experienced by those
Iberians who were capable of grasping the intense

excitement of novel world venture and the inevitable accompanying alarms and anxieties.

THE BIOGRAPHICAL CONTEXT OF ANDRADA'S TRACT

The writer and his tract

Manuel de Andrada Castel Blanco (to give him the Spanish form of his name, as it appears on the tract) is not known for any other writings and our knowledge of his career is drawn almost exclusively from what he tells us in his tract.[6] The earliest reference to his career he cares to supply is to the year 1560, when he left Portugal on a ship bound for India but appears to have stopped off at Bahia in Brazil. He was presumably already a priest, since we gather that during most of the 1560s he served as a missionary somewhere in Brazil. For an unstated reason he left America around 1570 and went to Spain, where, at Seville, he played some part in the organisation of an expedition to a struggling Spanish settlement in the River Plate. Despite his being awarded an ecclesiastical post in the expedition, he had abandoned it by the time the ships called in at the Cape Verde Islands, and he then returned to Portuguese service. During the mid 1570s he held a parochial benefice in the islands, and also assisted the bishop as his

---

[6] Andrada tells us that he is writing - or perhaps intends to write - a 'book ... in the service of God, about the four-fold division of the universe, which is intended to encourage many religious to decide to go out to preach the Gospel' (f.26v). It does not appear that this work was published and perhaps it was never completed. The reference to the 'religious' perhaps indicates that Andrada was critical of the religious orders, as no doubt many secular clergy were, in understandable response to the general contempt of the religious for the seculars.

vicar-general, perhaps visiting the Guinea mainland. He fails to reveal where he was in the 1580s but implies that he moved among influential lay circles at Lisbon, and perhaps also among the same at Madrid, the major seat of Philip's government. By 1590, when he is writing his tract, he is not only tutor to a Spanish nobleman but a royal chaplain, with apparently some, albeit perhaps very limited, degree of access to the court. (This summary skates over very thinly evidenced areas of Andrada's career - these are examined in more detail below.)

The tract is printed but lacks date and place of publication, and no copy other than the one we have seen appears to be extant.[7] This raises the possibility that it was never published and that only a handful of copies was printed. If so, what we have is a writing intended, as the tract itself states, to be seen by the monarch - in person or vicariously through the eyes of his officers - but not intended to be circulated elsewhere. Apparently it was to be presented by Andrada's patron, Don Felipe de Albornoz, to King Philip.[8] The single copy

---

[7] I have been unable to trace the work in the standard bibliographies of Spanish literature (including the bibliography of works by Portuguese authors), or in the catalogues of West-European national libraries, and in 1984 Professor Ursula Lamb reported that "no other copy has been found in London, Paris, Germany, Portugal or Spain, nor have I found mention of the author".

[8] The title-page states as follows: **Ofrecela Don Felipe de Albornoz. Compuesta y ordenada por ... Manoel de Andrada Castel Blanco.** This ambiguous wording could mean that the author is Albornoz and that Andrada is simply ordering the material and helping with the drafting. But since indubitably the autobiographical content relates to a cleric (and **componer** was used to describe at least the composing of poetry), it must mean that Andrada wrote the work and is using Albornoz as an intermediary to present the work to the king. (I am indebted to Dr García for these comments on the wording.) The D.Felipe de Albornoz in question has not been adequately identified. An individual of that name, one of a family of distinguished brothers, was brought up at the royal

has on its otherwise blank end-pages a portion of a manuscript letter or note in Portuguese, in a contemporary hand, partly illegible because of show-through. But what is written in the parts that can be read unfortunately does not seem to have any reference to the tract or to provide any proof that the letter was written by Andrada.[9] The single copy of the tract has been in English hands since at least the later decades of the seventeenth century. It almost certainly formed part of a collection of Spanish material made by Dr William Bates (1625-1699), a Nonconformist divine, whose library was acquired by another learned minister, Dr Daniel Williams (?1643-1716), and added to his own; the tract was listed in the first printed catalogue of Dr Williams's Library in 1727. Nothing has been discovered about the history of the tract between c.1590 and its acquisition by Bates.[10] (For a note on the Spanish material in Dr

---

court in the 1590s, being at one time a page there, and is known because in 1627-1632 he served as a disastrous governor of Tucumán in Argentina (Enrique Udaondo, **Diccionario Biográfico Colonial Argentino,** Buenos Aires, 1945). But although Andrada may well have been tutor to a child or youth (and might even have influenced him to develop an interest in an overseas career), it seems doubtful whether even Andrada would have considered a juvenile an appropriate person to transmit an **aviso** upwards at court. Andrada refers to 'certain gentlemen in whose hands this **aviso** may fall' and who may ridicule it (f.35v) - he is presumably indicating members of the royal councils.

[9] I am grateful to Miss Ann Mackenzie for her work in deciphering and translating what can be read of this letter.

[10] If the tract was indeed a semi-official, 'confidential paper', printed only in a few copies, one wonders how a copy escaped from the archives, eventually to pass into English hands. It seems unlikely that it was captured aboard a Spanish vessel, as some official papers were. Perhaps it was obtained by an English spy in Spain. If an indecipherable but seemingly English signature on the title-page could be read, its transmission might be revealed. The surname begins 'Ba', and at one time I hoped that this might indicate Sir Nicholas Bacon,

Williams's Library, see Appendix C, contributed by Dr
A.M. García.)

The date of writing of the tract can be established with
fair ease.   At one point reference is made to the
'present year, 1590', and other references suggest that
by 1591 and not later it had been completed.[11] As stated
above, Andrada's own experiences went back to 1560, but
he included in the tract a number of references to events
earlier in the sixteenth century, as well as an undated
reference to Vasco da Gama's 1498 voyage and a wrongly-
dated reference to the 1450s discovery of the Cape Verde
Islands.

Andrada claimed to have spent 'thirty-one years to date'
gaining knowledge and experience of the matters he wrote
about (f.23v).[12] Presumably this was the period between
1560, the first date in his career he mentions, and 1591,
the year he was writing this section of the tract.   He
implied, however, rather more: that during this period he

---

an Elizabethan spy-master whose spies collected material in Spain.   But the
signature almost certainly continues 'Bak..' (Baker ?).

[11]   Andrada was alarmed at Drake's penetration into the Pacific Ocean via
Magellan Strait, but mentions the later English penetration of the Indian Ocean
from the West only once, and then in a wording which suggests that he considered
it only a potential threat, not an actuality (f.5v).   The first English vessels
passed the Cape of Good Hope in 1591, and although the survivors did not return
to England until 1594, it is likely that news of the passage reached Portugal
much sooner, perhaps by 1592.   Andrada's lack of knowledge of the English
penetration would seem to indicate that he was writing in 1590 or very soon
after.

[12]   Hereafter the references given in the Introduction are to the foliation
of the original, as indicated in the translation of the tract that follows.   The
reader's attention is drawn to the associated annotation of most of the passages.

was engaged in maritime and overseas activities, or even that in all these years he was sailing the seas. In fact, the least concrete claim was the most correct one, since he was serving on land during most of the 1560s and 1570s, and was probably not overseas during the 1580s. As we shall see, Andrada is explicit about his career only to a limited extent, and indeed is at points evasive about his life-history and not a faithful witness to it.

Andrada in Brazil

Andrada's earliest personal reference relates to the year 1560. He was already a **clérigo**, a secular priest, and since he joined a fleet sailing to India presumably he intended a career in the East. The ship unexpectedly put into port at Bahia in Brazil, and when it sailed again was wrecked in the Indian Ocean, off Sumatra (ff.19v-20, 25). Despite Andrada's categorical claim to have been one of the survivors, it is clear that he left the ship at Bahia and never saw the East. His tract includes no personal reminiscences relating to Asia, and no information about any part of that continent he could not have acquired from his reading.

Although he fails to say so, it seems that this was his first visit to Brazil. Like many other of the passengers, he stayed on after the ship left. His motives for doing this are not known, but perhaps at Bahia he was offered and immediately obtained a clerical post. He now spent a period of years in Brazil. He must have visited the southern part of the territory, since he records an episode 'when I was on the coast of Cananea' (f.31).

His fullest statement about residence in Brazil is the following. 'For nine years I preached the Gospel in their own language to the Brazilians ... I instructed many Lutherites who were converted, because I knew how to administer the sacraments to them in the midst of wars. Some I instructed by means of the language of the Indians' (ff.23v-24).[13] This statement represents the evidence that Andrada was a priest on arrival in Brazil, while its reference to 'Lutherites' can only apply to the Portuguese campaigns against the French - as is confirmed in a later reference. 'When the fortress of Rio de Janeiro was won from the Lutherites ... and the governor was Mundo de Saa, among the books and records we captured ... were thousands of papers [evidencing their plans], and I also saw many Frenchmen' (f.36-36v). Governor Mem de Sá captured the French fort in Rio de Janeiro in early 1560. But we know that the ship in which Andrada was travelling reached Bahia some months later, therefore Andrada cannot have taken part in the campaign. He may have seen the Frenchmen either when Mem de Sá returned in triumph to Bahia with prisoners, or else during a later campaign.

Among the named 'captains, governors and admirals' with whom Andrada claimed to have 'sailed the entire ocean' (f.23v), were three notables with exclusively Brazilian military connections - Estácio de Sá, who arrived in 1563 and died in 1567, leading a further campaign against the French in Rio de Janeiro; Crístovão de Barros, who arrived with reinforcements in 1567 to complete the campaign, and then served in high offices in Brazil until the 1590s; and D. Pedro Leitão, the second bishop of Brazil, who served from 1556 to 1573. It thus seems likely that Andrada took part in the 1565-1567 campaign,

---

[13] Like his fellow Iberians of the period, Andrada calls all Protestants **Luteranos**, literally 'Lutherans', even when specifying French Protestants who were, of course, not Lutherans in the strict sense, but Calvinists. The translation therefore instead uses the term 'Lutherites', which expresses in English the derogatory and omnium gatherum sense of the Spanish.

since all three notables were associated with this, and that he met his 'Lutherite' Frenchmen then. Perhaps for a time he served as a chaplain on one of the ships involved in the campaign. But since Estácio de Sá recruited parties of Indians from as far down the coast as São Vicente, it is just possible that, instead, Andrada, serving as a missionary in the South - hence, perhaps, the reference to Cananéia - accompanied his Indians to the war.

The history of the few secular clergy in sixteenth century Brazil has been almost totally overshadowed by the history of the self-publicising Jesuits. Perhaps significantly, Andrada never mentions the Jesuits in Brazil, nor does he mention the fact that the hero of the Sumatra shipwreck was a Jesuit (unless this is merely further evidence that he was not involved in the disaster). Again, discussing a famous marine disaster, he fails to note the feature which attracted most attention in Iberia, the massacre by the attackers of a party of Jesuit passengers (f.22). His only mention of the Jesuits is a hostile one - they collect a levy on seamen in order to build a Lisbon church (ff.38-39). A contemporary writing a similar tract of advice to the crown called for the Jesuits to occupy ports in western Africa: Andrada, too, wants missionaries in Africa but does not name the Jesuits.[14] Andrada does not tell us why he left Brazil, or why he returned, not to Portugal, but to Seville; given the scathing comments of the Jesuits on the behaviour of the secular clergy in Brazil, it is conceivable that he left after a controversial pastoral episode or after local criticism.

---

[14] Domingos Abreu e Brito, **Um inquérito á vida administrativa e economica de Angola e do Brasil**, Coimbra, 1931, p.91.

If it is correct that Andrada arrived in Brazil in 1560 and if thereafter he served nine consecutive years (and there is no evidence otherwise), then he left Brazil in 1569 or 1570. This agrees with his claimed participation in the preparations for the 1572 Zárate expedition to Río de la Plata (River Plate), on one of whose ships he travelled as far as the Cape Verde Islands. After leaving the islands and crossing the Atlantic, the expedition halted at Santa Catarina Island (in modern southern Brazil but at that time in silent dispute between Portugal and Spain), and again Andrada lets the reader suppose that he travelled as far (f.22v). In fact, he was only in America during his single stay in Brazil in the 1560s. The later events in Brazil he mentions, such as two marine disasters in 1570 and 1571 (ff.21v, 22) and the alarming English attack on Bahia in 1588 (f.26), were probably common knowledge in Iberia. However, Andrada shows some detailed knowledge of Brazil of the kind most probably only to be gained from close personal experience. He comments on the topography of Bahia (f.26-26v) and Rio de Janeiro (f.28v), he lists the localities of the southern coast (ff.7v, 32), and he names the Amerindian peoples (at least as they were distinguished and named by the Portuguese) (f.6). He appears to have some knowledge of the route to the interior from São Vicente (ff.30v-31) and it is just possible that he may have visited Santa Catarina Island from the mainland. He claims to have spoken an Amerindian language, presumably the **lingua geral** extensively studied by the Jesuits, Tupi.

There is no evidence that Andrada visited Brazil after the 1560s, therefore some of his references to that territory may have been out of date by the time he came to write his tract. It cannot be said that his knowledge of post-1560s events involving Brazil shows a continuing interest in the colony, since these mostly represent

general knowledge. But he does show a flicker of
interest in the 1584 defeat of the French on the Paraiba
and the foundation there of 'Philip's City' (f.5v). Yet
his apparent intention of returning to America in 1572,
to work in the Río de la Plata region, presumably among
Indians as well as among the settlers, may indicate a
genuine missionary vocation. Be that as it may, he never
returned, and his geographical references to the interior
between colonial Brazil, Asunción, and Río de la Plata
are fairly vague and not entirely sound.

The significance of the Zárate episode lies partly in the
fact that, ten years before the union of the crowns, the
Portuguese Andrada was prepared to work for the Spaniards
in America. His apparent willingness to move southwards
from Brazil to Río de la Plata perhaps directed his
attention towards Magellan Strait, and certainly in his
tract he echoes the sudden and almost panic-stricken
concern that arose in Spain after Drake's 1578 irruption
through the Strait, a concern that was re-aroused by
Cavendish's 1587 repetition of the English success.
Andrada's frequent references to the Strait reflect the
anxieties of his later Spanish masters.

Andrada in the Cape Verde Islands and Guinea

Andrada states that, after nine years in Brazil, he
'later was for five years in Guinea' (f.23v). He adds
elsewhere that he was 'serving as provisor and
vicar-general for King D. Sebastião' when the renegade,
Bartolomeu Bayão (Andrada mistakenly names him Pedro
Bayão), was 'captured in Guinea', and that he saw Bayão
(ff. 40v-41). This second statement raises problems.
Bayão was indeed captured 'in Guinea', near Cacheu. He
was then transferred to Santiago in the Cape Verde
Islands, the administrative centre, and in August 1572
sentenced to death (see note 3 to Chapter 15). But it is

difficult to see how Andrada can have encountered him.

According to Andrada, when Ortiz de Zárate was appointed governor of Río de la Plata, 'he was taking me with him as his Vicar-General, in consideration of my organising for him ... the pilots and sailors. We sailed as far as Cape Verde, at which point the governor took other counsel ...' (f.22v). No confirmation of the claimed official appointment to the Zárate expedition has yet been traced. However, a single independent reference appears to confirm that Andrada sailed on the Zárate fleet, and also that he left it at Santiago (see note 8 to Chapter 8). But the fleet only reached Santiago in December 1572, that is, several months after Bayão's death sentence. It follows that either the sentence was not carried out immediately, which is difficult to equate with the documentation; or else that Andrada was being untruthful in claiming to have actually met Bayão.

Nevertheless, there is no reason to doubt that Andrada worked in the Cape Verde Islands for some years (and these islands might reasonably be considered to be 'in Guinea'). He was most probably the 'Manuel de Andrade' who in November 1573 was appointed vicar of the church at

Praia in Santiago Island,[15] Praia being a major town of

---

[15] Our man was not the Dr Manuel de Andrade (the Portuguese form of the surname) who also served in the Cape Verde Islands, but as **corregedor** (magistrate) from the 1550s up to the appointment of António Velho Tinoco in 1570. Instead he was - almost certainly, if we can discount what he seems to be saying at one point, that he was provisor and vicar-general when he allegedly met Bayão - the Manuel de Andrade who became vicar and preacher of the church of Nossa Senhora da Graça in the town of Praia on Santiago Island in November 1573. The document registering his presentation to the double benefice, noted in A. Brásio, **Monumenta missionaria africana**, 2nd. series, vol.3, Lisbon, 1964, p.467, has been examined in a photocopy kindly supplied by the Archivo Nacional da Torre do Tombo, Lisbon. It introduces the appointee as **'natural** [crossed out] **maestre na dita ylha do Cabo Verde**, i.e., 'native [crossed out] master in the Island of Cape Verde' [i.e., Santiago Island]. It may be inferred that Andrada was not a native of the islands (despite a measure in 1570 intended to give preference to native clergy, it appears that only one native cleric in the later sixteenth century can be traced: Brásio, op.cit., pp.3-4; António Brásio, **História e missiologia**, Luanda, 1973, p.893). The exact significance of the term **m(a)estre** is uncertain. If an academic title, it would surely have appeared in full (e.g., **mestre em teologia**) and on Andrada's title-page. Assuming that it instead refers to Andrada's previous post, he is unlikely to have been a mere secular schoolmaster. The reference is therefore probably to a clerical post, and if so probably to the post of **Mestre-Escola do Cabido** (Master of the Chapter School), rather than to the lesser post of **Mestre de capela da Sé** (Cathedral Chapelmaster), which, if not a sinecure, presumably called for a musician. Both were posts for clergy, and ones from which other individuals were eventually promoted to the senior post of canon (ibid., pp.468-9; vol.4, pp.214,326,500). Another man was appointed vicar of the church at Praia in September 1577 (ibid., vol.3, p.468), and may have been Andrada's successor, if it was only at this late date in his stay that Andrada was promoted to provisor and vicar-general - it is almost certain that he had to give up the parish benefices when he became provisor and vicar-general. Praia, a major port of the main island of the archipelago, in 1572 had thirty households of 477 'souls', probably not counting minors as 'souls' and certainly not counting a probably much larger number of slaves (ibid., pp.38,101). Our Lady of Grace was its only parish, an outlying chapelry having been hived off in 1572 (ibid., pp.51,57). A sheaf of documents relating to ecclesiastical affairs in the Cape Verde Islands during the years 1570-1573 has been published by Brásio, and indicates a re-organisation, perhaps a reform, of the local clergy attempted in these years, probably inspired by a bishop who died in 1571. From these

the archipelago.[16] The post of 'provisor and vicar-
general', that is, assistant to the bishop, certainly
existed, so that although there is apparently no record
of Andrada's promotion to this post or service in it we

documents we learn some details relevant to Andrada's career in the islands.
Allegedly to encourage native candidates, candidates for dignities and benefices
were from 1570 to be canonically examined (ibid., p.3) - an oft-repeated,
oft-needed and oft-ignored universal injunction, perhaps therefore not unduly
critical of the state of the local church. Allegedly because of inflation, the
salary of the preacher at Our Lady of Grace was doubled in 1570, from 20,000 **reis**
to 40,000 **reis**; and the vicar's salary of 17,400 **reis** (which was added to by the
silver collection at the regular masses for the soul of the Infante D. Henrique,
alias 'Henry the Navigator'), was raised in 1572 to 30,000 **reis**, on condition
that the vicar ceased also to hold the post of treasurer, which had been worth
20,000 **reis** (ibid., pp.14,38,55). Thus, as vicar and preacher Andrada earned
70,000 **reis**, perhaps still plus the silver collection. (If his previous post was
that of Mestre-Escola, he was being paid much more, since thirty years later the
Mestre-Escola's salary had only risen to 45,000 **reis**: ibid., vol.4, p.214).

[16] The town of Praia was several times sacked and burned by enemies in the
decades immediately after Andrada left, perhaps during an attack by French,
English and Portuguese forces supporting the Portuguese pretender, D. António,
in 1582, certainly by Drake in 1585, and again by the English in 1598 (ibid.,
pp.131-5,408-27). The church (it dated from at least 1526, when it was either
under construction or was being extended: ibid., vol.2, pp.192-203) was most
probably looted and damaged in all of these attacks, as well as in later ones -
in the next century it was rebuilt at least twice (Brásio, op.cit., vol.1, p.192;
vol.4, pp.337,648; vol.5, pp.431,472 - for its site, see the eighteenth-century
plan of the town in vol.4, and it is probably the large building on the extreme
left of the raised site in the mid nineteenth century drawing of the town in
vol.2; M.F.Keeler, **Sir Francis Drake's West Indian Voyage 1585-86**, Hakluyt
Society, London, 1981, pp.149,233 - the town of Praia is depicted, perhaps
schematically, and with no church distinguishable, on the English plans showing
the attack on Santiago, see p.185 below; but a church is shown on a later Dutch
engraving, see p.91 below). Andrada must have known of the damage done to Praia
in 1585 (and perhaps 1582), and this no doubt lent spice to his interest in Drake
and to his feelings about the English.

need not doubt that he held it.[17] However, contrary to
what Andrada states, it is unlikely that he arrived in
the islands in 1572 as provisor and vicar-general, and
more likely that he gained the post at a later date: his
recollection of the whole Bayão episode seems confused.
It was a responsible and well-paid post, principally
entailing ecclesiastical administration, but it is
conceivable that one of its duties was to participate in
the pastoral and disciplinary visitation of Portuguese
settlements on the mainland (annual in theory, almost
certainly infrequent in practice) - such visitations by

---

[17] The fragmentary records (as published by Brásio, vol.2, pp.xiv-xv;
vol.3, pp.465-71) do not detail all appointments, retirements and vacancies, but
Andrada may have succeeded a named individual who in 1567 was referred to as
provisor and vicar-general (ibid., p.466). In August 1573, the provisor and
vicar-general was addressed by the king, but was not named (ibid., p.68).
Andrada's arrival in the islands may have had something to do with the appointment in 1572 of a new bishop, Bishop Bartolomeu Leitão (I have been unable to
discover whether he was a relative of Bishop Pedro Leitão, under whom Andrada had
served in Brazil). However, in August 1573 the king was writing to the provisor,
which indicates that the new bishop had not yet taken up residence in his
diocese, and when he actually arrived in the islands is not clear (ibid., p.68).
It is therefore possible that Andrada was promoted when, or perhaps as soon as,
the new bishop arrived. The salary of the provisor and vicar-general was in 1570
raised to 100,000 **reis** - in comparison, the bishop had 200,000 **reis** (ibid.,
pp.5,59-61). In 1581 this bishop was denounced for misbehaviour, the less
serious charges being that he had conferred parish churches on unworthy
individuals and had been blind to the excesses of his subordinates - Andrada may
have been one of those complained about, on each count. However, Brásio argues
that the charges were only standard skirmishing against an unpopular bishop, who
in this case retained his post and made a voluntary retirement only in 1594
(ibid., vol.2, pp.xii-xiv; vol.3, pp.86-7). Since benefices in Guinea were
formally appointments of the Order of Christ, of which the king was head, Andrada
could reasonably claim that by holding ecclesiastical posts in the Cape Verde
Islands he was 'serving King Sebastião'.

other senior clergy being known.[18] It is possible that Andrada's fairly detailed information on the Sierra Leone estuary was based on experience of an actual visit there. If so, this may have been in the course of a visitation. Alternatively, he may have travelled to Sierra Leone as a chaplain on the expedition headed by Governor António Velho Tinoco which took place in either 1574 or 1577 (see note 4 to Chapter 6). However, Andrada says little about other places he would surely have visited on an ecclesiastical visitation and which certainly were visited by the expedition, notably Cacheu and Guinala, and this raises doubts about his travel to the mainland. He notes at one point that he has been to Bezeguiche Bay (Dakar Bay), travelling directly from Lisbon (f.3v): this is impossible to fit in with his known movements, and if he did visit the bay he is more likely to have done so from the Cape Verde Islands.

Andrada states that he was serving in the islands 'in the years 1576 and 1577', when Drake arrived and 'we fought him and his fleet and drove them away' (f.9v). Drake sailed through the islands, with hardly any counteraction from the Portuguese, actually in January-February 1578 (see note 2 to Chapter 4). Since Andrada arrived in the islands in late 1572, his departure after 'five years' could well have come about in mid 1578, allowing him to experience the local alarm during Drake's passage. Andrada regularly recalls the Drake voyage, particularly in relation to its penetration to the Pacific coast of Spanish America, which obviously impressed him very much; but he has little to say about the Cape Verde Islands or his experiences 'in Guinea'. Why he left the islands is

---

[18]   André Álvares de Almada, **Tratado breve dos Rios de Guiné** [c.1594], Lisbon, 1946; annotated English translation by P.E.H.Hair and J.Boulègue, 2 vols., Department of History, University of Liverpool, 1984; chapter 9, paragraph 9; Brásio, op.cit., vol.3, p.379; vol.4, p.258).

not known, any more than it is known why he previously left Brazil.

Andrada in Portugal and Spain

Where Andrada graduated as a **licenciado** has not been discovered, nor where he gained any further training as a priest. His capacity in Spanish may indicate that he was educated in Spain, rather than in Portugal. At the other end of his career, what he did after his return from the Cape Verde Islands, probably in 1578, is not clear. The knowledge he shows of events in the 1580s does not locate him specifically in Portugal, Spain or overseas, nor does it indicate any close personal involvement with the events - he is merely reporting the gossip among the Iberian well-educated. However, he speaks of offering advice, on the subject of the 1581 despatch of an expedition to Magellan Strait (f.23), to D. Cristóvão de Moura, Philip's leading Portuguese supporter, 'at Lisbon'; and of again offering advice to the same notable before one of Drake's attacks on the Iberian peninsula, either that of 1587 or that of 1589 (f.17v), by which dates D. Cristovão may have been located either in Lisbon or in Madrid. Thus it seems that Andrada was resident in either Portugal or Spain during the 1580s, and it was most probably during this decade that he became 'tutor in mathematics' to D. Felipe de Albornoz.

He implies that he had access to high places, and this may indicate that he was living at Madrid. It is difficult to say whether his post as royal chaplain means that he had in fact gained a foothold in the corridors of power - the post may have been largely honorific. It is plausible, however, that D. Felipe was in attendance at the royal court, and Andrada clearly believes that his patron provides a route to the monarchy. At one point

Andrada writes - 'This I shall further demonstrate to the point of conclusiveness, as Your Majesty has always commanded me to do' (f.29). This might indeed indicate a personal contact with the monarch, but it is perhaps more likely that it is only a general reference, indicating a desire to be loyal to the crown's presumed wishes. Alternatively, it might however indicate that Andrada had previously sent similar memoranda to the crown and had received back - allegedly from the monarch but actually from a weary minister or official - a polite directive to be more concise and clear. Again, in one obscure passage the wording is such that Andrada would seem to be offering to assist the king in the selection of suitable knights to settle St Helena (f.37-37v). But it is difficult to believe that this is what he really meant to say, or meant to be understood. In sum, although Andrada may have had a measure of entrée to the royal presence, it is unlikely that he was a person of any significant influence with the king.

Even on the supposition that Andrada went overseas after very limited clerical experience in Portugal, at his arrival in Brazil in 1560 his age must have been not far short of thirty. Hence the writing of his tract took place when he was, at the least, close to sixty, elderly by contemporary standards. This might explain some of his lapses of memory and confusion. What became of him after his tract was written and printed, and when he died, are not known.[19]

---

[19]   Another Manuel de Andrade, although flourishing c.1590 and also in direct contact with D. Cristóvão de Moura and distant contact with King Philip, is patently not our man: he appears in page after page of the English state papers as a double agent spying for Philip at the court of D. António, the Portuguese pretender, then in England; and he was married (M.S. Hume, Treason and plot, London, 1901, 115-164; P.B.Wernham, **After the Armada**, London, 1984, 104,120,314,443,526).

Andrada's ocean strategy

Andrada's ocean strategy involved pressing a solution to a Portuguese problem on a king more concerned about Spanish problems. Whereas the Spanish **Carrera de (las) Indias** mainly shunted treasure between the Caribbean and Iberia, so that the solution to its difficulties in the later sixteenth century was to strengthen the convoys and armed fleets on a limited Atlantic course, the Portuguese **Carreira da Índia** traversed two oceans and tapped trade in a third. Immediately after their arrival in the Indian Ocean, the Portuguese evolved a strategy of seizing strongpoints at its narrow entrances and exits, in order to keep out enemies and turn the ocean into a Portuguese lake. Thus, Ormuz and Malacca were seized, and Aden was attempted; while a halfway base was established at Mozambique. The strategy succeeded, at least to the extent that a degree of control over Asian shipping was gained for more than a century, and Portuguese naval dominance maintained until the arrival of other Europeans after 1600.

Andrada reflects on the importance of the Malacca Straits (which he terms 'Cabo de Sabão'), both as giving control over the sea route to China and as holding back Islamic advance in South-East Asia. He wants the Portuguese position in the straits strengthened: his geography is weak but he appears to be calling for a strongpoint at Johore additional to that at Malacca (ff.6v-7v). On the other side of the Indian Ocean, he regrets the failure to capture Aden and to hold its off-shore outpost, Socotra, as a defence against the dreaded Turks (f.34v). He fears that if the heretics of Europe were ever to break into the Indian Ocean from the West, and there ally with the Moslems of Aden and Mombasa, then the Turks would be able to sally out of the Red Sea and join their local co-religionists in expelling the Portuguese from their bases in India (f.5-5v). Andrada recollects that the Portuguese were besieged in Goa as recently as 1570 (f.5v). Ormuz he fails to mention, but he is aware that the Persians are hostile to their fellow Moslems, the Turks (f.34v) - a stroke of fortune for the Christians. Not knowing that the English were just about to test it, and were to be followed more decisively by the Dutch, Andrada does not express concern about the southern entrance to the Indian Ocean, at the Cape of Good Hope. He appears to think that this cape would only be passed if the heretics first had a half-way house in the Atlantic, at St Helena (f.5-5v).

The Indian Ocean strategy of seizing peripheral strongpoints, which Andrada wants to see maintained and strengthened, particularly to forestall Islamic advance, he now also wishes to see applied to the southern Atlantic Ocean, where the **Carreira** faced a more recent, more dangerous threat, the advance overseas of the 'Lutherite' French and English. (He counts the French as Protestant, as indeed so many of France's Atlantic seamen were.)

The defence of the South Atlantic had exercised the minds of other Portuguese before Andrada. As early as the 1530s, the arrival of French and English ships in Guinea and Brazil had led to an unsuccessful attempt to establish a Portuguese strongpoint at River Sess on the Malagueta Coast (in modern Liberia).[20] (The existing

[20] A.Teixeira da Mota, 'Duarte Coelho, Capitão-Mor de Armadas no Atlântico (1531-1535)', **Revista de Ciências do Homem**, vol.4, sér.A, 1971, and Série separatas, Agrupamento de Estudos de Cartografia Antiga, Lisbon, no.68. Proposals from 1556 to establish a Portuguese fort at or near the Cape of Good Hope were designed to provide a place of refreshment and refitting for crews and ships of the Carreira da India, rather than a base against enemy action (Maria Emília Madeira H. Santos 1969, 'O carácter experimental da Carreira da Índia -

Portuguese base in Guinea, the fort of São Jorge da Mina on the Gold Coast, was too far out of the path of the major winds for an ocean strategy.) Again, in the early days of the **Carreira**, on the outward journey to the East Portuguese vessels which missed the Cape Verde Islands slipped into Dakar Bay to water and rest (f.10v). But this tactic seems to have fallen out of use, perhaps as the ships learned to make a wider sweep to the South-West. Yet, in the later decades of the sixteenth century, Bahia in Brazil was forbidden to the **Carreira**, for mercantilist reasons, although it remained available as a port of refuge in an emergency - genuine or fabricated - and was indeed so used by the ship in which Andrada travelled in 1560. But Bahia began to be threatened by the English in the 1580s, and it then became clear that its fortifications, built a generation earlier, were rudimentary (ff.25,26v-27).

On the return journey, the **Carreira** made regular use of the isolated mid-ocean island of St Helena, both as a port of refuge and as a refitting base, and some slight facilities for the sick aboard the ships were eventually provided there. But the island had no permanent population and was unfortified. By the later 1580s the despoilers of the **Carreira** were wont to lurk off St Helena; and consequently in 1592 - just after Andrada had completed his tract - King Philip forbade Portuguese vessels to call at the island.

Andrada argues for either the establishment or the strengthening of a Portuguese presence at six localities in the South Atlantic. One is the island of St Helena,

um plano de João Pereira Dantas, com fortificaçao da Africa do Sul (1556)', **Revista da Universidade de Coimbra,** 24, 1969, and Série separatas, Agrupamento de Estudos de Cartografia Antiga, Lisbon, 1969).

the others are localities on the East and West shores of the ocean. In western Africa, the locality of 'the Jalofo' (the Dakar district of the 'Little Coast' of Senegal) and more specifically 'Bezeguiche' (Gorée Island), and also the locality of Sierra Leone (at that date meaning the estuary of the Sierra Leone River), are to be settled and fortified (ff.10-11v,42v-43). On the other side of the Atlantic, the fortifications of Bahia are to be updated, and those of 'the City of Sebastian' (Rio de Janeiro) to be extended (ff.26-26v,44v). Further to the South, the island of Santa Catarina is to be occupied (ff.31-31v,45-45v) - since this was disputed territory Andrada tactfully does not speak of settlement from Brazil but only of settlers sent by King Philip via Brazil (f.45).

Although Andrada manages to think of local trading advantages in each case, the establishment of a permanent Portuguese presence at Bezeguiche and St Helena was basically intended to provide ports of refuge for shipping either distressed by long voyages and storms or threatened by heretic pirates. For the latter reason, settlement is linked to 'fortification', a military presence. Andrada seems to include Sierra Leone in the same category, although its value to shipping traversing the Atlantic was less plausible, its fine natural harbour being further off the normal routes than was Bezeguiche. It lay along the route to Mina, however, and Andrada probably saw a naval base there primarily as a shield for the gold trade from Mina.

At both African localities there were already small (notionally illegal) settlements of Portuguese traders, and Andrada knew about these places from his contacts in the Cape Verde Islands with the local trading community, if not from personal experience. Moreover, it is possible that Andrada was acquainted in the 1570s with an

Islands trader, André Álvares de Almada, who in 1581 was to call for a Portuguese settlement of Sierra Leone, and who in a work of c.1594 drew attention to the strategic importance of 'Bezeguiche' and suggested its fortification.[21] It would seem therefore that Andrada's proposals for West Africa were borrowed from the current thinking of the Cape Verde Islands trading and administrative community. The proposals were reasonably realistic. In fact, some fifteen years after Andrada completed his tract an attempt was made to establish a Portuguese settlement at Sierra Leone; and later in the seventeenth century Gorée Island was actually fortified - but by the Dutch, not the Portuguese.[22] Contrariwise, Andrada's proposal for St Helena was armchair strategy and unrealistic - the island was never to be fortified, either by the Portuguese or by the other European nations who in later centuries called there.

Turning to the other side of the Atlantic, Andrada's proposals for strengthening the fortifications of the Brazilian towns of Bahia and Rio de Janeiro were conventional, although in both instances Andrada showed some knowledge of the local topography, a knowledge most probably gained rather from personal experience than from maps (ff.26v,28v,44v-45). His proposal for settling Santa Catarina Island was more novel but not very realistic - the island was never given a fortified base

---

[21] Almada, op.cit., p.2 and chap.2/7: an Islands contemporary of Almada also proposed a settlement of Sierra Leone, André Donelha, **An account of Sierra Leone and the Rivers of Guinea of Cape Verde**, ed. A.Teixeira da Mota and P.E.H.Hair, Lisbon, 1977, p.73.

[22] On the attempted Portuguese settlement of Sierra Leone (and an alleged attempt to build a fort there), see P.E.H.Hair, 'The abortive Portuguese settlement of Sierra Leone 1570-1625', in **Vice-Almirante A. Teixeira da Mota in memoriam**, Lisbon, 1987, pp.171-208.

(f.45-45v). However, all these West-Atlantic proposals had a similar prime motive, the intention being less to rescue distressed shipping, than to deprive Lutherite incursions into the Iberian world-space of essential calling-places and bases. Bahia and Rio de Janeiro had only to be better defended against enemy attacks, but Santa Catarina Island was open to instant Lutherite seizure, at least as a temporary base.

If Andrada's proposals for Bahia and Rio de Janeiro were in defence of the Portuguese empire, the inclusion of Santa Catarina Island was a gesture to Madrid, being in defence of King Philip's Spanish empire. Andrada's strategy at this point was totally in keeping with Spanish official strategy, both of them being Drake-obsessed. Shaken by Drake's irruption through Magellan Strait, in 1581-1584 the Spaniards borrowed a leaf from the Portuguese Indian Ocean strategy and tried to seal off the Pacific by establishing a fortified base in the strait. The attempt failed disastrously. Although it is not clear whether Andrada knew this when he was writing, he proposed a second line of defence. Since he understood that enemy ships attempting the strait used Santa Catarina Island as a jumping-off point, he proposed its fortification; and he added that this would assist the Spanish settlement of Río de la Plata, a process he had himself almost shared in, in 1572 (f.45v). If any part of Andrada's tract was capable of arousing the interest of King Philip and his Madrid counsellors, it was this proposal.[23]

---

[23] For a more or less contemporary representation of Spanish nervousness about Drake and his English successors in the South-West Atlantic, as experienced on the spot in the Rio de la Plata and Peru regions, see the epic poem **Argentina** by Martín del Barco Centenera, published in Lisbon in 1602 (the poet was Andrada's fellow-traveller on the Zárate expedition of 1572). Archdeacon Barco Centenera devoted part of his Canto XXII to a narration of Drake's activities in

Andrada's other proposals

Like many Iberian contemporaries, Andrada was convinced that the increasing losses at sea were due to mismanagement. While the king could provide more refuges from storm and pirates around the Atlantic, the pilots of Spanish and Portuguese vessels needed better training in order to guide their ships successfully between the bases. Here Andrada's proposals were fairly commonplace and in the direction of developments already under way in both countries (ff.34,35) The autodidact lays great weight on an understanding of the cosmographical principles that governed the winds and currents of the oceans, but his exposition of these principles is weak, not only because of the inadequate scientific knowledge of the age, but because his own powers of explanation are limited (ff.23-23v,33-34).[24] Nautical mathematics - what was later called the science of navigation - should be taught, he argues, in Iberian universities and in the

---

1578-1579, part of Canto XXIV to the Spanish reaction, the attempt to establish a base in Magellan Strait, one verse in Canto II to the Fenton expedition of 1582, and all of Cantos XXVI-XXVIII to the activities of Cavendish on the Pacific and Atlantic coasts of lower South America in 1586-1587 and 1591-1592.

[24] Ursula Lamb concedes rather more practical value to the tract than I do. "Among the intellectual skills which Andrada cultivated were mathematics and cosmography. He claimed to be self-educated in the theory but practiced through his many voyages in the art of navigation. His text bears him out with respect to the former which concerns knowledge of the sphere and the globe. He considered this knowledge essential and requested that it be taught to all sailors. A brief sample of his explanation of the various motions of the sea and atmosphere under the twelve signs and the seven planets, etc, makes it clear the pilots and sailors may have been spared a good bit of confusion. However, when he discusses the need for practical experience of tides and winds, of currents, monsoons and calms, the importance of local information,and consideration of seasonal variations at sea, he speaks from bitterly won experience, repeatedly and accurately."

sea-ports (ff. 15v,34). However, Andrada has also picked up some common popular notions which he repeats - that the surrender of great ships to English attackers is due to cowardice (f.35v), that men of humble birth are not fit to be captains of vessels (f.39v), and that the ordinary sailors of the **Carreira da Índia** are demoralised because of lack of adequate pay and rewards, hence to some extent because of a Jesuit levy on their liberty chests (f.38v). As a typical cleric, Andrada thinks 'greed' is to blame for much, and he criticises merchants (ff.32v,39v) - but the profit of the crown is sacrosanct.

The character of Andrada ?

From his tract one gains only a very general idea of Andrada's character. He was certainly a patriot - as his career required - and as such a supporter of Catholic world-empire and an enemy of "heathen" Lutherites (ff. 2,42v). How attached he was to the finer points of religion it is difficult to say. Apart from clichés about the defence of the Catholic church, he says little in detail about religious practice. However, at a few points he notes his own missionary activity and advocates active evangelization of non-Christians (ff.11v-12,23v-24,26). His call for preachers in the Colleges of Spain to remember their vocation and preach the Gospel (f.13v), presumably in the mission field, although it echoed a frequent appeal from churchmen to the crowded convents of Iberia for mission volunteers, may well have been sincere.

Andrada is proud of his self-instruction, and of the width of his knowledge as well as of his experience; but he promises much more than he can deliver. Almost certainly he is not altogether truthful about the width and depth of his experience. If he seems vain, over-ambitious and egotistic in his tract, these characteristics, like the defects in the presentation of his material, may have been partly the failings of senescence.[25] But it is, after all, the old who reflect, sadly and nostalgically, on the past - and do not hesitate to draw dubious lessons from it.

---

[25] Note, however, that it is probable that Andrada was rather younger than his monarch, Philip II.

CHRONOLOGY

and

MAP

Dates supplied by Andrada, and his personal episodes, are in bold print. Corrected dates and significant events not mentioned by Andrada are added in square brackets.

DATE	**PERSONAL EVENTS**	OTHER EVENTS
1472 [1444]		Cape Verde discovered, allegedly by D.Henrique (f.3)
1505		King Manuel gives sailing instructions to Afonso de Albuquerque (f.10v)
1507-11		Portuguese occupy Socotra (f.34v)
1515 (f.38v)		crown permits liberty chests to seamen
temp. King João III (= 1521-1557)		India ships allegedly water at Sierra Leone (f.19v)
temp. Emp. Charles V (= 1519-56)		alleged voyage to River Plate of 'Diego de Mendoça'
1540 [1549]		Bahia fort established (f.25)
1549 (see **1540**)		
1550 [1557]		governor of Brazil, Mem de Sà, delayed at sea (f.21v)
1550-1590		French allegedly plan to settle St Helena Island (f.5)
1552		Manuel de Sousa [Sepulveda] shipwrecked (f.25v)
1553		Palma in Canaries sacked by French (f.41v)
1556		India ship 'Flamenca' lost (ff.21v,37v)
1556-73		D.Pedro Leitão, [bishop of Brazil] (f.23v)
1557 (see **1550**)		
1559		fleet of Jaime Raschin wrecked at River Plate (f.22)
1559 [1560]		French fort on Rio de Janeiro captured, Lutherite books seized (ff.6,36-36v)

1560 (see **1559**)

1560   Malacca galleon lost off Sumatra (f.39v)

1560   **travels to Bahia on 'S.Paulo' (ff.25,26), ship wrecked off Sumatra (ff.19v,25v,39v), stays in Brazil**

1560s   **spends 9 years in Brazil, preaches to Amerindians, serves under bishop Leitão** (see 1556-73) **(f.23v), meets Araucanian in Cananéia (f.31)**

1562 [1564]   Diogo Lopes de Mesquita wrecked (f.25v)

· 1562-7 (see temp. King Henrique, 1578-80)

1564 (see **1562**)

1564-7   **serves under Estácio de Sá in Brazil (f.23v)**

1565-7   [Estácio de Sá leads and is killed in campaign against French]

1565-95   [Cristóvão de Barros in Brazil, supports and succeeds Estácio de Sá in 1565-7 campaign]

? 1565-7   **serves under Cristóvão de Barros (f.21v) [? in 1565-7 campaign]**

1565-7   French defeated on Rio de Janeiro, City of São Sebastião founded (f.6-6v)

? 1565-7   **interrogates French prisoners about plans (f.36v), converts Lutherites (f.24), French were allegedly planning to settle St Helena Island (f.36v)**

1565 (see **1569**)

1566   Funchal in Madeira sacked by French under Caldeira (f.41-41v)

1566 (see **1567**)

1567 [1566]   Arguin captured by Lutherites (f.8v)

1567   foundation of 'Sebastian City' (Rio de Janeiro) (f.6)

1569 [1565]	French in Florida defeated by Pedro Menéndez (f.10)
? 1569	**[leaves Brazil]**
1570	D.Luís Fernandes, governor of Brazil, suffers disaster at sea (f.22), [and Jesuits massacred]
1570	siege of Goa (f.5v)
1570	Lutherite fleet defeated at Cape Verde (f.17)
1570s	**spends 5 years in Guinea, as vicar-general for unstated period (f.23v,41), serves under Tinoco (f.23v)**
1570-7	António Velho Tinoco governor of Cape Verde Islands
? 1570-2	**at Seville, recruiting for Zárate expedition to Río de la Plata, appointed vicar-general (f.22v)**
1571	Don John of Austria, Doria, 'Marco Antonio' (f.35v) [win battle of Lepanto against Turks]
1572	Bartolomeu Bayão captured in Guinea, [executed at Santiago]
1572	Zárate sails fleet to Río de la Plata, encounters difficulties (f.22v)
1572	**[leaves Zárate fleet at Cape Verde Islands], claims to observe Bayão (ff.40v-41)**
pre-1577	Tinoco defeats Lutherite fleet at Cape Verde (f.16v)
1573-?6	**[vicar of church at Praia in Cape Verde Islands]**
1573	Luís de Alter lost off Brazil (ff.21v-22)
1574	Lisbon Jesuits given royal grant of levy on imports (f.38v)
? 1574 (see 1577)	
1576-7	**serving in the Cape Verde Islands (f.9v), ? now vicar-general**

1576-7 [1578]	Drake passes through the Cape Verde Islands (f.9v)
1577 [? 1574]	Tinoco defeats French fleet at Sierra Leone (f.16v)
1577 [? 1574]	**[? visits Sierra Leone with Tinoco]**
1578 (see 1576-7)	
1578	[Portuguese defeat in Morocco, King Sebastião killed]
? 1578	**[leaves Cape Verde Islands]**
1578-80	Drake passes Magellan Strait, attacks shipping off Peru, seeks Northwest Passage, allegedly returns via Atlantic [but actually circum-navigates] (ff.7v-8,9v-10)
temp. King Henrique (= 1578-80) (but perhaps temp. regency, 1562-7)	Mina sailors not favoured (f.40v)
1578-86	galleys sent to the Caribbean (f.4)
c.1580-1591	Iberian fleets take roundabout routes to avoid attackers (f.32v)
1580-81	[Portuguese succession dispute, King Philip wins, D.António flees]
1580 [1582-3]	supporters of D.António attack Cape Verde Islands (ff.8v-9)]
1581	expedition under D.Diego Flores de Valdes leaves for Magellan Strait, early difficult-ies (f.25)
1581	**in Portugal, advises D Cristóvão de Moura on sailing date for Magellan Strait expedition (f.25)**
during 1581-9	**warns de Moura about future English assaults on Iberia (f.17v)**
1582	Gaspar de Brito lost, [dies when wintering in East Africa] (f.25v)

c.1582	Malacca galleon turns back (f.21v,39v)
1582	marquis of Santa Cruz (f.35v) [defeats a French fleet and the supporters of D.António in the Azores]
1582	[French fleet at Mina]
1582	[English expedition under Fenton at Sierra Leone]
1582-3 (see **1580**)	
1584	defeat of French at Paraíba in Brazil, establishment of Philip's City (f.5v)
1585-9	[D.António in England]
1586-8	[Cavendish circumnavigates]
1587	conquest of Johore by D.Pedro de Lima [after siege of Malacca] (ff.6v-7)
1587	English attack Cadiz (41v)
1587	Drake captures the 'S.Felipe' (f.39v), and attacks Cadiz (f.41v)
1587	Lutherites attack islands in the Azores (f.41v)
1587 (see **1588**)	
1587-9 (see 1588)	
1588 [1587]	English attack Bahia (f.26)
1588	English attack 'Spanish Armada' (f.41v)
1588 [1587-9]	Francisco Giraldes, governor of Brazil, sails, but voyage aborted (f.18)
1588	Diogo de Azambuja attacked by French pirates (f.25v-6)
1589	English attack Lisbon vicinity (ff.37,42)
1589	[D.Pedro de Lima shipwrecked and dies]

1590	most of India fleet under Matias de Albuquerque turns back (ff.18,39)
1590	returning India ship under Bernardino Ribeiro Pacheco has to winter in Brazil (ff.18,38)
1590	**'the present year' (f.5), tract being written**
1591	[a Moroccan army, partly of Portuguese captives, conquers in West Africa and occupies Timbuktu]
1591	[the first English fleet passes the Cape of Good Hope]
1590-1	**now tutor in mathematics to D.Felipe de Albornoz and royal chaplain**

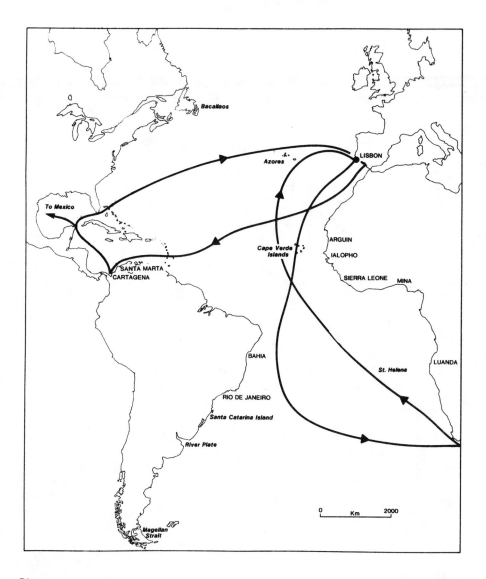

The sea routes shown were typical routes of the Spanish
Carrera de Indias and the Portuguese **Carreira da Índia**.

TEXT

in translation

with notes

INSTRUCTION

GIVEN TO YOUR MAJESTY,

THAT YOU MAY

COMMAND

THAT THE OCEAN SEA BE FORTIFIED

AND DEFENDED AGAINST ALL ENEMY PIRATES,

WHETHER FRENCH OR ENGLISH,

IN ALL THE NAVIGATIONS OF YOUR ROYAL CROWN

WITHIN THE TROPICS.

Presented by Don Felipe de Albornoz.

Composed and set out by
his Tutor in Mathematics,
Licentiate MANOEL DE ANDRADA CASTEL BLANCO,
Chaplain to Your Majesty.

[no place of publication or date]

THE COURSE OF ARGUMENT

throughout this **INSTRUCTION,** which is

about the importance of

UNDERSTANDING NAVIGATION and

ACTING AGAINST THE LUTHERITES.

It deals with the fortification -

: Of the **Kingdom of the Ialophos** - its
  settlement and the advantages

: Of **Sierra Leona** - its site and the
  advantages

: Of the **City of San Salvador** and **Brazil,**
  and of the entrance of the channel
  to the city

: Of **Sebastian City** in the Rio de Enero
  [Rio de Janeiro], captured from the
  French

: Of the **Island of Santa Catalina,** [as
  a safeguard for] Río de la Plata,
  Magellan [Strait], and Charcas
  [province] of Peru

: Of the **Island of St Helena,** with
  reference to [its importance for] the
  East Indies   **/f.2/**

[Enemy attacks on the Empire, and the remedies]

FIRST it must be taken into consideration that the whole of the Ocean Sea that is navigable, in every direction of the four winds, belongs to Your Majesty, and that you rule with complete legitimacy all the kingdoms and conquests [therein], being Defender of the Faith. For this reason the heathen English and French attack and rob the Defender of the Faith, over the entire Ocean Sea, in all its shipping routes, those of the East as well as those of the West. By these means they become rich and powerful, in order to maintain wars against the Catholic Church and against Your Majesty's Crown. For the defence of which, I shall identify all the remedies [for these problems], and they will be stated below. They are deduced mathematically, with respect to the dimension of the globe, the fourfold division of the /f.2v/ rising and setting sun, and the movement of the tides, which by their nature have their own individual and varied effects.

CHAPTER 1

[West Africa : the Jolof kingdom and its port, Bezeguiche]

At 15° North, on the opposite coast of Africa, lies a kingdom called the kingdom of the Ialopho, who in his own tongue is called Gudumel, meaning something like 'Grand Duke'. He is very powerful and rich, but for his defence lacks artillery and ships, although he has many cavalry forces.[1] At precisely the same latitude lies Bezeguiche, which means in his language 'great bay or headland', a city where his court resides. /f.3/ This city is called Cabo Verde by the Portuguese.[2] The Infante of Portugal, D. Enrique, discovered it in person in the year 1472, being the first navigator to, and discoverer of, all the adjacent islands to the West, which are San Felipe, Santiago, San Nicolas, San Anton, Santa Lucia, San Vicente, Isla de la Sal, Isla de Mayo, Isla Brava, and the Islands of Cabo Verde.[3]

1. IALOPHO An African polity, located on the coast of Guinea between the Senegal River and Cape Verde and known as Kajoor or 'Kayor', whose inhabitants formed a section of the Wolof people, was in earlier centuries commonly known as 'Jalofo' or 'Jolof' (Gamble 1957, 11,17; Boulègue 1987, passim). (In 1592, Abreu de Brito also used the term 'Jalofo', but in a very loose and inaccurate sense, apparently to connote the whole western coast of Guinea up to Sierra Leone: Abreu de Brito 1931, 3,82,91.) This polity was frequently discussed by early Portuguese sources, which sometimes instead referred to it as 'Budumel', from **bur** 'king', and a specific title of the ruler, **damel**, in the Wolof language (Almada 1984, chap.1, notes 3,6-8; Boulègue 1987, 15). Andrada gives a variant, 'Gudumel' (cf. 'Guodumel', in a 1582 text as the personal name of a Jolof ruler, Brásio 1964, 97). Thus the meaning of 'Budumel' was not very far from the one suggested by Andrada. The precise relationships, during the later sixteenth century, of this polity with its former overlord in the interior, the 'Grand Jolof', and with the other Wolof polities further South on the coast, are far from clear; and it is possible that Andrada, rightly or wrongly, thinks of the 'kingdom of the Ialopho' as rather wider than Kayor. Wolof armies included considerable cavalry forces (Almada 1984, chap.1/14,16-17). Andrada later proposes an embassy to the 'King of the Ialophos', with a gift of harnesses for horses (ff.43v-44).

2. BEZEGUICHE Early Portuguese sources gave the name 'Bezeguiche', first to an African notable encountered near Cape Verde, then to his town and port in the bay (now Dakar Bay) to the South of the cape (and occasionally to the island in the bay later known as Gorée Island) (Pacheco Pereira 1956, n.100; Hakluyt 1598, 2/2:188; Donelha 1977, 279,ns.203,204; Boulègue 1987, 110-111,127). Andrada's interpretation of the term is original but probably fictional. It is doubtful whether the Portuguese ever called any town in this vicinity 'Cape Verde', and also doubtful whether the 'Jolof' ruler regularly held court in any seaside town, his base being in the interior.

3. D. ENRIQUE Andrada's history is inaccurate. The Infante D. Henrique, the 'Henry the Navigator' of British historians, never sailed on the African voyages he is credited with inspiring, and he died in 1460. Cape Verde was, however, reached by Portuguese vessels in 1444, during the Infante's lifetime, while the Cape Verde Islands were discovered in the 1450s and then settled in the 1460s. Andrada names the major islands but omits Boavista, and he uses an alternative name for Fogo, São Filipe (cf. Fernandes 1951, 114). By the 'Islands of Cabo Verde' Andrada presumably means, not the Cape Verde Islands which he has just named individually and which lie far out in the ocean, but the tiny islets off Cape Verde, the Madeleines.

CHAPTER 2

[The French at Bezeguiche - pirates in the
Caribbean and on the Guinea coast - the threat
to St Helena - if the English reach the East -
pirates in Brazil]

[The French at Bezeguiche]

In Bezeguiche, the capital of the kingdom of
the Ialophos, there is a gulf and bay, very
large, roomy and beautiful, in which 100 or
more high-sided ships /f.3v/ and more than 200
galleys with all their boats and smaller
vessels (**baxeles**) can anchor.[1] The route and
voyage is so short and easy that, having set
out from Lisbon, one arrives in thirteen days,
as I have experienced.[2] The Lutherites from La
Rochelle, Bordeaux, Havre de Grâce, and all of
Brittany, and other pirates belonging to the
province of Gaul and its shipping fleets, make
port and call here, without anyone stopping
them. They carry to France much gold, ambergris, ivory, hides, and various kinds of valuable musk in great quantities.[3] They leave behind for the Ialophos, who are adherents of the
sect of Mohammed, an abundance of instruments
of war, such as lances, daggers, swords, cut-
lasses, shields, and all else that is forbidden
[to be sold to Muslims] by the [papal] bull **De
la Cena.**[4] Here the pirates take on water while
they stock up with provisions. /f.4/

1. BEZEGUICHE BAY Contemporary Portuguese sources also spoke highly of the facilities afforded to shipping by this bay (Donelha 1977, 127; Almada 1984, chap.1/6).

2. ANDRADA AND THE BAY Andrada implies that he had himself visited and observed the bay, on at least one occasion, after sailing there from Lisbon in thirteen days. The sailing time is correctly represented (Sierra Leone could be reached from Lisbon in 15-16 days, according to Almada 1984, chap.19/3). Yet on the only voyage from Lisbon Andrada records his having taken, his 1560 voyage to Brazil, the ship did not go near Cape Verde and had not even reached the latitude of the cape by the thirteenth day (Boxer 1968, 61). On his 1572 voyage, the ship sailed, not from Lisbon but from San Lucar, it did not go near Cape Verde, and it only reached the latitude of the cape after several months of voyage. It seems unlikely that Andrada ever sailed from Lisbon to Cape Verde, but possible that he visited the bay when working in the Cape Verde Islands during the 1570s. Hence, when writing his account, he confused information and personal experience, deliberately or by misrecollection.

3. FRENCH TRADE Writing in the early 1590s, André Álvares de Almada, a trader of the Cape Verde Islands, recorded that the bay was "regularly frequented by the English and the French. ... Through it pass most of the ships of our enemies, whether going to Serra Leoa, to the Malagueta Coast, to Brazil, or to the Indies of Castile ... treating the bay as if it were one of the roadsteads of England or France" (Almada 1984, chap.2/6-7). The French had developed a trade with this area since the 1560s, the export trade being mainly in hides; the English, with some support from the Portuguese pretender, D. António, began regular trading there in the late 1580s (Hakluyt 1598, 2/2:189; Nunes Costa 1953). Andrada throughout assumes that the French are all 'Lutherites', that is, Protestants, whereas in fact the majority were Catholics, the French objection to Iberian monopoly of Atlantic trade being more political than theological. Writing in 1592, Abreu de Brito (whose knowledge of the region was admittedly very second-hand) thought that the Jalofos traded with "pirates and corsairs" because formerly the Portuguese had given them only "sashes of little value", in exchange for very valuable ambergris and gold, while the foreigners offered a wider range of goods, "Rouen cloth, beads, knives, coloured cloths, and some iron" (Abreu de Brito 1931, 83).

4. ISLAM AND WEAPONS At this date, only certain sections of the 'Jolof' had been fully Islamized, but the ruling lineages of Kayor considered themselves Moslem (Boulègue 1987, 93-99): Andrada himself later minimises the extent of Islamization (f.11v). The papal bull 'De la cena', annually promulgated 1364-1774 on Maundy Thursday (**in Coena Domini**, hence its name), consisted of a catalogue of anathemas against transgressors, including those who provide infidels with arms. (The Portuguese, however, occasionally obtained special dispensations to sell arms to friendly non-Christians, for instance, to the rulers of Makassar - p.c. John Villiers.) A constant theme of Andradas's thought is that the enemies of Spain and Portugal sell weapons to non-Christians and thus support them against Christian Iberians. But although the French and English of this period paid for the products they bought from Africans and from Amerindians by selling European

[Some pirates disperse to the Caribbean coasts]

From this port they sail grouped into fleets. Some are bound for the coast of La Burburuata, where at Cavo de la Hacha they trade with the Spaniards for gold, worked silverware, and other valuables such as emeralds and many cornelians. And these are the people who plunder the coast, and the seas off Cartagena and Nombre de Dios.[5] To defend that coast, Your Majesty assigns galleys which are consumed by worms and are excessively expensive, without being of any use, because in a rough sea they cannot engage high-sided ships, which roam this area extensively all the year round.[6] For these pirates, by using the sea conditions of April, when the Northwesterlies are weak, set out to pursue their assault and robbery from the Equator [northwards]. After devastating and plundering they return with the South West and West winds, in all this following the principles of navigation, /f.4v/ which, when followed, sustain them at sea.[7] At this same port, other corsairs split off [to head] for the islands of the West, such as Trinidad, Margarita, Santa Marta, Santo Domingo and Havana, and others for Puerto Rico, Vera Cruz and Honduras, this being the Mexican shipping route, robbing everywhere they sail.[8]

manufactures, and although these frequently included iron tools and metal containers, it is unlikely that, in either Africa or America, large quantities of weapons were handed over. Further, see note 4 to the Epitome.

5. CARIBBEAN RAIDS AND TRADE The references are to the SE coast of the Caribbean, the localities named ranging from Burburuata (in modern Venezuela, West of Caracas) westwards to Río de la Hacha (Colombia), Cartagena (Colombia) and Nombre de Dios (Panama). Burburuata (**"el pueblo de las minas de la Burburuata"**, Vellerino 1575), a settlement so frequently raided by corsairs that it was vacated temporarily in the 1550s and abandoned permanently towards the end of the sixteenth century (López de Velasco 1971, 76; Andrews 1978, 28), here gives its name to the coastal region of western Venezuela. By 'Cavo de la Hacha' Andrada presumably means Cabo de la Vela, on the tip of the peninsula to the NE of the settlement on the Río de la Hacha. The gold and emeralds of the interior (López de Velasco 1971, 180) were reported as reaching the coast in the 1580s account of Lopes Vas, but the same account emphasised that earlier depredations on the coast were mainly the work of the French, not the English (Hakluyt 1598, 3:781-2). Andrada fails to mention the pearls collected on the coast (which gave the name to the island of Margarita), and instead mentions cornelians - a slip, since cornelians, normally a product of the East, do not appear in a contemporary list of products of Spanish America (López de Velasco 1971, 13).

6. GALLEYS Galleys were sent to Cartagena, Santo Domingo and Havana between 1578 and 1586, in the belief that these vessels would be the answer to the raids of corsairs. Although at first the galleys scored some successes, in 1590 an official wrote that they were "a useless extravagance" (Andrews 1978, 102-5; Hoffman 1980, 179-193).

7. PRIVATEERING SEASONALITY "The privateering season in the Caribbean was more or less fixed by the weather and the movements of Spanish shipping converging on Havana during June and July. Most of the privateers therefore left in March or April" (Andrews 1959, 28-29).

8. CARIBBEAN TARGETS Since none of the previously named American localities was specifically termed a port, 'this port' must refer back to Bezeguiche. Andrada lists various Caribbean islands - Trinidad, La Margarita (on the coast of Venezuela), Santo Domingo (i.e. Hispaniola) and Havana (i.e. Cuba) are individual islands, while Santa Marta was a locality on the mainland (between Cartagena and Río de la Hacha) whose port lay between two islets (Hakluyt 1598, 3:782; López de Velasco 1971, 192). This group of American localities represented the course of ships entering the Caribbean from the extreme SW; Puerto Rico represented a more northern course; and Honduras and Vera Cruz a course extending to the NE, that is, as Andrada says, to Mexico. By 'Honduras' Andrada means the port of Puerto de los Caballos in the Gulf of Honduras, a port "subjected to attack year after year from 1592 to 1597" (Andrews 1959, 38). For French and later English **corsários** attempting to trade at or otherwise attack these localities during the half-century between the 1530s and the early 1590s, see Andrews 1978, 65-66,74-79,135-156.

[Other pirates plunder the Guinea coast]

Others again turn South, to plunder the whole
coast of Guinea, that is to say, they rob Your
Majesty's **Casa de Contratación** located on Rio
de Santo Domingo.[9] And they plunder even Rio
Grande itself, which is the river of the
Bujafras, and from there they go to Sierra
Leona, to make their way along the entire coast
of Mina.[10] This lies within the equinoctial
zone at 6°, and corresponds on the face of the
globe, according to the latitudes and longitudes of the **Cosmographia,** to the opposite coast
of /f.5/ Argel [Algiers] and Fez and to its
meridian[s].[11] They proceed until they reach
the islands of Príncipe and São Tomé, committ-
ing great robberies and crimes, and by loading
up those obscure kingdoms with weapons, they
arm infidels. Very severe losses to Your
Majesty result from this.[12]

9. RIO DE SANTO DOMINGO The Rio de São Domingos, later known as Rio Cacheu (in modern Guiné-Bissau), contained a royal **Casa do Contrato**, an office for crown administration of the royal monopoly and commercial dues, from at least the 1550s, albeit perhaps intermittently operative. This **Casa** was originally at the Portuguese settlement at Bichangor but in the 1580s was moved to Cacheu (Blake 1937, 141; Hair 1970, 6).

10. RIO GRANDE 'Rio Grande' was a name applied by sixteenth-century sources on Guinea to Rio Jeba, to Rio Balola, or to the wide estuary from which both can be entered (all in modern Guiné-Bissau). The 'Bujafras' or Biafada, who lived between the two rivers, were the ethnicity most accepting of cooperation with the Portuguese in this region of Guinea.

11. COAST OF MINA Andrada is correct: the central point of the 'coast of Mina', the Portuguese fort of São Jorge da Mina (at modern Elmina, in Ghana) was located close to 6° N, and midway between the longitudes of Fez and Algiers.

12. EASTERN GUINEA French and English trading on the eastern coast of Guinea was up to the 1590s much more limited than the trading of the same nations on the western coast. Attempts to break into the Mina gold trade in the 1550s and 1560s had largely failed (Hair 1988). But in 1582 the Portuguese fort at Mina accepted for a short period the commercial visit of a French fleet, the garrison temporizing while considering the most suitable patriotic reaction to the news of Philip II's accession to the throne of Portugal. In the same year, the island of Príncipe attempted to declare for the pretender, D. António (Vogt 1979, 129-135). The more important equatorial island of São Tomé, which declared for King Philip, had had occasional earlier hostile contacts with the 'Lutherites'. Probably the first French visit was an attack on the island in 1567, while probably the first English visit was not until 1589, when a small outlying island was assaulted (Purchas 1625, 2/7:970). (The Dutch do not seem to have visited until they attacked the island in 1599.) Andrada thus appears to exaggerate the extent of the past 'Lutherite' threat to eastern Guinea but is correct in predicting its future increase.

[The threat to St Helena, particularly should the English reach the East]

Others again sail to Angola, the Congo, and the Island of St Helena, where they take on water between September and March, using the regular motions [of the sea] in order to enter and leave the Torrid Zone or Equinoctial. In this zone they have proposed to raze by fire this island, which they would have done if God had not blinded them. And if [instead] they had settled it, as indeed they have desired to do from the year 1550 up to the present year of 1590, this would have been the ruin of all the East.[13] For the Moors of Arabia and Mombasa, and those on the island of Zocotorá [Socotra] and in the /f.5v/ strong and populous city of Aden at the mouth and entrance of the Red Sea, would have conspired with the English. And having been provided with a port the English would then make their way past the Cape of Good Hope more easily than they pass the Cape of Magellan.[14] Against such an evil there would be no remedy. The Turk would seize the opportunity, and India would break out in rebellion, as was attempted in the time of Viceroy Don Luys, when the capital, Goa, was besieged.[15]

13. ST HELENA For St Helena, see note 1 to Chapter 13.

14.   MOORS AND ENGLISH Andrada, having previously denounced the French, now refers to the English. It seems that he does not know of the first English voyage to the East via the Cape of Good Hope, in 1591. But since the English have rounded South America, by passing through Magellan Strait - the reference being to Drake in 1579 (he nowhere specifies the subsequent passage by Cavendish in 1587) - he foresees, correctly, that they will now attempt the other gateway to the East, the Cape of Good Hope. He argues that, since the Portuguese, when sailing to the East, and after passing the Cape of Good Hope, sometimes called at their base of Mozambique before proceeding to India, the English will have need of a similar port of call, and may therefore visit the Islamic ports of Mombasa, Aden or Socotra. He was partly correct. In 1591-2 the first English voyage wintered at Zanzibar, an Islamic port (Hakluyt 1598, 3:571). But later English (and Dutch) voyages to the East instead made use of harbours near the Cape of Good Hope or on Madagascar, points outside both Portuguese and Islamic control. In chapter 12 Andrada returns to the subject of the threat from Islamic Aden, but after the present reference he does not again mention the possibility of the English reaching the Indian Ocean from the Atlantic.

15.   GOA Goa was besieged in 1570, unsuccessfully, when the viceroy of the 'Estado da Índia' (that is, all Portuguese possessions East of the Cape of Good Hope) was D. Luís de Ataíde, viceroy 1568-1571 and 1578-1581 (Serrão 1980, 3:140).

'The Castle of Mina', as shown on a Portuguese map of
c.1575 - to the left, the lion on the mountain
indicates Sierra Leone (f.4v)

[Other pirates disperse to Brazil and thence to Magellan Strait]

Other pirates again head towards and reach the Sea of Pernambuco in Brasil, on the West, after they too have crossed the equinoctial zone. Here is located Philip's City (**la ciudad Filipina**), which your Majesty now possesses, having won it from the French.[16]   And the pirates trade all along the coast of Brazil, reaching as far as the famous city and capital of the kingdom called La Bahia de Todos Santos, the City of San Salvador, which corresponds in the same degree and /f.6/ parallel to Cuidad de los Reyes in Peru, to Santa Marta and to Cuzco.[17]   They then descend in a North/South direction by latitude, distributing weapons throughout the kingdoms of the Pitiguares, the Tupinambas, the Tupinaquins and the Tamayos, and by reaching the Tropic of Capricorn, as far as the coast of Cananea, the waters of Río de la Plata, and Magellan Strait.[18]

16.   CIUDAD FILIPINA In 1584, a joint Spanish-Portuguese force, after sinking French vessels at Paraíba in northern Brazil, and driving off the Amerindian allies of the French, established a fort named 'São Felipe'. The name of the fort probably led to the subsequent Portuguese settlement in the same locality being named 'Cidade Filipina', or 'Philip's City' (Varnhagen 1959, 1:384). (For Iberian concern in the early 1580s about French plans to establish bases in northern Brazil and the Amazon, see Lorimer 1989, 15.) In 1592, "Cidade Felipesa called Paraiba" was one of four Brazilian localities recommended for fortification (the others being Pernambuco, Bahia and Cape St Augustine) (Abreu de Brito 1931, 85).

17.   SAN SALVADOR The city located in the Bahia de Todos os Santos (All Saints' Bay), the capital of colonial Brazil until 1763, was originally called Sao Salvador but soon was known simply as Bahia. The district around formed the Captaincy of Bahia, but the 'kingdom' to which Andrada refers was presumably what he later terms (inaccurately) 'the kingdom of Brazil' (f.30), hence he is supplying both names for its capital. Bahia and the two towns in Peru that are named, Ciudad de los Reyes and Cuzco, are indeed almost on the same latitude, approximately 13° S. But Santa Marta (which Andrada has mentioned earlier) is in Colombia, not Peru: perhaps Andrada was confused by the fact that the latitude of Santa Marta is approximately 13° N.

18.   AMERINDIAN 'KINGDOMS' Andrada gives the names of four of the Amerindian groups of coastal Brazil distinguished and so designated by the Portuguese in the later sixteenth century.   The Pitiguares/Petiguares were found on the most westward part of the coast, between Rio Grande do Norte and Rio Paraíba, in the North of the colony; the Tupinambas and Tupinanaquins/Tupiniquins (perhaps same people under different names) further South, from Bahia towards Rio de Janeiro; and the Tamoyos around Cabo Frio and Rio de Janeiro (Varnhagen 1959, 1:28; Lussagnet 1953, 18,299).   The 'coast of Cananea' (modern Cananéia) lies between the Santo Amaro and São Francisco rivers, a little to the South of the Tropic of Capricorn.

CHAPTER 3

[The French defeated in Brazil 1559 - Portuguese successes in Malaya 1587 - the Lutherites
pass and repass Magellan Strait - the English
on the African coast - seizure of Arguin 1567
- rebel Portuguese attack the Cape Verde
Islands 1580]

[The French defeated in Brazil]

It should be noted that, on the site where
there has now been established Sebastian City
(**ciudad Sebastiana**), there used to be a strong
fortress, which was garrisoned with 1,800 men,
French Lutherites, under Monsieur de Vide Galã
[Villegaignon], **/f.6v/** supreme field marshal of
the King of France (whose field marshal was
nephew to a Monsieur who was a Knight of the
Order of Rhodes). And from his hands, in the
year 1559, Your Majesty's aunt, the Lady Queen
D. Catalina of sainted memory, won it, together
with much heavy artillery and munitions.[1] And
together with it she gained the Island of La
Palma. This was to the great credit of the
Portuguese, the Captain General of the Sea being then Bartolome de Vasconcelos, a religious
of the Order of Avis.[2]

1. CIUDAD SEBASTIANA AND THE FRENCH   Nicolas Durand de Villegaignon (1510-1571), after commanding French forces in the Mediterranean and Scotland, in 1555 established a French settlement in Brazil, in Guanabara Bay, better known as Rio de Janeiro. Villegaignon's ancestry is uncertain but he was alleged to be the nephew of the forty-third Grand Master of the Order of St John of Jerusalem (i.e. the Knights of Rhodes, later of Malta), and he himself became a knight of the same order (Heulhard 1897, 2; **Dictionnaire Biographique Française**). The blood-relationship with the Grand Master seems to be what Andrada is referring to in a garbled clause. The major French base in Brazil was captured in March 1560 (not 1559), during the regency of Queen Catarina (widow of King João III, whose sister was the mother of King Philip - hence 'Your Majesty's aunt').   The Portuguese were led by Governor Mem de Sá and Bartolomeu de Vasconcelos, the latter having commanded the fleet sent from Portugal to evict the French. The Portuguese settlement founded in the bay in 1567 by Mem de Sá was named 'São Sebastião do Rio de Janeiro', in honour of the child-king Sebastião (Julien 1948, 188-217; Varnhagen 1959, 1:304-6,325; Serrão 1980, 3:135-6). Andrada refers to the 1560 episode again (f.36-36v).

2. LA PALMA Andrada later refers to a 1553 French attack on La Palma Island in the Spanish Canaries (f.41v). Of course this does not fit the reference, yet I cannot trace any other relevant activity involving this or any other La Palma Island during the relevant period. The phrase 'to the great credit of the Portuguese' probably refers back to the conquest in Brazil.

A Portuguese ocean vessel **(nau)** of the mid
sixteenth century

[Recent successes in Malaya]

In the year 1587, in Your Majesty's East
Indies, D. Pablo de Lima, a Portuguese knight,
destroyed and razed the stronghold of the
Emperor of Dachen, [a state] in the imperial
island of Tapobrana [Sumatra]. For at the same
time that the French were equipping in order to
settle the Island of St Helena, a city was
being settled and fortified in the strait of
Cabo de Sabão, /f.7/ on the fringes of the
kingdom of Sion [Siam], a kingdom that troubles
the sea-route to China. And at this place he
seized, by war and naval battle, many galleys
and smaller ships, and on land in the interior
he killed more than 30,000 men, Moors and
Turks, taking from them more than 30,000
arquebuses and 5-6,000 pieces of heavy
artillery, and he fired their forts, and razed
the city to its foundation.³ All the mischief
which the Lutherites have practised in the
Western Ocean for so many years past, the Moors
in East India have joined in, with the [mutual]
intent of appropriating the ocean for themselves, in opposition to Your Majesty, by settling and fortifying the two most threatening
and important of the ocean ports, these being
the Island /f.7v/ of St Helena in the West and
Cabo de Sabão in the East.⁴

3. CABO DE SABÃO 'Sabão' (Sabang), a locality to the West of Singapore, perhaps to be identified with Kundur Island (Pires 1944, 150), gave its name to a passage between Sumatra and off-shore islands at the southern end of the Malacca Strait (for references to 'Estreito de Sabão' in sixteenth-century sources, see Bourdon/Albuquerque 1977, 156). Hence 'Cape Sabão' indicates the tip of the Malay Peninsula. 'Tapobrana' should be Taprobana, from Taprobane, the Graeco-Roman name for Ceylon, which in the sixteenth century was mis-applied to Sumatra. In 1587, the Portuguese base in the peninsula, at Malacca, was under attack from the ruler of the neighbouring Islamic polity of Johore (Jor). D. Paulo de Lima Pereira commanded a Portuguese expedition which relieved Malacca and captured, sacked and razed the town of Jor (Johor Lama). The Portuguese claimed to have killed 3,000 of the enemy and to have seized 800 bronze cannon, 1,500 muskets and more than 1,200 vessels of various sizes (Couto 1903, caps. xxiv,xxx, pp.108,134; Macgregor 1955, 88-112) - Andrada exaggerates the numbers. He wrongly thinks the stronghold attacked was in 'Dachen', that is, in the Islamic polity of Aceh in northern Sumatra, on the opposite side of the Malacca Strait, which had frequently in the past challenged the Portuguese and attacked Malacca, but in fact was not involved in the 1587 war - Andrada's geography is confused. (The form 'Dachen' occurs in an account of the 'São Paulo' shipwreck, an episode in which Andrada gives the impression that he was involved, but not in the account published contemporaneously which he may have read: Álvares 1948, 35, 'Dachẽes'.) Andrada mentions Siam because this kingdom had exercised nominal suzerainty over part of the Malay Peninsula in earlier centuries. But under Islamic influence, Malacca had broken free from Siam shortly before the Portuguese arrived in South-East Asia (Pires 1944, 253). Siamese trade with China to some extent competed with Portuguese trade to China via Malacca, but probably the sea-route to China was 'troubled', not by Siamese state action, but by Siamese, Indo-Chinese and Japanese pirates. Andrada's view of the geo-political situation in South-East Asia was not original: a Portuguese attack on Aceh, to synchronise with a Spanish attack on Siam from the Philippines, was proposed by the bishop of Malacca in 1584. Andrada may have been influenced in referring to this region by his having read a work of 1585, Jorge de Lemos' **Hystoria dos cercos que os Achems e Jáos puzeram á fortaleza de Malaca** ('History of the sieges of Malacca by the Achems and Javanese'). This work had pointed out the dangers if the Islamic polities of the region, possibly with Turkish help, blocked the Malacca Strait (Boxer 1985, reprinting Boxer 1969a, 422-3, and Boxer 1969b, 119,125,128). The hero named by Andrada, D. Paulo de Lima, came to be remembered principally in connection with the 1589 shipwreck of the 'São Thomé' on the coast of eastern Africa and the subsequent epic northwards march of the survivors, during which D. Paulo died (Macgregor 1955, 118-120; Boxer 1959, 51-104). This episode cannot have been known in Iberia until 1591 or 1592, and Andrada's failure to refer to it may be significant in respect of the dating of the composition of his tract.

4. LUTHERITES AND MOORS The notion that the 'Lutherites' were acting in alliance with Islamic polities against the Catholic powers and their imperial possessions in the East was a constant Iberian suspicion in the later sixteenth century. It had been given substance by the Franco-Turkish alliance in the Mediterranean in the 1530s (Julien 1948, 55). A contemporary of Andrada in Brazil, the distinguished Jesuit, Manuel de Nóbrega, claimed in 1560 that "the

[The pirates, defeated further North, threaten the Pacific via Magellan Strait]

It results from all this that the Lutherites, having been rooted out from Florida, and from Rio Parayba and Rio de Janeiro[5], cross the equinoctial zone and go down Brazil to Rio de los Patos and the island of Santa Catalina, which is next to Río de la Plata and the kingdom of the Carijos, robbing the entire coast and the shipping of Cabo Frio, Biriquioca and San Vicente.[6] They threaten to assault Las Charcas del Peru, a route to which begins in this port, via Rio Grande, a fresh-water river, which is navigable into the interior, more than 200 leagues [on].[7] And water can be procured there from its watering-places, and also victuals, for the passage of Magellan Strait, and in order to sail into the Ocean of Peru on the coast opposite to Brazil.[8] They can return /f.8/ by the same strait and repair their ships in the above-mentioned ports. And whoever says that they take another route, by the northern parts, by Bacallaos [Newfoundland] or Tierra del Labrador and the Cortes Reales, does not know the globe or the dimensions established by cosmographers, nor has he sailed there; and I will demonstrate this any time I am asked to do so.[9]

King of France was allied with the Turk, promising him the conquest of India and the Portuguese ships that come from there" (Leite 1955, 369).

5.   FLORIDA AND PARAIBA French settlements were destroyed in Florida and on the Rio de Janeiro in 1565-7, and the Portuguese in the mid-1580s conducted a successful campaign on Rio Paraíba, in northern Brazil, against an Amerindian group that had remained loyal to the French (Julien 1948, 219; Varnhagen 1959, 381-7).

6.   BRAZILIAN LOCALITIES Cabo Frio is near Rio de Janeiro, the other localities mentioned are on the southern coast of modern Brazil. São Vicente (modern Santos, 23° 57' S) was an early Portuguese settlement; 'Biriquioca' (Brikioca, Britioga, Buriquioca, etc, in contemporary sources, see Cardim 1978, 244-5, modern Bertioga) is a locality near São Vicente where in the 1550s a Portuguese fort was sited (for a detailed and colourful first-hand description of the district by Sir Richard Burton, see Staden 1874, iii-xxv). In the sixteenth century São Vicente was the southernmost point of effective Portuguese administration in Brazil, and the coast to the South was claimed by Spain - hence early toponyms are in Spanish (López de Velasco 1971, 279,284). Santa Catarina Island (27° 40' S) is 'next' (or 'near') River Plate (cf.p.31v) only in the sense later explained by Andrada, that it was often the final stopping-off point for ships from Europe heading for the river, 1,200 km to the South. For the 'kingdom of the Carijos', see note 6 to Chapter 11. The name 'Río de los Patos' ('River of Ducks'), although often applied by contemporary map-makers to a river well South of Santa Catarina Island (Dominguez 1891, xxvi), was stated in the 1580s to refer to a river, **'muito grande'**, emerging opposite the island, therefore probably not the tiny Rio Mass(i)ambu (Soares de Souza 1851, 103; Lussagnet 1953, 320, n.2; Laguarda Trías 1972). Associated, apparently, with Río de los Patos was Puerto de los Patos. A rutter probably supplied by Lopes Vas c.1580, as translated and printed by Hakluyt in 1589, stated, regarding "the river of Patus", that "the mouth doth shut with an Island, called S.Katherins"; while the revised version of the rutter printed by Hakluyt in 1600 omitted the river but stated that "hard by even with this island is Porto de Patos" (Hakluyt 1589, 803; Hakluyt 1598, 3:723). According to a Spanish source, "Puerto de Patos is the same as Puerto de Santa Catalina, or is near it, to the South, so that they are considered more or less the same" (López de Velasco 1971, 284). Later in the same sentence (the next sentence in the translation), Andrada's reference to 'this port' may indicate 'Rio de los Patos and the island of Santa Catalina', alias Puerto de los Patos.

7.   LAS CHARCAS AND RIO GRANDE Las Charcas del Peru, a Spanish administrative unit, established in 1559 and governed from La Plata (Sucre in modern Bolivia), covered the whole vast inland territory between the estuary of the River Plate on the South-East and the eastern slopes of the Andes as far North as Peru (López de Velasco 1971, 250; Haring 1947, 92-93). Las Charcas provided an overland route between the South Atlantic and Peru almost always preferred to the dangerous sea-passage through Magellan Strait. As a Spaniard reported in 1590, "from this harbour [of Buenos Aires] all kinde of Spanish and Portugall commodities are caried to this citie of Potossi in carts and on horses: for it is but 10. or 12. dayes journey, and the countrey is very plaine for carts to

[The English on the African coast between Morocco and Senegal, and a seizure of Arguin]

I must warn that any delay in this matter may do much harm, and the brief time in hand must be usefully employed. Note that when one hundred and more ships leave England several times in one year, and we do not know where they disappear to, the explanation is that when they leave England they make for all the [Atlantic] coast of Spain, the Canary Islands, Madeira, Larache del Estrecho, and Cabo de Aguer. And they supply weapons to the Africans, until they reach the Tropic of Cancer and the coast of Arguin, and enter **/f.8v/** the aforementioned port of the Ialopho.[10] This port is at the forefront of, and could be the protection for, the Ocean of the Spanish Indies, the Eastern Ocean of Ethiopia, the Western Ocean of Brazil, and Magellan Strait. And among the more important strongpoints in Your Majesty's possession, for the defence of your crown, it could be the major one. In the year 1567, the Lutherites, who had reassembled themselves in the port of the Ialopho, left to assault the ancient fort of Arguin, its neighbour, and they seized it and took all its artillery.[11]

travaile" (Hakluyt 1598, 3:563). The reference to Las Charcas and Rio Grande is part of a sentence occupying 38 lines in Andrada's text, and the sequence of thought is difficult to follow. Andrada is arguing that the enemy might assault Peru by an overland route from the East, through Las Charcas, 'this port providing access by Rio Grande'. Assuming that 'this port' is 'Puerto de los Patos' (see previous note), then 'providing access by Rio Grande' almost certainly means that the overland route begins on the coast of southern Brazil, up a large river near Santa Catarina Island. Andrada's locating of Las Charcas at '200 leagues from this river' is a fair estimate for an interior territory some 1,000-1,200 km inland. For further discussion of 'Rio Grande', see note 5 to Chapter 11.

8. 'THERE' 'There' refers to the port under discussion, either Santa Catarina Island or Puerto de los Patos, which provides a jumping-off point for Magellan Strait.

9. NORTHWEST PASSAGE This refers to attempts to discover a presumed 'Northwest Passage' around the American continent, balancing the southern passage via Magellan Strait. It is unclear whether Andrada's 'other route' means the use of the Northwest Passage to effect an entry to the Pacific, or otherwise an exit from it. But probably Andrada has especially in mind Drake's 1579 voyage up the Pacific coast of America as far North as California (or perhaps further), which was generally presumed to have been an abortive search for such an exit (Quinn 1977, 378). By Andrada's day it was assumed that the eastern entry to any Northwest Passage would lie to the North of the St Lawrence, that is, beyond Newfoundland ('Bacallaos', so-called after the **bacalhau** or stockfish obtained there) and Labrador. The coast North of Newfoundland was explored c.1500 by Portuguese seamen, João Fernandes Labrador and the brothers Corte Real (ibid., 112,121-4) - hence the name Andrada gives to this region. In respect of Drake's intentions, Andrada probably knew that Spanish sources stated (wrongly) that Drake had claimed that "he was bound to return by the Estrecho de Bacallaos [Newfoundland Strait]' which he had come to discover" (Quinn 1979, 1:463).

10. LARACHE - ARGUIN 'Larache del Estreito' and 'Cabo de Aguer' are Larache and Cape Guir (near Agadir) in Morocco. The 'coast of Arguin' is the Saharan coast around Arguin (in Portuguese, Arguim) Island, at 20° 35' N, in Andrada's day the site of a Portuguese fort.

11. ARGUIN CAPTURED This 1567 capture of the Portuguese fort at Arguin ('ancient' because built in the 1450s), carried out by 'Lutherites', who would most likely be French, is not mentioned in a detailed history of Arguin (Monod 1983). However, it was reported in Spain in 1566 that three French ships had attacked the fort and taken away 80 'Moors' and some bronze guns (Archivo General de Indias, Seville, Patronato leg.265, ramo 5, ff.4,7v,8). Although these French ships appear to have reached Arguin from the North, and not from the Jolof port, this is probably the episode to which Andrada is referring. His interest in Arguin may have been aroused by two other events. At an uncertain date, perhaps in the 1560s, a Portuguese renegade who had earlier assisted Spanish interlopers from the Canary Islands to trade in Guinea in defiance of the Portuguese, and who was imprisoned at Arguin, led an uprising which for a time took over the fort and

[Portuguese rebels attack the Cape Verde Islands]

In the year 1580, a Portuguese, a native of the Island of Madeira called Cabeças, sailed from the Terceras [Azores] under the orders of the tyrant Manoel de Silva, brother of the pirate Antonio de Silva - who married and lives in La Rochelle -, and he invaded the island of Santiago de Cabo Verde, which is ancient, Catholic, and renowned. He sacked and ruined it, burning it down, this being brought about by /f.9/ a cleric or clerics, and by laymen who at that time by sea and land bargained with the Lutherites, a crime which until now has not been punished, nor has it been ascertained who they were, as was done in the case of those from Tercera.[12] Patently [nothing has been done], for otherwise these seizures of ships and goods, and many seizures like them along the whole coast of Guinea, would not have occurred, nor in this region would the tunny-fishery grounds (**almandravas**) of Arguin have been lost to Your Majesty over these many years.[13]

disposed of the artillery - or so he later claimed (Teixeira da Mota 1980, 234-5). Again, in 1582, a Franco-Portuguese force supporting D.António attempted to seize the fort (it was eventually captured by French Huguenots in 1595) (Frias 1955, 200-204; Serrão 1979, 4:30-1; Monod 1983, 32-9). Andrada makes only one further reference to 'Your Majesty's fortress, the castle of Arguin' (f.42v). Although Andrada does not lay great weight on the importance of Arguin, in 1580 it was suggested to King Philip that the Spaniards should seize the fort and evict the Portuguese, while a later anonymous Lisbon petition addressed to the king argued at length against a proposal to abandon the fort (probably the proposal made in 1586, Brásio 1964, 133-5), partly because of its value in deterring foreign pirates (Fernandes Asis 1943, items 1043-4; Monod 1983, 25-8).

12. SANTIAGO ATTACKED Manuel da Silva Coutinho, created conde de Torres Vedras and governor of Terceira Island in the Azores, and the Cabeças, a family of New Christian merchants settled in La Rochelle, were supporters of D.António, the pretender to the Portuguese throne, who, after being driven out of Portugal by Philip II of Spain, had his main base in Terceira. António da Silva 'the pirate' is mentioned again (f.26). In 1582-3 (not 1580), Manuel da Silva organised a Franco-Antonine attack on Santiago Island in the Cape Verdes which did damage, as Andrada states, but was ultimately unsuccessful. The attack was led by Manuel Serradas, a New Christian and a native of Madeira, but as far as is known neither Baltezar Cabeças nor Gaspar Barbosa Cabeças was involved: Andrada appears to have confused the Cabeças with Serradas (Frias 1955, 187; Serrão 1959, 126,147). To support his cause, in 1582 King Philip had sent reinforcements to Santiago, but there was some sentiment for D.António among the Portuguese of the islands and the Guinea coast. An English expedition visiting Sierra Leone in 1582 was informed by the Portuguese traders there about the ambivalence of the islanders, and the Bishop at Santiago was thought by the 1583 attackers to have been sympathetic to their cause - D. António certainly had clerical supporters in his entourage (CSP Foreign 1583, 178-9; Frias 1955, 236-9; Madox 1976, 179; Serrão 1979, 4:28-9,228-9). Since Andrada had himself served in a clerical post in the islans up to 1578, his references to 'a cleric or clerics' probably referred to some of his former colleagues. They may have included Bishop Leitão, who still held the see in 1583, and whom Andrada may have been responsible for his retirement from his post and the islands. In 1583, after the forces of King Philip had conquered those islands in the Azores that had supported D.António, the Antonine governor of Terceira and his lieutenants were executed (Serrão 1979, 4:32).

13. ARGUIN FISHERIES The Saharan coast provided rich off-shore fishing for Iberian fishermen from at least the fourteenth century - in the sixteenth century the Portuguese crown, which licenced fishing in various parts, issued licences for fishing around Arguin (Serrão 1979, 4:367: Monod 1983, 49). The petition calling for the retention of Arguin (note 10 above) emphasised the importance of the fishing there (Monod 1983, 26). Many sixteenth-century English and French accounts document attacks on Portuguese and Spanish fishing vessels off the Saharan coast, and in the later decades of the century French fishermen began to fish the Arguin banks extensively (Roncière 1923, 4:92,98).

CHAPTER 4

[Drake's voyage into the Pacific 1577-1580 -
the necessary fortification of Bezeguiche and
the religious and commercial advantages - to be
matched by the seizure of Aden - the Lord of
the World and the clergy reformed]

[Drake reaches the Pacific 1578 - but decides
against fortified settlement, allegedly warned
by French failure in Florida]

To express the whole truth regarding these
events, we can affirm that the Lutherites range
powerfully over the sea because they are very
skilled /f.9v/ in the art of navigation. They
take the latitudes of all kingdoms, provinces,
and localities very exactly, and they navigate
in a sure manner, without sustaining losses
comparable to ours.[1] With the art of mathemat-
tics, Francis Drake became such a perfect
navigator and corsair that in the years 1576
and 1577, when I was serving Your Majesty in
the Cape Verde Islands, and when we fought with
him and his fleet and drove them away from the
land, he sailed off with seven galleons to rob
and destroy Spanish shipping over almost the
whole sea as far as Magellan Strait, which he
passed through.   Then in the South Sea
[Pacific], he stole many talents of gold,
because he found the ships of the Ocean Sea of
the South unprepared for war and without
artillery.[2] That was the first voyage which he
made after he became a pirate.[3] /f.10/

1. LUTHERITE NAVIGATION   Andrada is unfair to his own side.   In fact, the non-Iberians not only were slow to follow up the Iberian out-thrusts overseas but depended for long on Iberian navigational aids.   By 1590, however, there was little to choose between the various West-European nations in high-seas skills: Andrada is over-impressed by the recent (admittedly dramatic) English advances and challenges, and over-depressed by recent Iberian losses.

2. DRAKE'S VOYAGE TO THE PACIFIC   Andrada is particularly impressed by Drake's seamanship in gaining the Pacific in 1578.   Drake sailed through the Cape Verde Islands in January-February 1578, and en route captured a Portuguese vessel, bringing his fleet up to seven ships, as Andrada correctly states.   But the claim that Drake was fought and driven off is exaggerated: according to the English, "our ships ... sayled by the Island of S.Iago, but farre inough from the danger of the inhabitaunts, who shot and discharged at us three pieces, but they all fell short of us and did us no harme" (Hakluyt 1589, unnumbered page after 643). 'Your Majesty' is a slip: Andrada served the King of Portugal, but Philip was not king of Portugal until 1580.

3. DRAKE'S CAREER   Andrada regards the circumnavigation of 1577-1580 as Drake's 'first voyage after he became a pirate'.   Perhaps he did not know of Drake's participation in the 1572 joint French-English attack on Nombre de Dios (but see note 3 to Chapter 15).   At an earlier date, Drake had played only a minor role in the 1567-8 Hawkins expedition to Guinea and America which had culminated in a Spanish success at San Juan de Ulúa.   (It is curious that, given Andrada's personal knowledge of Guinea in the 1570s, he never names Hawkins or specifies the English Guinea voyages of the 1560s.)

In the same year he took with him in his fleet much artillery and many noblemen, with the intention of establishing himself in remote provinces. However he did not do this, because he changed his mind after he saw the ships laden with gold. He returned via the same strait and headed to northern parts, after having dared to sail into the second hemisphere. He was motivated by greed, and he scoffed at Joan Ribao [Jean Ribault], the famous corsair, who had [once] fortified himself in Florida, which is on the coast of the kingdom of Mexico and is a sterile and swampy country, because Ribao was defeated there by the good captain Pero Melendez, general of Your Majesty's galleons in the **Carrera de Indias**, who destroyed him in the year 1569.[4]

4. DRAKE'S AIMS Although it has been argued that "the ulterior aim [of Drake's 1577-1580 voyage] was undoubtedly colonization, looking in the first place to the Plate estuary, the strait, Arauco, and in the long run to Peru" (Andrews 1982, 63), it is very unlikely that during the voyage Drake ever considered 'establishing himself in remote provinces'. But since 1570 the Spaniards had feared an English seizure of Magellan Strait, and a project to "pass the Strait and establish settlement" became known to them (Taylor 1935, 87; Andrews 1981, 9; Andrews 1982, 62) - so Andrada's inference was not absurd. Because Andrada wants to make the point that Drake was more interested in gold than in settlement, he interpolates that Drake 'scoffed' at Jean Ribault - an individual with whom Drake had in fact no known personal connection. Ribault established in 1562 a French settlement in Florida that was finally destroyed in 1565 (not 1569) by the Spanish general Pedro Menéndez de Avilés, previously commander of trans-Atlantic fleets on several occasions (Fernández Duro 1896, 2: passim; Julien 1948, 228-48; Chaunu 1955, 3: passim). Note that Andrada implies that Drake returned by Magellan Strait and therefore does not credit him with circumnavigation. English official circles kept the circumnavigation secret until 1589, and although Spanish official circles knew about it, they did not trumpet it - hence some incredulity persisted elsewhere throughout the 1580s (Wallis 1984, 133-141). For instance, the French cosmographer, André Thevet, when discussing the Pacific in his unpublished writings of c.1590, mentions Drake only in relation to the American coast. However, Andrada at a later point (f.31v) notes that from Magellan Strait 'the Lutherites plan and make their navigations to the rivers and ports of the Orient', a reference that implies circumnavigation and which more probably points to Drake than to his successor in circumnavigation, Cavendish, whom Andrada never names.

Profile of part of the passage through Magellan
Strait, drawn by Sarmiento de Gamboa, 1583 (ff.22v-23)

[The importance of the Jolof port as a refuge long known - how to form a fortified settlement there]

And in order that the Lutherites may now lose the desire they have to settle and live in Your Majesty's kingdoms and discoveries, **/f.10v/** it is very important that this port and watering-place of the Ialophos be fortified and won over. And also because it is capable of supporting and victualling fleets of Your Majesty which make port there. On account of its capacity as a port, King D.Manuel, King of Portugal, gave permission to his generalissimo, Alfonso de Alburquerque, who was admiral of the fleet bound for the East Indies, that in case - despite keeping to the nautical ordnance and leaving Lisbon in the month of March - he could not cross the Equator by St John's Day [24 June], then in order not to waste the voyage he could refit there; and this he did, being the excellent pilot he was.[5] Since then for more than seventy years up to the present day, Portuguese seamen have engaged in trade with this Ialopho king. He has always wanted his land to be fortified and settled by Christians.[6] For since the inhabitants **/f.11/** of the Cape Verde Islands originate themselves from that kingdom, [the two sets of people] have a liking for each other, are neighbourly, and get on very well together.[7]

5. ALBURQUERQUE AND BEZEGUICHE Afonso de Albuquerque, the most famous governor of the Portuguese 'Estado da Índia' (1509-1515), commanded a section of the 1503 India fleet (Serrão 1980, 3:110). The fleet left on 6 April, and it followed King Manuel's instructions by re-assembling and watering at 'Biziguiche', according to Baião 1914, 19-20; but Baião does not mention the conditions cited by Andrada. Similarly the 1507 fleet was instructed to water either at the Cape Verde Islands or on the 'coast of Bezegiche' (Albuquerque and Madeira Santos, 1988, p.167). In fact, although India fleets at first used Bezeguiche (Teixeira da Mota 1968b; Rau 1972, 14-16), by 1510 they were instructed not to water either at the Cape Verdes or at Bezeguiche "where previously all the fleets went, lest the voyage be lost because of the delay" (Boxer 1972 in Boxer 1984, 34). In 1510 and 1512 the islanders, in petitions, pointed out that Albuquerque on a return voyage, and others too, had been saved from disaster by using the islands as a port of refuge (Brásio 1963, pp.39,58). Perhaps reference to Albuquerque in arguments about ports of refuge was something Andrada had picked up when on the Cape Verde Islands. As governor, Albuquerque carried through a strategic plan, partly conceived in Lisbon, for controlling the Indian Ocean by setting up Portuguese bases at key-points such as Ormuz and Malacca - a strategy of naval key-points now advocated by Andrada.

6. SEVENTY YEARS The period from Albuquerque's 1503 departure for the East up to c.1590, when Andrada was writing, was almost ninety years, not a mere seventy years. In further correction, the Portuguese had visited the Cape Verde area since the mid 1440s; and India fleets had called there in the 1500s (as Vasco da Gama also did on his 1498 return voyage). Like almost all African rulers, those in Senegal welcomed European trade, and as early as the 1450s there was trade with 'Budumel' (Cadamosto 1966, 49). By the 1590s, a small population of Portuguese (some however refugee Jews and New Christians) lived in towns on the 'Little Coast' of Senegal, South of Cape Verde, with the permission of the ruling groups (Donelha 1977, 283,n.212; Almada 1984, chap.2/8-9; Moraes 1972, 38-9). But there is no evidence that the 'Jolof king' welcomed or would have tolerated extensive white settlement, or that he ever asked for a Portuguese fort. For the ambivalent attitude to European forts of sixteenth-century African ruling groups elsewhere in Guinea, see Hair 1988.

7. ORIGINS OF THE CAPE VERDE ISLANDERS This sentence may be garbled in the original. That the inhabitants of the Cape Verde Islands originated from the African mainland - which is what it seems to be saying - is a curious notion. The islands were uninhabited before the Portuguese discovered and settled them. But by Andrada's day the white population had been joined by larger numbers of black slaves, and there were many families of mixed extraction. (Thus, André Álvares de Almada, the most distinguished islander of the later sixteenth century and author of a famous description of the Guinea coast, was denied an honour because his maternal grandmother was a black woman.) Nevertheless the Portuguese-speaking freemen on the islands claimed that they originated from Portugal, not Africa; and the black slaves, who had of course no say in affairs there, in fact came from many parts of the nearer African coast and not merely from the 'Jolof' kingdom opposite.

If this port were fortified, together with the
port of Sierra Leona - as will be suggested
below - the revenue Your Majesty obtains from
Guinea would increase by more than 50 **cuentos**
(millions), and what is now taken by the Lutherites would, more happily, come to Spain. As
for the fortification of this port, it could be
done quite easily, because Santiago Island has
many adventurous and enterprising people, all
of them mariners, who long to expel the Lutherites from the district.[8] It should be noted
that the fortification must be built in the
specific locality which I shall indicate. At
the inlet of this bay is a rocky islet on
which, if Your Majesty were to construct a
strongpoint manned by a garrison, it would then
be impossible for any enemy to enter the port
without **/f.11v/** being sent to the bottom by
[fire from] those on the islet. Equally,
enemies would be sunk [by fire] from the point
of the mainland, which would form part of the
city which Your Majesty would command to be
established and built on that site. This city
would be impregnable there, because on the sea
side it is strong, and on the inner side the
bay continues, which makes it stronger. On the
North side, the island is so secure and so en-
closed that no ship could assault the entrance,
if perchance any had this intention, on account
of the sharp rocks.[9]

8.   FORBIDDEN FOREIGNERS It was tactful to tell the king that the inhabitants of the Cape Verde Islands were hostile to foreigners. André Álvares de Almada, who was writing at the same time as Andrada, implied much the same. But he also drew attention to a small number of Portuguese living on the coast, as adventurers (**'lançados'**, literally 'runaways'), who cooperated disloyally with foreign traders (Almada 1984, chaps.2/6,9/4 - on the **lançados**, see Boulègue 1989). Even this was less than the truth. While no doubt many elements on the islands were loyal to King Philip and patriotically xenophobic, the trading community had long resented the Portuguese crown's commercial system which favoured the metropolis at the expense of the imperial periphery, and had reacted against crown monopoly by trading secretly, and even at times openly, on the mainland coast with the forbidden foreigners. Moreover, Portuguese vessels, some from the Cape Verde Islands, had a long tradition of trading illegally with the Spanish Indies, so their owners must have had post-1580 reservations about the union of the two crowns. Conversely, the Spaniards of the Canary Islands traded illegally with Guinea - for Portuguese attempts to stop this trade, see Teixeira da Mota 1980. Hence, to the traders of the Cape Verde Islands the Spaniards were almost as much rival foreigners as the Lutherites. Andrada, who had lived in the islands during the 1570s, must have known all this.

9.   GORÉE ISLAND The island that Andrada suggests the Portuguese should fortify is Gorée Island. Since a contemporary living in the Cape Verde Islands made a similar suggestion c.1594, this was perhaps an idea common among the Portuguese in Guinea (Almada 1984, chap.2/7). But the island was only fortified after the Dutch acquired it in the 1620s (and gave it the name that became 'Gorée'). The site of the proposed 'city' appears to be within the area now occupied by the actual city of Dakar (population one million), capital of modern Senegal, a settlement developed only after 1850. Indeed, Andrada's location between the sea and an inner bay (the site of the present-day port) fits the precise area where modern development began (Church 1980, 205-7). The details of the fortification are repeated in ff.42v-43, which enlarges as follows. 'With security provided by the fortification of the islet and the city on the mainland, there would be no [enemy] fleet which could enter the port, because all ships seeking an entry would have to pass under the guns of either the city or the islet, and could be sent to the bottom'. Andrada also goes into more details about the settlers (f.43-43v). In 1592 Abreu de Brito called for the fortification of "all the ports there are from Arguin Fort and in all Jalofo and skirting Sierra Leone", or at least "all suitable ports" along this coast, but was no more specific (Abreu de Brito 1931, 3,83).

[Missionary advantages of this settlement]

By fortifying this port, Your Majesty would gain its inhabitants as friends and vassals, and [also] their souls, through the baptism you would command to be preached to them, in order that they might accept the Gospel. For the entire Kingdom of Ialopho, although visited by Mohammedans, consists of heathen who have no Koran or mosques, and truly only /f.12/ the king is a Moor, together with some of his nobles who join him to make their prayers.[10] Nevertheless they ask for [spiritual] bread, yet as long as a fortification is lacking there is no one to distribute to them the word of God. Because of the delay in anyone going to preach to them, African **cacizes** (Islamic teachers) visit there, to corrupt them with statements about their own false sect, whereas if there were religious from here, who were supported by this fortress and who instructed them in the faith, I believe that they would all be baptized and converted.

10. ISLAM IN SENEGAL Sixteenth and seventeenth century sources testify to the gradual conversion of the Wolof to Islam, but Andrada here exaggerates the limited progress by his day. See note 4 to Chapter 2.

'The king of the Jalopho', an imaginary portrait, 1575 (ff.2v,11v,44)

[Commercial advantages from trade via the Sahara with North Africa]

Once Your Majesty has the friendship of the Ialopho King - for he is bound to become a friend - he would be very useful to Your Majesty, on account of the trade and the contracts [that would follow] throughout Ethiopia and its sea. For this king is lord over all of the interior of Africa to the border of Morocco, and in the other direction, towards the East, lord to the border of the kingdom of Tremecen [Tlemcen].[11] /f.12v/ By the sea-coast, he is lord of the Berbeçin king and the famous Rio Çanaga [Senegal] which separates to the North the [hills called] Montes Claros, and [to the South] the kingdom of Fulo Barbaro and the kingdom of great Tumbucutum [Timbuktu] of Egypt. This is the famous city which has the trade of the Schyo in the South, in the interior of Africa, in lands overflowing with gold, ivory, ambergris, herds of elephants and lions, and many unicorns. It is a healthy land which enjoys the influence of a benevolent heaven, being [on] the Tropic of Cancer in the latitude of Persia, Mesopotamia, and Mexico.[12] From this fortress of the Ialopho, Your Majesty will be able to pursue trade with all these heathen kings, in order that, acting with them, the treasures conveyed from Tumbucutum to Argel [Algiers] for the Grand Turk can be obstructed, and [instead] used to ransom and save thousands of Christian captives from Morocco, /f.13/ Fez and Argel, captives who escape overland by fleeing in the caravans of the Berbers.[13]

11. IALOPHO EXTENT Andrada grossly exaggerates the extent of the domain of the ruler of Kayor, and even that of the 'Grand Jolof' in the interior, who at one time had had some control over the coastal territories but who had lost this control in the course of the sixteenth century. The various polities of the Wolof, however delimited at the time that Andrada was writing, did border the Senegal River on the North, but stopped at the interior territories of the Fula people ('the kingdom of the Fulo Barbaro' - see note 13 below) on the North East. Wolof rule, although not Kayor rule, did extend as far down the coast as River Sine ('Berbeçin'). But Morocco and Tlemcen (in modern Algeria) to the North, and Timbuktu to the East (if that is what Andrada is implying), were far beyond Wolof rule and influence (Boulègue 1987, p.12, map). The 'Montes Claros' were hills between Morocco and Senegal which kept appearing on early maps and in early descriptions of Africa, but which were either misplacings of the Atlas Mountains or entirely imaginary.

12. TUMBUCUTUM Timbuktu, situated on the River Niger where it passes closest to the Sahara Desert (but nowhere near 'Egypt'), after a distinguished history in earlier centuries as a trading, administrative and intellectual centre, in the later sixteenth century was in decline (Saad 1983). It first became known to Europeans when an account of northern Africa by the North African trader known in Christendom as Leo Africanus was published in Ramusio's 1550 collection of voyages. Leo Africanus' somewhat rhapsodic description of Timbuktu influenced later European writings, and Andrada appears to have picked up echoes from secondary sources. But Portuguese attempts to reach Timbuktu in the 1560s via River Senegal were known in the Cape Verde Islands, and no doubt also influenced Andrada (Teixeira da Mota, 1970). At 16° 49' N, Timbuktu is a little further South than Mexico City but much further South than Mesopotamia and Persia.

13. SAHARAN TRADE The best-known trade between Timbuktu and North Africa was the export trade in West African gold. Andrada supposes that this trade was directed solely to Algiers, which at this date formed part of the empire of the Ottoman Turks, the main Islamic threat to Christendom. He suggests that the trade be obstructed and re-directed southwards to the Guinea coast, where the gold would be purchased by the Portuguese. In fact this re-direction had been happening since the arrival of the Portuguese in Guinea in the fifteenth century - in a famous dictum, 'the caravels replaced the caravans' (at least to some extent). Andrada complicates his argument by adding that the gold could be used to ransom the Christians who were captives in North Africa. He was no doubt thinking particularly of the survivors of the disastrous battle of Alcaçer-Quivir in 1578, when 15,000 Portuguese were captured in Morocco, only a small number of whom were subsequently ransomed. It seems, however, that he is not suggesting that the ransom should be paid to the Moslem captors in North Africa, but to those who help the Christian prisoners to escape southwards across the desert, in 'the caravans of the Berbers', and thence to the coast. (Note that **Barbaro** is here translated 'Berber', which makes sense, and may apply in 'Fulo Barbaro' above. But this assumes some confusion on Andrada's part, since the Spanish term for 'Berber' is berbero - hence **barbaro** is elsewhere translated 'savage'.) While Andrada was writing, a Moroccan army, made up partly of Portuguese captives who had submitted to Islam, was crossing the desert to attack the state of Songhay on the Niger, which it conquered in early 1591, occupying Timbuktu. By 1594

[The fortification of Bezeguiche to be matched
by the seizure of Aden, saving the Empire and
the Church, and stirring up the Spanish clergy
to become missionaries]

For the reasons I shall give, and on the evidence, I state the following. If it were settled, this port on the West would be the remedy
for Spain and the confusion of the Lutherites.
In the East, God willing, Your Majesty might
gain the city of Aden, which is located at the
entry to the Red Sea, and you would be the Lord
of the World, superior to any Caesar, Alexand-
er, Darius, Mogore [Moghul], Sophy, or Turk,
since Aden is their gateway, through the equinoctial zone, to India.[14] These [two] ports by
themselves encompass [in strategic terms] the
entire globe, and their position gives hope
that through Spain the Catholic Church may
maintain itself and be augmented by the life
and support of Your Majesty, who follows in the
footsteps of your saintly /f.13v/ Catholic
forefathers and ancestors (**padres y aguelos**),
Charles V, and King D. Manuel, Your Majesty's
grandfather of immortal memory; to the end that
a halt be called to so many evils, robberies
and heresies.[15] Your Majesty would benefit your
kingdoms and vassal states, and the Catholic
Church would grow, because there is no room for
preachers in the Colleges of Spain who do not
reflect on the purpose of the habits they wear,
their income and their profits - the purpose
[of all these things] being [for them] to
preach the Gospel, and not to hide away their
talents and thus give rise to much ridicule
from depraved Lutherites.[16]

English traders in Morocco were witnessing the arrival there of "thirty mules laden with gold", tribute from West Africa (Hakluyt 1598, 2/2:192-3; CHA 1977, 414). Presumably Andrada would have mentioned these relevant events if he had been writing any later than 1591.

14. ADEN The Portuguese recognised that Aden was the key to effective control of the Red Sea. At the beginning of the sixteenth century, the grand strategy of Albuquerque included the matching of his conquest of the Indian Ocean key-points of Ormuz and Malacca with a seizure of Aden. But he failed as regards Aden and had to be content with a short-lived occupation of Socotra, a less effective key-point (see note 1 to Chapter 12). The intention had been, not only to control the spice trade passing up the Red Sea to Egypt, but also to halt the southward expansion of the Turks, and perhaps even to threaten the Islamic holy city of Mecca, at least by a blockade that thwarted the annual pilgrimage. A second attempt to control Aden, made in the 1540s, also failed (Serrão 1980, 114,117,128). Andrada refers again to Aden (f.34v).

15. CATHOLIC FOREFATHERS The Emperor Charles V was the father of Philip II of Spain/Philip I of Portugal, and Manuel I of Portugal was Philip's maternal grandfather.

16. CALL TO MISSIONS As a former missionary in Brazil, Andrada is scornful of clerical colleagues who fail to be active evangelists, whether at home or in the mission field. In this context, as in several later contexts, 'Spain' means Iberia. In the 1580s, a Spaniard writing in Lisbon proposed the founding of royal colleges where "the tongues of the infidels in Persia, Malacca, Angola, Congo, Brazil and Peru will be taught", so that the students could go out to convert the world (Goodman 1988, 10).

At ports near 'Bezeguiche', Portuguese ships attacked by a Dutch fleet and defended by Africans in canoes, 1601

CHAPTER 5

[Knowledge of the winds and of their cosmic
determinants essential for navigation - past
navigations and conquests - need to teach
mathematics for navigation]

[The cosmic forces explained]

If, out of contrariness, Your Majesty is told
that, should this port be taken away from the
Lutherites /f.14/ they will not fail to find
another, we shall respond as follows. The
Ocean Sea is large and has, in geometrical
terms, a spherical shape and equidistant para-
llels; [one of which,] the Equator, divides the
world into two halves, as stated by Ptolemy, by
Aristotle, and by everyone else, including
myself who has sailed the ocean. It has two
tropics and two circles, and there are four
meridians, so that, on account of this fourfold
division, there actually come to be twelve
equal parts, corresponding to the twelve signs
[of the zodiac] and the planets in the sky. By
their influence these [planets] move the waters
of the sea, and govern the rise and fall of the
tides. The tides turn, and ebb and flow, as
lifted up and moved by the force of the seven
planets below the regiment of the sun, and the
sun, acting with energy, by its procreative
power regenerates the earth, sending to it
winters, summers, autumns /f.14v/ and springs.
The seasons of the globe create the motions of
the four winds, that is, the northern, southern, eastern, and western winds. These, under
the Zodiac, comprehend at their centre the
Elemental Sphere, which is the Ocean Sea, the

87

Nao ſam Paulo.

¶ Viagem & naufragio da Nao ſam ſPaulo que foy pera a Jndia o anno de mil τ quinhentos τ ſeſenta. Capitão Ruy de melo da camara Meſtre Joam luys, ſPiloto Antonio Dias.

☩

Com licença Jmpreſſo.

'The voyage and shipwreck of the "São Paulo", 1560'
(ff.19v-20,25-25v) - the woodcut not original

exhaler of the winds, which are as many as
there are degrees of longitude and latitude in
the Zone or Zodiac, which comprises, according
to the teaching of Ptolemy, 360 degrees. By
the variations of these winds and exhalations,
men navigate in either hemisphere, not when
they wish it, but only when the winds blow.
Those of us on this side [of the earth] who
sail against the wind, or those who sail
against it in the Antipodes, become lost, unless possessing [first,] considerable skill,
and [secondly,] ports where repairs can be done
and shelter had.[1]

1. COSMIC FORCES AND NAVIGATION Andrada argues that other ports will not be as useful as the 'Jolof' port, because of the prevailing winds. But he, Andrada, understands the wind-systems because he knows the cosmographical explanation of winds. He therefore enters into a rambling and unoriginal digression on the alleged relationship between the planets and other cosmic phenomena and the winds. (The moon does, after all, control the tides, and it was only beginning to be realised that the planets are vastly more distant). But this amounts to little more than saying that the winds vary in direction in different parts of the globe and at different seasons. Andrada therefore shifts the argument, by implying that only those - such as himself - who have learned about the winds and other sea-conditions in practice, by long experience at sea, can expound an effective global marine strategy.

A Portuguese vessel in the South Atlantic, 1547

[Fortifying to save the conquests made by past great navigators]

This [need for skill and suitable ports] is the conclusion I lay stress on in this paradox,[2] **/f.15/** this brief compendium on the subject of fortification, a matter essential for [the future of] the Catholic Church. It is inherent that it would suffice to fortify only the principal ports, because these would protect all the lesser ones, and the routes would be shorter and more easily navigated. The Christians would not fear to venture out to seek a livelihood and, in between [the times of] preaching the Gospel, would enrich themselves and their country, as did the immortal captain of Your Majesty, Al[f]onso de Alburquerque, and [also] D.Vasco de Gama. These distinguished themselves among men on earth by their navigations and discoveries, and their conquests subjected to Your Majesty so many empires and kingdoms, in order that Your Majesty should cultivate [these lands] like a true father of the families of our Roman Capitol, and a true father of the vineyard of the Lord **/f.15v/**.[3]

2. PARADOX The older and more correct meaning of the term 'paradox', here used by Andrada, was exactly expressed in a work of the 1550s, **Paradoxo ou sentença philosophica: contra a opinião vulgo** ("Paradox or philosophical judgement contrary to vulgar opinion"). Coincidentally or otherwise, the author of this work, Jean Bolés, was a French theologian who, after deserting from Villegaignon's settlement on Rio de Janeiro and joining the Portuguese under Mem de Sá, was later imprisoned in Brazil on a charge of heresy brought against him by the Jesuits (Sousa Viterbo 1900, 258; Julien 1948, 217-8). It is likely, therefore, that by reputation Bolés was known to Andrada.

3. IMPERIAL HEROES Andrada selects two Portuguese imperial heroes but does not name, here or elsewhere, any of the Spanish conquistadores. Albuquerque was of course neither a discoverer nor a great navigator, and neither he nor Vasco da Gama lived long enough to be a 'captain of Your Majesty', although both served the dynasty eventually represented by Philip.

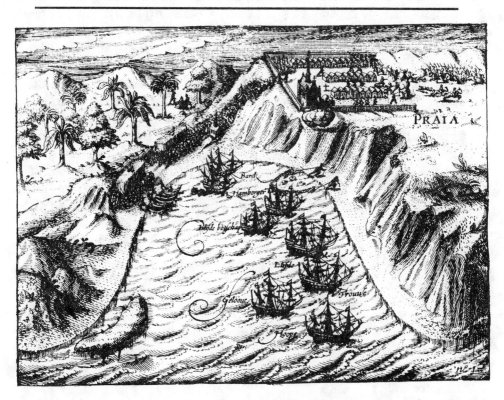

The town of Praia in the Cape Verde Islands, under attack by the Dutch, 1598 - note the church (Introduction, note 16)

[Nautical mathematics should be taught - Bezeguiche should be fortified]

[As to improving skill,] Your Majesty should order navigational-mathematics to be very seriously taught in all your cities and maritime ports.[*] For mathematics is the science of dirrection and demonstration. By it, the military man sees and picks his way, and at sea he battles for his religion, his king, and his country - and when these are [invoked] together, terror falls on our adversaries. Seeing our condition, God will favour the cause of Your Majesty, since you are the defender of His Catholic Church. To sustain its sons and the baptized peoples in the East and West, He entrusted to Your Majesty the navigation of the whole world. Hence, just as, for so many reasons, it is fitting that, with all possible secrecy, the port of Ialopho should be settled, so it is right that, after that, Your Majesty should order the fortification of Sierra Leona, the kingdom of the Zapi, which is on the same **/f.16/** mainland and coast of Guinea.

4. NAUTICAL MATHEMATICS By 'navigational mathematics' (**las Matematicas navegatorias**) Andrada means the theory and practice of calculating positions at sea, by the use of navigational instruments, astronomical tables, and maps. On mathematics as an essential aspect of contemporary nautical science, especially in the training of navigators and pilots, see Teixeira da Mota 1969, 32-36; Albuquerque 1985, 8/264.

5. ZAPI 'Zapi' or 'Sapi' was a term loosely employed by Portuguese writers on Guinea to denote the inhabitants of the coast between Cape Verga and Sierra Leone, and hence it covered a varying number of separate, but perhaps to some extent related, ethnicities and polities (Almada 1984, chap.15/6 and note on Sapes). Andrada, however, appears to limit the 'Zapi' to Sierra Leone, by which he means essentially the district of the Sierra Leone estuary.

Drake seizes a Spanish ship, the 'Cacafuego', in
the Pacific (f.9v)

CHAPTER 6

[Sierra Leone as an enemy base - a 1577 success of the Portuguese - renegade sailors - a further attack on Spain itself - marine disasters 1588 and 1590 - the need for West African ports]

[Sierra Leone described - the French defeated there]

Sierra Leona is very rich in gold, as much and more so than the whole region of Peru. This Sierra Leona stands in 6° North of the equator.[1] It has a prolific population of blacks and an abundance of everything necessary for human existence. It has gold, crystal, sugar, brazil-wood, ambergris, elephants, buffalo, lions, tigers, gazelle, deer, and a pepper called **mantibilia**, of better quality than the pepper from India. The **sierra** has enormous rivers of fresh water, in which gold is found in quantity.[2] One /**f.16v**/ of the rivers, a very famous one called Tagarin, is where the great India ships of Portugal very expeditiously take on water and all else that is necessary.[3]

1.   SIERRA LEONA 'Sierra Leona' (Portuguese **serra leõa** 'leonine range of hills') often meant to sixteenth-century Portuguese not only the Sierra Leone estuary and the land immediately around it, including the hilly peninsula to the SW which originally gave the district its name, but also a lengthy stretch of coast to the North (Hair 1966). However, Andrada's references concentrate on the estuary, which provided an ample and safe harbour for shipping, and around which, for over a century before 1590, a small number of Portuguese traders, mainly from the Cape Verde Islands, had made semi-permanent homes. The estuary actually lies at 8° 31' N. Abreu de Brito referred to the ports "skirting the Serra Lioa" (**as fraldas da serra Lioa**) (Abreu de Brito 1931,3).

2.   SIERRA LEONE ABUNDANCE This rapturous account of Sierra Leone resembles what was said, at greater length, by two contemporary writers, André Álvares de Almada and André Donelha, both traders of the Cape Verde Islands (Almada 1988, chap.19; Donelha 1977, chaps.1-4). These islands are in part very arid, making extended settlement difficult. Moreover, by the 1590s the Portuguese towns on the islands were suffering from regular enemy assaults. Faced with these difficulties, Almada proposed that the islanders migrate to Sierra Leone (Almada 1988, chap.19/2). But even in the 1570s a source connected with the islands had described Sierra Leone as "the most highly prized of all the land"' of the mainland coast (Donelha 1977, 352). Hence an exaggerated view of Sierra Leone's productive capacity and suitability for settlement was apparently common in the islands - and was shared by Andrada (Madeira Santos 1988). In fact, Sierra Leone had limited supplies of alluvial gold, only a legendary possession of crystal, only sugar in the form of wild cane, and only those varieties of 'pepper' which, contrary to Andrada's statement, were considered inferior to the corresponding Asian spices by the European palate and market.

3.   THE WATERING-PLACE 'Tagarin' was one of the names used by sixteenth-century Portuguese to designate the Sierra Leone estuary (Hair 1966). The estuary contained a very handy and much-used watering-place (Donelha 1977, 199,n.29). The belief that ships on the **Carreira da Índia** watered at Sierra Leone was also expressed by Donelha (Donelha 1977, 74). Portuguese ships travelling to the East normally watered either at the Cape Verde Islands or at Cape Verde. Occasionally they took a course which passed down the Guinea coast as far as Cape Palmas, but even then did not normally call at Sierra Leone. Andrada specifies that in 1582 the Malacca galleon, in distress, put in at Sierra Leone (f.21v); but a more reliable source states that the port of refuge was River Sess (modern Liberia) (Paez 1937, 77). On the return voyage, while the ideal course lay in mid-Atlantic, ships which needed attention sometimes called at African ports. A Spanish source of c.1580 stated, when discussing Sierra Leone, that "the ships of Portugal when they were coming back from India used to refit here, but because the land is unhealthy, and there was much sickness, and many died, and in order to avoid tornadoes, they abandoned this course" (Sarmiento 1944, 111). Andrada later claims that 'in the time of King D.João III [1521-1557], ships from India often watered in this watering-place' (f.19v). While it is certain that Portuguese vessels travelling to the eastern parts of Guinea and those engaged in coastal trade watered at Sierra Leone, there is no direct evidence that ships of the **Carreira da Índia** ever called at Sierra Leone.

It is there that the English and French regularly come to refit, in order to ravage the Ocean, as already stated, and from here they rob the trade of Your Majesty in the navigation of Cape Verde and that of the whole sea. They did just this in the year 1577, when those from La Rochelle arrived to seize the **sierra**. King D.Sebastian - may God pardon him - sent a fleet of galleys and all kinds of ships to drive them out, under the command of Captain Antonio Vello Tinoco, who, before winning this battle, had been victor over another fleet anchored within the kingdom and port of the Ialofos. And the ships of the Lutherites were many and were very full of munitions, /f.17/ weapons and merchand- dise.[4] In the same manner, during the year 1570, Captain Melchior Montero with his galleys dispersed and defeated another Lutherite fleet in the port of the Ialofos, which lies nine de- grees of latitude North of Sierra Leona, at 17 1/2 leagues per degree.[5]

4. FIGHTING FRENCH FLEETS Elsewhere Andrada states that he served in ocean ships under António Velho Tinoco (f.23v), and also that he was in the Cape Verde Islands when Drake passed through (i.e., in early 1578). António Velho Tinoco was made chief magistrate and effectively governor of the islands in 1570: he continued in this post until late 1577, but was in Lisbon by January 1578 (Donelha 1977, 337,341). Andrada, who was 'provisor and vicar-general [bishop's deputy/assistant] in Guinea' (f.41) during some of the middle years of the 1570s, must have held this post during at least part of the period of Tinoco's governorship of the islands. Andrada exaggerates the extent to which English vessels made use of Sierra Leone in the half-century before 1590 (although Hawkins visited thrice in the 1560s), and probably also exaggerates the French presence there (Hair 1969). But his view was not original: in 1582 a Portuguese writer complained that the trade of "the rivers of Sierra Leone" was being lost because of "many French ships which go there to rob and to buy many slaves" (Brásio 1964, 3:106). In 1592, Abreu de Brito did not specify Sierra Leone as a corsair base but stated that "the sea-ports, bays and anchorages from Arguin to Sierra Leone", were used by Lutherites to make assaults on passing Portuguese vessels that were "limping or light", as well as to trade with the heathen of the locality (Abreu de Brito 1931, 82). There is independent evidence that French vessels trading in the Sierra Leone estuary (but not attempting 'to seize the **sierra**') were attacked by a fleet of Portuguese galleys commanded by António Velho Tinoco, and allegedly sunk (Donelha 1977,115-6,265,339-41). The author of this reference, Donelha, apparently an eye-witness of the episode, stated elsewhere that he was in Sierra Leone in 1574 (ibid., 78). A modern editor (Teixeira da Mota), quoting two documents of 1575-6 which refer to Tinoco's success in "driving away the French pirates whom he fought on the coast of Guinea", and also to his having, in "the Rivers of Guinea, defeated four pirate ships", has assumed that the documents refer to the episode at Sierra Leone, and concluded that it occurred in 1574, as Donelha's evidence seems to confirm. If this is correct, then Andrada's date of 1577 is wrong. However, since Andrada states that at an earlier date Tinoco fought enemy vessels off Cape Verde, then it is possible that actually this engagement was the 1574 episode. If we dare now assume that Donelha visited Sierra Leone on two occasions, and that the date '1574' was not intended to apply to the sea-battle episode, it would be possible to accept that the date Andrada supplies for the Sierra Leone episode, 1577, is correct. However, since Andrada is regularly careless in his dating, his date is the less likely. It is possible that Andrada sailed on the Sierra Leone expedition. He claims to have served at sea under Tinoco - but on ocean ships, whereas Donelha states that the Sierra Leone expedition consisted of "a fleet of galleys" (ibid., 114). No other details are known of either the earlier success of Tinoco or the 1570 sea-battle off Cape Verde. Since, as far as is known, no English fleets visited Cape Verde c.1570, the 'Lutherites' on both occasions must have been French, and French activity in the region is known. French ships visited Sierra Leone in 1565 and 1566, and perhaps in 1567, and in 1566 were attacked and sunk by a Portuguese fleet (Hair 1969, 1032-3, correcting Roncière 1923, 4:82). In 1564, a Portuguese vessel approaching River Senegal fought a French vessel, and in 1570 a ship from Dieppe was attacked in the Gambia by "many Portuguese" (Santarem 1843, cxxxv,391,511; Teixeira da Mota 1970, 5-6,13).

5. MELCHIOR MONTERO In 1565, a Melchior Monteiro was captain of a Portuguese

**[The English use of renegade sailors - the
threat to Spain - a previous warning]**

So, continuously, and now more than ever before, the Lutherites have brought over to their
side many Spanish mariners and captains, contrary to their service to Your Majesty and contrary to your laws.[6] England is full of hope
that it can disturb the peace of Christendom,
and it has the favour of the adherents of Don
Antonio, the Prior of Crato as was.[7] If Your
Majesty does not maintain your sea-power actively and systematically, so that God can help
us to begin to fortify and settle, /f.17v/ I
fear that within days the Lutherites, being
skilled sailors, will make some damaging
assault upon Spain itself. If nothing is done
about such serious perils, there will come to
pass what happened after I gave warning to Don
Cristoval de Mora of similar events. He will
testify that I gave the same warning that I now
repeat - nothing being then done about it -
that speedy remedial action must be at once im-
plemented, to prevent future evils.[8]

slave ship robbed at the Ilhetas (near Cacheu) by an English vessel commanded by Bartolomeu Bayão (Public Record Office, London, State Papers, Foreign, Elizabeth, vol.95, ff.260-261v). The 'port of the Ialofos' near Cape Verde, at 14° 42' N, was actually just over six degrees North of Sierra Leone.

6. RENEGADE PILOTS A steady trickle of Portuguese pilots had transferred to French and English shipping throughout the sixteenth century. While this was eventually regarded as desertion and treachery by the Iberian authorities, early in the century transfer between the nations had been more lightly regarded - perhaps partly because of the example of the Italians employed by Portugal and Spain, for instance, Columbus and Cabot. Portuguese pilots had worked for Spain long before the union of the crowns, for instance, Magellan. Further, if most 'renegade' pilots had transferred for mercenary reasons, a few were religious refugees (for instance, the pilot of the 1553 English voyage to Guinea).

7. DON ANTONIO The linking of England with D.António suggests that Andrada was writing at a period when England was thought to be still the pretender's chief backer. After the fall of his base in the Azores, D.António lived in England between 1585 and 1589, and he participated in the unsuccessful English attempt to seize Lisbon in the latter year (Serrão 1979, 37-41). He then retired to France, more or less in obscurity, until his death in 1595: Andrada is clearly writing before that date. Until he was proclaimed king (according to the Antonine party) or until he was stripped of his honours for rebellion (according to the Philippine party), D. António had held the honorific title of Prior of Crato.

8. WARNINGS OF DISASTERS Andrada is writing after Drake's 1587 attack on Cadiz and 1589 attacks on Vigo and Lisbon, and it is presumably one of these episodes that he is hinting that he previously warned about. He now predicts a further assault, and in fact a joint English and Dutch fleet attacked and sacked Cadiz in 1596. D. Cristóvão de Moura, a Portuguese grandee and the leading supporter of Philip in the succession dispute, was one of the most influential men in Lisbon c.1590, and therefore worth claiming the acquaintance of, as Andrada does here and later (f.23). D. Cristóvão undoubtedly had the ear of the king and Andrada no doubt hoped that he would 'testify' to the writer's bona fides as part of a request to the king to read the **aviso.**

[Marine disasters since 1510 and their cost - recent disasters and the need for ports in West Africa]

As proof of what I say, consider the great loss of ships on the **Carrera de la India**, from the discovery of India [i.e., the East Indies], year by year for some eighty years up to now, a loss of more than one hundred ships, which either were forced to return to port or were wrecked, with very serious losses of men, and [also] of income to the Portuguese economy and Your Majesty's treasury.[9]   This must have amounted to more **/f.18/** than thirty **cuentos** of gold with the return to port in 1590 of the four ships which were under the command and in the voyage of the viceroy, Mathias de Alburquerque[10]; and with the disaster suffered in the same year by Admiral Bernardino Ribero, when he failed to make the Island of St Helena and was driven along the whole equatorial latitude as far as the Hispaniolas.[11]   Again, Francisco Giraldes, governor of Brazil, who left Lisbon in 1588, sailed for two years under the Tropic of Cancer, causing the destruction of his fleet without any escape, on account of a failure to make port in the Ialopho or at Sierra Leona.[12]

9. LOSSES AT SEA   Here Andrada exaggerates only a little.   In a shorter period, between the 1550s and 1590s, nearly 40 out of some 250 ships making round voyages in the **Carreira da Índia** were lost at sea, excluding half a dozen taken by the English (my calculation, from the lists in Paez 1937).   However, the vast majority of the losses in this period occurred in the Indian Ocean, whereas Andrada implies that Atlantic circumstances caused the losses.   He may have directed attention to the Atlantic because a king at Madrid had to consider Spanish losses too, and these were mostly in the Atlantic.   On the Spanish **Carrera de Indias**, in the same period 1550-1600, losses were higher in absolute numbers although lower proportionally - 96 vessels out of 4,147 departures (Chaunu 1955, 6/1:862).   But total Spanish losses were more damaging than the previous figures suggest: during the period 1534-1585, losses by corsair action to shipping in the Caribbean or between there and Spain amounted to over 350 vessels (Hoffman 1980, 26,66,113,211).

10.   MATHIAS DE ALBURQUERQUE   Matias de Albuquerque, appointed viceroy of India, sailed from Lisbon with five ships on the annual voyage in May 1590, but only his own ship, the 'Bom Jesus', reached India in May 1591, the others encountering difficulties in the Atlantic and returning to port in May and September (Figueiredo Falcão 1859, 179; Paez 1937, 83; Boxer 1959, 7-8).   Andrada later refers to the voyage again (f.39).   Abreu de Brito also mentions this set-back (Abreu de Brito 1931, 90).   **Cuentos** is Portuguese **contos** 'millions', the **conto** being one thousand **mil-réis**.

11.   FORCED WESTWARDS   Bernardino Ribeiro Pacheco commanded a fleet that left Lisbon for India in April 1589, but on the return voyage his own ship, the 'Madre de Deus', missed St Helena and had to winter in Brazil (not in the 'Hispaniolas' or Indies) (Figueiredo Falcão 1859, 178-9; Paez 1937, 82-3).   This was commented on contemporaneously.   "The Admirall of the Portugall fleet that came from India, having missed the Iland of S. Helena, was of necessitie constrained to put into Phernambuck [Pernambuco], although the king had expresly under a great penaltie forbidden him so to doe, because of the wormes that there doe spoile the ships" (Linschoten, as translated in Hakluyt 1598, 2:184).   Since Andrada cannot have known about this before 1591, it represents perhaps one of the latest references in his work.   He refers to the voyage again (f.38).

12.   ABORTED VOYAGE   Francisco Giraldes, the son of an Italian merchant settled in Portugal, was appointed governor of Brazil in March 1587.   He sailed the same month, but returned to Lisbon eighteen months later, in September 1589 (and promptly died).   His ship, having failed to cross the Equator, had had to seek refuge in the West Indies (Salvador 1965, liv.4, cap.23; Varnhagen 1959, 5:244).

Were these two kingdoms to be fortified, other ports in Guinea would be immediately settled without fuss, ports which I avoid prolixity by not discussing, as would Santo Domingo, where Your Majesty's **[Casa de] la Contratación** is located, **/f.18v/** and also the kingdom of the Buyafras on the mighty Rio Grande, from which two ports are nowadays taken to the West Indies all the slaves who extract the gold from the mines.[13]

13. SLAVE PORTS For the Rio de São Domingos, the Biafada and the Rio Grande, see Chapter 2, notes 9-10. The 'two ports' are Cacheu and Guinala on the named rivers (and not the Jolof port and Sierra Leone, as the clumsy wording at first suggests), since these did supply slaves to the Spanish West Indies, and if not 'all' of the slaves, as Andrada asserts, at least a substantial proportion, perhaps a majority (Rodney 1970, 96). Given that Andrada knew these ports and their Portuguese settlements, perhaps even from visiting them, it is curious that he does not recommend that they should be the first to be fortified and become ports of refuge for Atlantic shipping. Instead he recommends two less used localities, the 'Jolof' port at Cape Verde and the Sierra Leone estuary: the former was certainly a sound recommendation because of its western situation, but Sierra Leone, being further East than Cacheu and Guinala, was prima facie not to be preferred. A possible explanation is that Andrada knew that both Cacheu and Guinala were more difficult of access for ocean vessels than was the Sierra Leone estuary. A supplementary or alternative explanation is that he knew that the Portuguese settlers who already existed at Cacheu and Guinala, while anxious to develop their trade with the Spanish Indies, were also less than fully loyal to Philip, and were known to be so. In the 1580s, the Portuguese at Cacheu and Guinala had organised their own fortifications, allegedly against the French, but the crown had showed no enthusiasm to support their efforts (Almada 1984, chaps.9/2,11/17). Andrada may not have been aware of these recent developments at Cacheu and Guinala, since they occurred after he left Guinea. Nevertheless, he may have decided that it was unwise to refer to the fortification of these established ports, and safer to recommend for fortification, at least in the first instance, localities which from their initial establishment as official ports could be placed under direct crown authority.

CHAPTER 7

[How to fortify Sierra Leone - the advantages
to be gained - the natives and Portuguese
adventurers]

[The site for a settlement at Sierra Leone]

Since we have demonstrated the reasons why
Sierra Leona, as well as the Ialopho [port],
should be fortified, it is only fitting to declare the way in which, at little cost to Your
Majesty, this entrance from the sea can be settled and fortified. On the shore-line is a
high headland almost completely cut off and
surrounded by water. This could easily be isolated completely. It is a beautiful locality
where might be founded one of the most populous
/f.19/ cities in the world.[1] For this land of
Guinea and Zape, as well as producing all that
Spain produces from all its mining of the
earth, brings forth particularly fine gold.[2]

1. FORTIFICATION AT SIERRA LEONE Andrada may have visited Sierra Leone on the Tinoco expedition in the 1570s. Donelha, who was certainly on the expedition and did visit Sierra Leone, also suggested the building of a 'fine city' (Donelha 1977, 76) - the similarity of the suggestions of Andrada and Donelha may confirm that Andrada had actually seen his 'beautiful locality'. However, whereas Donelha recommends as a site for the city the flatter land behind the watering-place, situated some distance up-river (and approximately the site of modern Freetown), Andrada points to a 'high headland', which must be either the whole Aberdeen peninsula at the entrance to the river, or, more likely, within that peninsula, the headland of Cape Sierra Leone. Both sites do in fact control the deep-water entrance to the estuary, the channel of which runs immediately below the headland (during the 1939-1945 war a boom was swung across the channel from the rocky shore of the headland). This was probably the site chosen for artillery c.1615 when - if the story is true - the Portuguese made an unsuccessful attempt to establish a battery of guns to cover the entrance to the estuary (Hair 1987,pp.202-3). In Andrada's day, both sites appear to have been uninhabited. While the narrow and elevated headland would not provide a site for a 'city', the whole Aberdeen peninsula is slightly more spacious and could probably contain double its present-day 40 or so dwellings. The locality for the fortification is repeated on f.44.

2. GOLD The comparison with Spain makes little sense. If Andrada was really stating that Sierra Leone produced, as well as gold, all the metals mined in Spain, he was wrong.

Two profiles of Sierra Leone as seen from the sea, drawn by Sarmiento de Gamboa, 1580 (ff.22v-23)

[Portuguese plans for settlement - the extent of this kingdom - its Manding conquest]

This Sierra Leona is the one which King D. Sebastian gave to Don Antonio, Prior of Crato, to settle; and to repeat what I have heard from all the sailors when I was in Guinea, it was said that it would be appropriate, should the port be fortified, for him to be called Duke or King of Sierra Leona.[3] I affirm that, whosoever were to rule it, he would have a better kingdom than the kingdom of Fez or even the kingdom of Morocco. This is because it extends for more than 100 leagues of longitude on the mainland coast, which is the region of La Mina de Portugal, and in the interior it reaches to 17° of [North] latitude, and borders on the kingdoms of Nubia and Libia of the Sands, below the meridian of Fez. On the eastern side it reaches **/f.19v/** to the [land of the] King of Mandinga[4], otherwise called Çumba, that is 'King', whose wife and queen governs and is herself the conqueror of those lands. To her captains she gives an **habito** (garment of honour), which consists of a scarlet cloak (**chya de grana**) hanging about the chest, a novel [form of **habito**] discovered among barbarians.[5] She claims Sierra Leona because of the wealth in gold her **conquistadores** bring her [from there].

3. AWARD OF SIERRA LEONE In 1577 D. António was awarded by King D.Sebastião the **almandravas** (fishery rights) of the Moroccan and Saharan coasts (Sousa Viterbo 1900, 247-248). But I know of no evidence to support Andrada's statement that Sierra Leone was awarded to D.António. However, it is recorded that Governor António Velho Tinoco asked the king, shortly before both men were killed in Morocco in 1578, to establish a captaincy of Sierra Leone and present him with it (Donelha 1977, 116). Possibly Andrada - or gossip 'among the sailors' - confused the award to one António with the proposed award to the other. When the captaincy of Sierra Leone was finally established and awarded in 1606 to Pedro Álvares Pereira, it was stated that the matter had been discussed in the time of Philip II, that is, before 1598 (Hair 1987, 176-7). It would seem, therefore, that the notion that Sierra Leone might become the subject of a Portuguese crown grant was in the air during the later decades of the sixteenth century.

4. EXTENT OF SIERRA LEONE Andrada presents an absurdly exaggerated view of the extent of 'Sierra Leone'. The polities around the Sierra Leone estuary were tiny and lacked influence on the interior or on neighbouring coasts. However, Andrada is probably building on a view expressed by his contemporaries, Almada and Donelha, and therefore perhaps common among the Portuguese of the Cape Verde Islands. This was to the effect that the Sierra Leone polities were, by conquest, tributary to larger polities elsewhere. A later Dutch source expounded this view in more detail: Sierra Leone was linked by a chain of vassalage and tribute, first to a larger polity in the near-interior ('the kingdom of the Logos'); secondly, to a polity at Cape Mount, eastwards along the coast; and thirdly, via the Cape Mount polity, to a large deep-interior polity, that of the Mandinga (Almada 1984, note 16/4 on Mane tribute). Yet even if these alleged links are taken into account, Andrada's view is still a gross exaggeration. Very many separate peoples and polities lay between Cape Mount and the Gold Coast to the East ('the region of La Mina de Portugal'); while northwards, if the Mandinga polity almost reached the Sahara Desert (the latter actually at 17° N), this was hardly the same as having boundaries with 'the kingdoms of Nubia and Libia of the Sands' (the latter a creation of the mapmakers).

5. ÇUMBA At this point Andrada's information more or less matches that in the writings of Almada and Donelha, the Cape Verde Islands traders. Almada called the invaders of Sierra Leone c.1550 'Sumbas', otherwise 'Manes', the latter name clearly indicating an alleged Manding origin; and both he and Donelha noted that the leader of one army was claimed to have been a woman (Donelha 1977, 106; Almada 1984, chap.16/1,2,4,7 and notes). Andrada's interpretation of the term 'Sumba' is novel but probably only a guess; his reference to the scarlet cloak of honour is original.

[Sierra Leone as a port of refuge - as a naval base against pirates on the coast - as a safeguard for the transport of Mina gold]

To return to the fortification of that **sierra** and port, two full-flowing rivers enter the sea [there], one called Tagarin, the other Mitombo.[6] In the time of King D.Juan III, ships from India often watered in this watering-place, it having the capacity to offer protecttion and repairs to any number of fleets arriving there when they are unable to cross the Equator, so that they do not need to abandon the voyage.[7] If my captain, Ruy de Melo, when he was taking us to India, had made for there and refitted, we would not have been shipwrecked and /f.20/ lost in Bahia del Brazil, or in the next year, on Samatra [Sumatra].[8] Further on [from Sierra Leona], La Mina, which is Your Majesty's Castle of San Jorge, would maintain the defence in its own district, and away from this coast would be driven those pirates who have calling-places in Rio de los Cestos and in Bahia de las Gallinas, where the Lutherites trade with salt for pure gold, and carry off the gold without [us having] any redress.[9]

6. MITOMBO The Sierra Leone estuary (strictly, not an estuary but an arm of the sea) is watered by several streams, but the main river was known to the Portuguese as either Tagarin or Mitombo - Andrada wrongly considers these the names of separate rivers (Hair 1966).

7. INDIA SHIPS On India ships watering, see note 3 to Chapter 6.

8. THE 'SAN PABLO' VOYAGE The voyage and shipwreck are discussed again later - see note 3 to Chapter 9. The 'São Paulo' had to put in to Bahia but it was not 'shipwrecked and lost' there, as Andrada now rhetorically states.

9. CASTLE OF SAN JORGE The Portuguese fort of São Jorge da Mina (at Elmina in modern Ghana), although no longer as important as it had been a half-century earlier, still guarded a trade which suppplied a substantial part of Portugal's import of gold. Andrada names two localities lying between the Sierra Leone estuary and Mina, River Gallinas (in the East of modern Sierra Leone) and River Sess (in Liberia): Portuguese and non-Portuguese vessels called regularly at the latter, but River Gallinas was an uncommon calling point for any ship. Gold could, however, be obtained at River Gallinas, although only a very small quantity (Jones 1983b, 20) - none could be obtained at River Sess. The salt Andrada mentions would almost certainly be obtained at the Cape Verde Islands (known to the Dutch c.1600 as the 'Salt Islands', De Marees 1987, 17), Maio Island having salines where salt could be collected without payment (Jones 1983, 10). But Andrada may have confused his information about River Gallinas, since in its lagoons salt was produced locally and probably traded outwards (ibid.). 'Gallinas Bay' (**Bahia de las Gallinas**), instead of 'River Gallinas' (Portuguese **Rio das Galinhas**, 'Hens' River'), is an abnormal form, but an earlier French source noted that the river "runs into a little bay" (Hair 1976, 30). **Rio dos Cêstos** ('Baskets' River') was the original Portuguese name for modern River Sess. When Andrada repeats these toponyms (f.30v) he reverses **rio** and **bahia**.

Fortifying this place would bring many bene-
fits, and the best of these would be that all
the treasure from Mina, for which Your Majesty
annually uses a whole fleet, could come to
Sierra Leona from Mina in two or three light
frigates, without [so much] cost and danger.
From Sierra Leona to Ialopho, and from there
onwards, they would travel to Spain with all
the ships from Cape Verde and the trade of the
Guinea contract, in order not be captured by
pirates, as they are now daily, **/f.20v/** because
they sail singly and away from the [convoy]
route,[10] the men of La Rochelle having from the
outset plundered them.[11]

10. MINA FLEET During the greater part of the sixteenth century, it had been the practice of the Portuguese crown to send annually a small armed fleet to Mina, to collect the gold purchased there and stored in the fort (Vogt 1979, 37). By the 1580s this fleet was sometimes reduced to a single armed vessel. Meanwhile, from at least mid-century on, the Spaniards had formed Atlantic convoys for their ships carrying American treasure home, and latterly these had linked up in the Azores with Portuguese fleets returning from the East. The Spaniards were also experimenting with the use of fast frigates which, travelling singly, could outsail enemy attackers. What Andrada seems to be suggesting is the extension of the regular Atlantic convoy system to the Portuguese traffic from the Cape Verde Islands (Spanish shipping passed these islands when outward bound, but not when homeward bound). Earlier in the century, Portuguese alarm about gold losses had tended to be concentrated, not on seizures at sea, but on the rival and competitive trading of foreign ships on the coast. But by 1590 shipping on the route from Guinea and the Cape Verde Islands was under frequent attack, and interception of the Mina fleet or vessel seems to have become more frequent. One such capture by the French occurred in 1575, and there may have been similar episodes in 1577 and at a unrecorded later date before 1583 (Trocmé 1952, 46; Gray 1965, 19; Vogt 1979, 123). Apart from the assumed reduced cost, the advantages of the frigate system recommended by Andrada for the transit from Mina to the Cape Verde Islands were the division of the annual gold export among several ships, making capture of the whole less likely, and the tactical benefit of faster vessels.

11. LA ROCHELLE Both the Portuguese and the Spaniards often referred to La Rochelle as if it were the base for all French marine activities hostile to the Iberian empires. Andrada has mentioned La Rochelle earlier (ff.3v,8v,16v) and he refers to it again (ff.26,28,40v,41v) - the phrase 'the French Lutherites from La Rochelle' making his (false) point that, as with the English, the hostility arose out of religious heresy rather than secular challenge. This attitude was summed up in a notice alleged to have been posted by a Spaniard when he executed Frenchmen in Florida - "I do this not to Frenchmen but to Lutherites" (Julien 1949, 243).

[The friendliness of the natives - how to win over the Portuguese adventurers resident there]

Nowadays it is the English who would be obstructed in every way if Sierra Leona were fortified, which could be done easily and without war.[12] The Zape and Ialopho are seeking the friendship of the Portuguese [subjects] of Your Majesty, for many fugitives from justice in criminal causes now live in Sierra Leona, whose only wish is that Your Majesty should pardon them and allow them to settle in the **sierra**. These are the men who up to now have loaded cargoes for the pirates,[13] and traded with them for gold, ivory, ambergris, pepper and other commodities.[14]

12. THE ENGLISH AND SIERRA LEONE Although Andrada's anxiety in 1590 about an overall imperial challenge from the English is understandable, his relating the English to Sierra Leone is at first sight puzzling. In the 1550s and 1560s, English activity in Guinea had consisted of trading voyages, first to the Gold Coast, then to Sierra Leone, where Hawkins established non-hostile trading relations with the local Portuguese (Hair 1970; Hair 1988). But the limited success of these voyages led the English to turn in the 1580s to a nearer coast, that of Senegal. Records are fragmentary but I know of only one English trading voyage to Guinea between 1570 and 1590 that involved Sierra Leone, the voyage in 1572 piloted by the Portuguese renegade, Bartolomeu Bayão. However, Sierra Leone was visited during the 1580s by four English expeditions en route to further objectives, in 1580 and 1586 in the course of the circumnavigations of Drake and Cavendish, and in 1582 and 1586 by two expeditions proposing to reach the East (Madox 1976; Hair 1984). Drake visited only to water, and two of the other expeditions made no contact with the local Portuguese and carried out hostile acts against the local Africans. But the 1582 Fenton expedition, during a visit of eight weeks, established friendly relations not only with the local Africans but also with the local Portuguese (because of the English alliance with D.António) (Hair 1978, 82-90). These four English visits to Sierra Leone were all reported in Hakluyt's 1589 publication, but almost certainly Andrada did not know of this work, indeed he may not have known of all the visits (but surely must have known of some of them). Drake's visit, if he knew of it, may well have impressed him, because of his respect for Drake. But his association of Sierra Leone with English activities is most likely to have derived, either from knowledge he acquired when he was in Guinea during the 1570s about the 1560s visits (although he never specifies these) or about the 1572 Bayão visit, or else from knowledge acquired later about the 1582 visit, since he goes on to discuss how the crown should regain the support of the local Portuguese.

13. PORTUGUESE RESIDENT IN SIERRA LEONE Early in the sixteenth century, the Portuguese crown forbade its subjects in the Cape Verde Islands to settle or even to trade in Sierra Leone, perhaps because it was considered outside its effective jurisdiction (Rodney 1970, 74-5). But the legislation did not stop small numbers of islanders from trading to Sierra Leone and setting up semi-permanent homes there (Hair 1987, 171-2). By mid-century, although such **lançados**, or adventurers (see note 8 to Chapter 4), continued to be denounced in public discourse, the Portuguese authorities were resigned to their presence (Hair 1970, 6-7). It is clear that these 'Afro-Portuguese' traded with the English and French long before the political disturbances of the early 1580s, but they normally denied it to the authorities, claiming instead that they had been robbed. Andrada makes the significant admission that they traded freely with the enemy, inferring that they did so because of resentment at the official attitude. Andrada also states that many were fugitives from justice. That the majority of the Portuguese in Guinea were exiled criminals was a claim made previously by the English and French, in a spirit of derogation, and the Portuguese authorities certainly had a policy of banishing criminals to outposts of empire (for an instance of a man banished to Sierra Leone, see Ryder 1965, item 406, an undated document). However, as has been pointed out in relation to Brazil, "many had been banished upon the flimsiest of excuses, for in those days some of the best subjects of the realm were sent out into the wilderness" (Freyre 1946, 28). In fact, as far as Sierra

Having considered the true facts about the shipwrecks and robberies we have suffered, I have decided, for the good of my conscience, to offer to Your Majesty the following points of advice.

Leone was concerned, Andrada probably exaggerates. Most of the very few
Portuguese there in Andrada's day are likely to have been merely enterprising
traders, neither fugitives nor banished criminals. Perhaps Andrada was simply
intending to point out that notionally any Portuguese in Sierra Leone was there
illegally, although his terminology seems too strong for this explanation.
Perhaps instead he was intending a reference to another group of traders
operating elsewhere in Guinea, the Jews and New Christians who had fled to the
mainland to escape religious persecution, and who were commented on by other
Portuguese writers such as Almada.

14.   COMMODITIES The list of commodities bought by non-Portuguese traders at
Sierra Leone is correct. As well as these commodities, Portuguese traders also
bought wax, slaves, and a product solely traded up-coast to Africans, cola (cf.
Brásio 1964, 106). Since non-Portuguese vessels arrived much less regularly at
Sierra Leone than did Portuguese vessels, it is highly unlikely that there were
Portuguese resident in this district who made a living merely by assembling
cargoes for non-Portuguese ships, as Andrada implies. Rather it was the case
that the Afro-Portuguese traders residing and/or working in Sierra Leone, and
normally trading within the commercial network of the Cape Verde Islands, were
prepared on occasions to trade with non-Portuguese, if this was profitable.

The Sierra Leone estuary, as charted by an
Englishman, 1582 - note the headland on the West,
Andrada's proposed site for a city (ff.18v-19)

I state that only men who have already sought
refuge in Guinea should be the settlers in
/f.21/ these cities, since such men are cour-
ageous and experienced at sea, and Your Majesty's favour would mean much to them, as would
the opportunity to do God more service, because
they would be throwing themselves not only on
your grace but also on the grace of God.[15] For
since they have no church [there], some of
them, although laymen, baptize each other's
children and their concubines, and commit a
thousand sins. One Spaniard joined the Ethiopians in going as far as to eat human flesh
during their wars.[16]

15. PROPOSED SETTLEMENT Andrada's proposal for the official Portuguese settlement of Sierra Leone contrasts sharply with the proposal put forward by Almada, the latter being to the effect that the population of the Cape Verde Islands should transfer to Sierra Leone (Almada 1984, chap.19/2). Andrada argues instead that the illegal and criminal population of the mainland coast, having been pardoned, both by the crown and the Church, and being therefore more loyal henceforth to both, should become the settlers of the proposed 'cities' at Cape Verde and Sierra Leone. Andrada's proposal was unrealistic in the sense that a few score **lançados** could not compose an adequate base for a formal settlement, even if they could be persuaded to congregate at the 'cities' and actually 'settle'. Nevertheless, it can be commended as being unusually realistic in another aspect - in that it faced up to the problem of the **lançados**. Other writers were content to echo the out-dated proposition that these adventurers were bad men acting illegally, who should be publicly condemned and if possible punished - a wholly unrealistic scenario. Andrada proposes instead to make positive use of their experience and enterprise, for the good of Portugal. Yet it must be added that his logic can be challenged: he now suggests that 'these cities' should be populated with mainland **lançados**, whereas earlier he suggested that the Cape Verde settlement should be populated from the islands (f.11). The suggestion regarding the **lançados** is repeated later (f.43v), and enlarged as follows. 'In this land of Guinea there are many men who have fled there because they have committed illegal acts, but if Your Majesty were able to pardon them, they would accept pardon and give a fifth of their goods towards the cost of the fortress.'

16. PORTUGUESE IMMORALITY Andrada, being a cleric, might be expected to comment on the morals of the Portuguese living at Sierra Leone. In fact, his criticism is much the same as that of the layman, Almada (who wrote about the **lançados** more generally). By 1590, Cacheu had a church and (apparently) a resident priest, but elsewhere in western Guinea, as Almada lamented, the Portuguese were ill-served by the Church. Only occasionally did a priest visit from the Cape Verde Islands, to hear confessions and administer the sacraments. But the Bishop of Cape Verde organised (perhaps spasmodically) an annual disciplinary visitation of certain Portuguese settlements (seemingly on the lines of parochial visitation elsewhere in western Christendom). But these were "visitations producing fruit only in his treasury, while the adventurers continued sinning as before, without renouncing their sins or returning to their wives" (Almada 1984, chap.9/9; cf. Brásio 1964, p.379). That is, the Visitor fined the Portuguese found guilty of immoral behaviour, but then left again, so that the adventurers continued living in sin, some even in a state of mortal sin (ibid., chap.11/20). Almada hints that the commonest sin was concubinage, that is, the adventurers had black wives - as one would expect. Almada does not state that the visitation extended to the Portuguese at Sierra Leone, but in 1605 a Jesuit reported (maliciously) that those priests who had visited Sierra Leone before himself had only bought and sold, and not said Mass - this may be an oblique reference to a visitation (Hair 1970b, 22,n.1). Elsewhere in Christendom, an episcopal visitation was often carried out by the bishop's senior administrator, the vicar-general - and Andrada states that in the 1570s he was vicar-general in the see of Cape Verde (for Andrada's clerical career in the Cape Verde Islands, see the Introduction and notes 14-16). As such, he may therefore

The natives of this **sierra** are idolators, and
having little understanding (**juysio**) and no
guidance (**direction**), they serve only the sun
and moon, and will be converted the day the
Gospel is preached to them.[17] Their weapons are
bows and arrows.   They have mines in their
possession; and there are those among them who
extract iron from the hills, or are blacksmiths, carpenters and silversmiths.[18]   If the
inhabitants of this **sierra** had the capacity to
found artillery, they would be /**f.21v**/ comparable to the men of Malabar in India, who are
sailors [too].   Throughout this land there are
mountains with a thousand kinds of trees, and
with wild oranges and natural sugar cane.

have himself carried out visitations of the mainland, although he says nothing
of this. (He may even have visited Sierra Leone in the Tinoco expedition, if not
as chaplain, then as vicar-general - certainly a priest travelled with the fleet,
as did a choir and musical instruments (Donelha 1977, 114). If so, he may have
been the first priest to say Mass in Sierra Leone. But this is tenuous
speculation.) As a zealous cleric, Andrada notes, not so much that the Sierra
Leone Portuguese live in concubinage, as that they themselves baptize their
concubines, as well as their children. But in fact baptising children in the
absence of priests is barely a church offence. Infants in extremis could (and
still can) be baptised by a layman if no priest is at hand - by extension, might
not lay baptism be applied to a child living in a land without clergy but where
it may suddenly die unbaptised ? As for baptising one's concubine, this might
be thought more an act of religious commitment, albeit naive and technically
invalid, than one of demerit. Andrada can be read as inferring that these are
acts of indiscipline rather than serious sins. The offence of eating human flesh
is in a different category of misbehaviour, that of un-human action condemned by
'natural' feelings; its relevance here is its reflection on the local Africans
- other Portuguese sources maintained that ritual cannibalism was practised by
the Mane invaders of Sierra Leone, in order to terrify their enemies (Almada
1984, chap.16/2 and note on Sumba cannibalism).

17.   CONVERSION The notion that the Africans at Sierra Leone could be easily
converted to Christianity was not original to Andrada. The account of Tinoco's
visit stated that "the people of this land are a good people, being gentle and
honest, and all of them prepared to receive the Christian religion. ... António
Velho Tinoco and those who live here have stated that if someone could be found
who would sow the Word of God among this people, it would grow in such a way as
to produce a hundredfold increase" (Donelha 1977, 353,354). Further, it was
thought that "if there was a settlement of Christians in the Serra, they would
very soon all be Christians" (ibid., 114). The Jesuits who began a mission in
Sierra Leone in 1605 started with the same notion, but eventually expressed
disillusionment (Hair 1987, 198,201).

18.   IRON It is likely that iron-mining was only carried out well to the
North of the Sierra Leone estuary, among the Limba and Susu peoples; but since
iron had been available in the region, most probably for many centuries, albeit
in small quantities, it is likely that there were indeed blacksmiths at Sierra
Leone (Almada 1984, chap.15/8 and note on iron; Donelha 1977, 106). It is
doubtful, however, whether silver was ever found in this region, hence unlikely
that there were silversmiths at Sierra Leone.

CHAPTER 8

[Marine disasters from 1550 onwards - failures
to settle River Plate and Magellan Strait - the
author's experience at sea and in the study of
navigation]

[Marine disasters in the South Atlantic from lack of a refuge at Sierra Leona]

The year Your Majesty was in Portugal, the
Malacca galleon, on its way to India, retired
to Sierra Leona, having been for eight months
on the verge of foundering, and it could have
proceeded on its way undamaged if it had been
repaired there.[1] And [similarly], in the year
1550, the governor of Brazil, the father-in-law
of the Conde de Linares would not have arrived
[there] in the state he did.[2] Nor would Luis de
Alter de Andrada /f.22/ have been lost with
his ship on the coast of Brazil, with only four
men being saved.[3] Nor would Don Luis, son of
Archbishop D. Hernando, have been lost.[4] Nor
would Don Diego de Mendoça, together with the
seven vessels he brought from Seville on the
orders of the Lord Charles V, the most mighty
Emperor, father of Your Majesty, when he passed
by Sierra Leona and was wrecked on the Island
of São Tomé.[5]

1. THE MALACCA GALLEON The galleon 'S. Francisco' left Lisbon for Malacca with the annual India fleet in April 1582; it turned back before reaching the Equator and took refuge on the Guinea coast, not in Sierra Leone, as Andrada states, but in River Sess (modern Liberia); and it returned to Lisbon in December 1582, a total voyage length of eight months (Paez 1937, 77).

2. THE VOYAGE OF THE GOVERNOR OF BRAZIL The reference is to Mem de Sá, third governor of Brazil, whose daughter and heiress married the third Conde de Linhares (Caetano de Sousa 1948, 5:153-4). Mem de Sá left Belem on 31 April 1557 (not 1550) but only reached Bahia on 28 December, the ship having been so driven off course that it touched at the islands of Príncipe and São Tomé in the Gulf of Guinea, where it lost many men from sickness (Varnhagen 1959, 1:299).

3. LUIS DE ALTER DE ANDRADA Luís de Alter commanded the 'Santa Clara', which left Lisbon with the annual India fleet in April 1573, but turned back in the South Atlantic and was lost off Brazil (Paez 1937, 71; Salvador 1965, liv.3, cap.21).

4. DON LUIS D. Luís Fernandes de Vasconcelos, a natural son of D. Fernando de Menezes, archbishop of Lisbon, was involved in two dramatic marine disasters. In 1557, he led a fleet setting out for India, but his own vessel had to winter in Brazil; on his return from India in 1559, he escaped from his ship when it was sinking and in a boat made land in Madagascar. In 1570, he was appointed governor of Brazil and sailed from Lisbon. His fleet, delayed in the Canaries to avoid being becalmed off Guinea, was ambushed by Huguenot privateers under Jacques de Sores, and a party of Jesuits aboard one vessel was massacred (Rumeu de Armas 1945, 1:511-518). Travelling on, the remaining ships were driven off course to the Azores and West Indies; and finally, his own vessel proceeding from the Azores to Brazil was attacked by other French ships under a lieutenant of Sores, and the governor was killed. At one stage Tagus fishermen had said that D. Luís was accursed at sea because his father had forbidden their fisherman's festival (Fonseca 1926, 274,280-3,308,327,350-1,369; Salvador 1965, liv.3, cap.5; Varnhagen 1959, 1:344,349-50; Southey 1822, 306-9; Roncière 1923, 4:116,119; Boxer 1968, 28,53; Gomes de Brito 1955, 1:191-226). Note that Andrada does not refer to the most sensational aspect of the final voyage, the killing of a large number of Jesuit missionaries.

5. DON DIEGO DE MENDOÇA I cannot trace an appropriate voyage of 'D. Diego de Mendoça' - Andrada must be confused. However, a voyage from Seville during the reign of Charles V (1521-1557) must have been a Spanish voyage; and a Spanish voyage which wandered as far off course as São Tomé can only have been proceeding to River Plate. Three out of the four episodes related by Andrada immediately after this one refer to River Plate, and the 1559 voyage of Jaime Raschin to River Plate is described as 'another such fleet coming after the previously mentioned captain', i.e. Don Diego de Mendoça. In 1535, D. Pedro de Mendoza led an expedition of eleven vessels to River Plate - but without loss, and via Brazil, not via São Tomé (Rubio 1942, 107-110). In 1549, Diego de Sanabria led an expedition of three vessels to River Plate, one ship of which went off course and, before reaching America, touched at Anobom Island, neighbouring São Tomé (ibid., 246-7). Finally, D. Diego de Mendoza led a Spanish fleet in which four

Nor would Jaime Raschin, with another such
fleet coming after the above-mentioned captain,
have been wrecked in Río de la Plata.[6] Nor
would the ship 'Flamenca', which was travelling
from the East Indies, have been destroyed at
São Tomé after it was unable to double Cabo de
Las Palmas, near Sierra Leona.[7] It should also
be borne in mind that after Jaime Raschin was
wrecked with his eight ships, he returned again
to Seville to put together another fleet, and
being a second time /f.22v/ foiled by the winds
and currents (**monciones**) near the Ialopho, he
might have saved himself, but for lack of a
port he went from there to Santiago Island,
where all his men died without a single one
remaining to him.

ships were wrecked, but this happened in 1558 - and not in the South Atlantic but off England (Fernández Duro 1896, 2:494). Can it be that Andrada has conflated elements from each of these episodes?

6. JAIME RASCHIN Jaime Raschin (Rasqui or Rasquin) commanded a fleet of three Spanish ships which sailed in March 1559 with orders to found settlements in southern Brazil and River Plate; but running out of food and encountering other difficulties, after great loss of life the fleet turned back and eventually two ships returned to Spain via the Caribbean (Fernández Duro 1896, 2:197-8; Gandia 1934, 241-311; Rubio 1942, 286-7; Chaunu 1954, 2:376,378). Not only is Andrada's account inaccurate in respect of the number of ships and their loss, but the subsequent reference to a second voyage by Raschin contradicts the known history of this man - after the 1559 voyage, he lived in Spain, in disgrace and penury, until his death in 1571 (Gandia 1934, 311-319). Perhaps Andrada was referring to another disastrous voyage which he wrongly attributed to Raschin, but that all the men on eight ships died at Santiago seems in itself a very tall story.

7. THE 'FLAMENCA' The 'Flamenga' sailed with the annual India fleet from Lisbon in 1554, but turned back and was damaged at São Tomé. In 1557, either the same ship, or one of the same name if the 1554 episode involved total loss, sailed from Lisbon, but on the return voyage from India was wrecked at Sao Tomé, although the crew were saved (Paez 1937, 60-1; Boxer 1968, 29). Andrada refers again to the loss of this ship , which he dates to 1556 and implies that it occurred while sailing between Angola and Brazil (f.37v).

From the **História Trágico-Marítima**

[The 1572 failure to settle River Plate - the 1583 failure to settle Magellan Strait]

Coming after these captains, in 1572 Your Majesty appointed Juan Ortiz de Çarate, the Biscayan, as **Adelantado** (governor) of Río de la Plata, and he was taking me with him as his vicar-general, in consideration of my organising for him, in Your Majesty's **Casa de la Contratación** at Seville, the pilots and sailors. We sailed as far as Cape Verde, at which point the **Adelantado** took other counsel (**mudo consejo**), and he came to a halt, in disorder, at the Island of Santa Catalina, below the Tropic of Capricorn, which was the reason why Río de la Plata was not settled as had been desired.[a]

8. THE ÇARATE VOYAGE Juan Ortiz de Zárate, appointed governor of River Plate in 1569, sailed with five ships and 350 settlers in October 1572. Considerable delays occurred on the voyage, partly owing to deficiencies in the preparations and to bad pilotage, and the fleet only reached the Canaries in mid-November and the Cape Verdes in mid-December, many desertions occurring at both points. After crossing the Atlantic, one ship sought port at São Vicente in Brazil, while the rest of the fleet had to winter at Santa Catarina Island, where many settlers died from hunger. When River Plate was reached, the remaining ships were wrecked and the survivors were attacked by Indians, before being rescued in 1574. Zárate himself survived these disasters and went on to found the town of San Salvador, but this settlement was abandoned shortly after he died in 1576 (Rubio 1942, 345-356). The Zárate voyage forms the central episode of the epic poem, **Argentina y conquista del Rio de la Plata** (published 1602), by Martín de Barco Centenera, who travelled on the voyage. The point that Andrada wants to make about the Zárate voyage seems to involve a shift of argument. Previous instances related to the lack of a port at Sierra Leone, but it is difficult to see how this could apply to the Zárate voyage. Instead, perhaps, this voyage should be related to the episode subsequently mentioned, which involves the seasonality of sailing. Some years later, a River Plate pilot reported that he had had to winter with Zárate because the voyage had started too late in the season (Chaunu 1955, 3:296). Andrada's somewhat surprising personal reference in relation to this voyage is intriguing. He states that, after being in Brazil in the 1560s, he was to be found in Spain c.1570, at Seville, acting as a naval administrator in conjunction with the crown **Casa de la Contratación**, the agency that organised the American fleets and trade. Zárate had difficulty in procuring settlers for his expedition, and from Seville he sent out recruiting 'captains': the recruits were later described, perhaps unfairly, as "mostly the scum of Andalusia" (Archivo Colonial 1916, 95,153). But the published sources neither mention Andrada when discussing the preparations for the voyage, nor confirm his claim to have been appointed vicar-general of the proposed settlement. His name is not included in an archive document listing settlers and crews, nor in another document naming three **clérigos** who also sailed (ibid., 50-113; Rubio 1942, 355; p.c. Ursula Lamb). Another document listing those prepared to sail noted that other **clérigos** who had been recruited, not having been paid, declined to sail (Garay 1899, 107; Gutiérrez 1912, xv). The last document was signed by 'Martín de Centenera'. One of the clergy who did sail was Martín del Barco Centenera, the nominated archdeacon of Asunción, a chaplain on the ships and the versifier of the voyage; and in a letter written to the **Consejo de Indias**, Barco Centenera does in fact mention Andrada. Writing from Santiago in the Cape Verde Islands, on 22 December 1572, and after noting that conditions aboard the ships were so bad that many persons had deserted the expedition, Barco Centenera added- "Manuel de Andrada, the Portuguese, wishes to be left (here), he being the **clérigo** about whom I wrote to Your Lordships that he was coming on this fleet" (Archivo Colonial 1916, 117). (Barco Centenera's earlier letter has unfortunately not been traced in the archives: Gutiérrez 1912, xvii). Although Barco Centenera must have known Andrada as a fellow cleric, he fails to refer to him as 'vicar-general'; yet the fact that he troubles to mention him suggests that Andrada was a person of some standing. This reference confirms Andrada's claim that he sailed on the 1572 voyage. But taken with the fact that Andrada supplies no personal information on the River Plate region, the reference makes it almost

And Captain Diego Flores, as a result of his
own bad voyage, did not achieve his purpose, or
settle Magellan Strait, **/f.23/** for he left San
Lucar against the seasonal wind (**moncion**).   I
advised Don Cristoval in Portugal, to the effect that Captain Flores was not going about it
the right way and would be lost if he detained
the fleet until the [season of this] wind, but
to no avail.⁹ And those far-away places in our
Antipodes will not be settled unless knowledge
of navigation spreads and unless the ships
leave with the proper wind.

certain that he abandoned Zárate and disembarked at the Cape Verde Islands. His statement that Zárate 'took other counsel' may be a veiled reference to a disagreement that persuaded him to leave the expedition.

9. THE MAGELLAN STRAIT EXPEDITION   D. Diego Flores de Valdes was the naval commander of a large fleet despatched to America in September 1581, with instructions to convey reinforcements to Chile through Magellan Strait, and also to found a settlement in the Strait designed to prevent English incursion into the Pacific by that route. Many difficulties were encountered and ships lost as the fleet proceeded via the Cape Verde Islands, Rio de Janeiro, and Santa Catarina Island; while Flores de Valdes quarrelled frequently with the bull-headed governor of the proposed settlement, Pedro Sarmiento de Gamboa, who blamed the naval commander for incessant delays.   The reinforcements were eventually landed in River Plate, to march overland to Chile, but after an unsuccessful attempt to enter Magellan Strait in early 1583, Flores de Valdes retreated to Santa Catarina Island and Rio de Janeiro, and then to Spain.   In 1584, Sarmiento de Gamboa with three ships returned to the Strait and founded the settlement. But its subsequent history was disastrous, and in 1589 the last survivor was rescued by an English vessel (Sarmiento 1895, xxviii,209-351).   It is curious that Andrada writes as if the settlement had never been founded, merely referring to the difficulties of Flores de Valdes.   By 1585 Sarmiento de Gamboa had returned to Spain, and hence it was known there by then, if not earlier, that the settlement had been established (but its collapse was most probably not known by the time Andrada was writing c.1590).   Although the settlement failed, it can be claimed that news of the Spanish attempt deterred English activity in the region, there having been a measure of English interest in the coast of South America from São Vicente down to Magellan Strait between the early 1570s and 1582 (Hakluyt 1598, 3:794-6; Andrews 1981 and 1982, passim). The trans-Atlantic passage of the Flores de Valdes fleet was in fact conducted fairly successfully, but at the very beginning of the voyage, when the fleet left San Lucar, five ships were lost, and Sarmiento de Gamboa's account complained that this was because the fleet had left at the wrong time of the month, "contrary to the opinions of good seamen [since] it would be right to wait until after the moon's conjunction". This account blamed the Duke of Medina Sidonia, who had had the fleet towed out to sea against the wind, despite the protests of the pilots and of Diego de Flores.   But Andrada's complaint appears to refer to the fleet leaving in the wrong season of the year, rather than in the wrong part of the month.   For D.Cristóvão de Moura, see note 8 to Chapter 6.   (for illustrations referring to Sarmiento de Gamboa and Magellan Strait, see p.75 above and p.161 below.)

[The need to understand the oceans - the author's thirty-one years of experience, including residence in Brazil and Guinea]

For within and without the tropics, the Elements in this world obey the Stellar Cycle, and navigation is so much more dangerous and arduous when practised improperly. When all is said and done, those who go out to sea leave their natural element [i.e., the land], which is why it is necessary to know the rules concerning navigation, the penalty for all who do not know what is appropriate in the art of navigation being that they are lost. **/f.23v/** Your Majesty, in service to God, should give me credit for what I write, because I discovered for myself almost all these things, not in the abstract, but by science and experience, from my observations during thirty-one years up to this day,[10] when I sailed the entire ocean with all the following captains, governors, and admirals: Jorge de Lima, Don Jorge Tubara (in the Azores), Pero Melendez, Juan Ortiz, Estatio de Saa, Cristoval de Barros, Antonio Vello Tinoco, Don Pedro Leitão, and others, all of these in ocean-going ships (**de altobordo**), also [I sailed] in galleys (**galeras**) with Fernandalvarez, Bernabe de Sosa, and Diego Lopez de Sequeira.[11]

10. THIRTY-ONE YEARS 'Thirty-one years up to this day' would seem to mean the whole of Andrada's career in which he had had any association with marine or overseas ventures. This may indicate a period from the earliest date of personal experience he supplies, 1560, up to a presumed date of writing, 1591. Or it may indicate a period beginning somewhat earlier, if Andrada's relevant career started in the 1550s, and if we may suppose that it terminated with some unstated event in the 1580s - perhaps his employment in Spain as a tutor. His marine career on 'the entire ocean' can only have been in virtue of isolated episodes during the thirty-one years, since most of his nine years in Brazil and later five years in Guinea, as a missionary and ecclesiastical administrator respectively, must have been spent on land.

11. ANDRADA'S CAPTAINS Three of Andrada's named commanders had served in Brazil in the mid 1560s: Estácio de Sá, nephew of the governor Mem de Sá, who arrived in Brazil in 1563 and died in a campaign against the French in 1567; Cristóvão de Barros, who arrived with reinforcements in 1567 and succeeded Estácio de Sá, later serving in high offices until the 1590s; and D.Pedro Leitão, the second bishop of Brazil, who held his office from 1556 to 1573. Andrada had left Brazil and was in Seville by 1570 or 1571 (f.22v, see note 8 above), and his earlier reference to António Velho Tinoco indicates that he was in the Cape Verde Islands in the mid 1570s (f.16v and note 4 to Chapter 6). Pedro Menéndez de Avilés (1519-1574), marquis of Santa Cruz, governor of Florida and Cuba, **capitán general de la Armada de la Guardia de la Carrera de las Indias,** was Spain's most distinguished admiral in the 1560s and early 1570s: his operations in the Atlantic and Caribbean included liaison with the Portuguese in the Azores, and since Andrada claims an association with the Azores perhaps this involved the admiral. I cannot trace Don Jorge Tubara (? Távora), but perhaps Andrada travelled back to Iberia from Brazil c.1570 with Tubara, perhaps as a ship's chaplain, perhaps via the Azores. A Diogo Lopes de Sequeira commanded a Portuguese fleet sailing to the Indies in 1551, but not of course in galleys and surely too early for Andrada; and the only Jorge de Lima I can trace as a Portuguese naval commander was even earlier (Fonseca 1926, 281,313; Paez 1937, 47). It is just possible that the Fernandalvares who commanded galleys (perhaps on the Tinoco expedition in Guinea), was the Fernão de Álvares who captained one of the ships that brought the supporters of D.António to Santiago Island in 1582-3 (Frias 1964, 99,240). I cannot trace Bernabe de Sosa, but if he was in charge of a galley, it is most likely that this was in Guinea waters, and therefore that Andrada knew him in the 1570s.

For nine years I preached the Gospel in their own language to the Brazilians, and later [I preached] for five years in Guinea. By the grace /f.24/ of God, in these provinces I instructed many Lutherites who were converted, because I knew how to administer the sacraments to them in the midst of wars. Some I instructed by means of the language of the Indians, which they knew, and others in Latin.[12] At the same time I managed to redouble my vigils in the study and art of the mathematics which pertains to navigation, and which is beneficial to the adventurous. This I did to serve Your Majesty, after the example of Saint Paul, who was shipwrecked three times while he spread the faith of our Lord Jesus Christ, **"qui non venit mit[t]ere pacem in terris sed gladium"** ("who came not to bring peace on earth but a sword").[13] Hence it is right for Your Majesty to command the fortification of the Tropics and all its lands, so that Moors, Ethiopians, Turks, French, and English may be disabused, for otherwise their only intent is to settle and despoil the equatorial realms of Your Majesty. They say that /f.24v/ they will persist, and in reply to whoever asks them why they pursue illicit wars, that our [fore-] father Adam died intestate, and so the world belongs to all men and not to the Spaniards [alone]. But the [real] reason for their persistence in this argument and in their evil conduct is simply that so far those sea-ports are without fortification, without the Church, and without religion.[14]

12. NINE YEARS IN BRAZIL, FIVE IN GUINEA The 'nine years' was almost certainly during the 1560s, probably from 1560 to 1569. The 'language of the Indians' was Tupi, which Portuguese missionaries put into writing, studied, and used in education. The 'Lutherites' who knew the language of the Indians were undoubtedly the French, against whose settlements and agents in Brazil the Portuguese conducted campaigns throughout the 1560s (Julien 1948, 208-218). Andrada cannot have known Tupi on arrival in Brazil in 1560, so cannot have communicated with the French prisoners in that language at that date, although conceivably he may have communicated with some of them in Portuguese, Spanish or Latin. His communication in Tupi most likely occurred during or after the 1565-1567 campaign against the remaining French in the Rio de Janeiro, a campaign in which Andrada apparently participated, since he claims to have served under the leading Portuguese, Estácio de Sá and Cristóvão de Barros (f.23v). Some of the French did not need to be 'converted' since they were already Catholics; but of course the Portuguese preferred to believe that all were heretics. The 'five years in Guinea' began when Andrada reached the Cape Verde Islands in December 1572, and he claims to have been still there in February 1578 (a date, however, he gives wrongly as 1577) (f.9v), so presumably he left 'Guinea' shortly after the latter event.

13. ST PAUL Andrada seems to be making a forced analogy between himself and St Paul, by hinting that he was in Brazil because of a shipwreck. But the wreck of the ship that brought Andrada to Brazil occurred in Sumatra, long after Andrada had disembarked - however, the ship had been brought to Brazil by unexpected circumstances at sea.

14. ADAM'S WILL Andrada repeats a famous comment reported to have been made by Francis I of France when charged by Spain with sending ships to invade the part of the globe allegedly entrusted to Spain by papal decree - "he would much like to see Adam's will, to learn how he had divided the world" (Julien 1949, 146).

CHAPTER 9

[Bahia and the disrepair of its fortifications
by 1560 - marine disasters 1562, 1588, etc -
the threat to Bahia - the renegades again]

[Bahia fortification]

Because the Lutherites call to collect water in
Brazil, and rob the whole coast, it would be
very appropriate for Your Majesty to fortify
those places which are most important and most
capable [of providing] for the defence of the
sea, such as La Bahia de Todos Santos, a populous and rich city. /f.25/ Bahia, situated at
15° South, is the best port of any in the equatorial region.[1] At the entrance to the bar the
port has an islet which adversely affects the
entrance, in such a way that, although the
entrance is three leagues wide, no ocean ships
can enter this port without passing within
cannon shot of a fortress which in 1540 King
D.Juan erected on the point of the mainland.
This was its defence from the Lutherites of
France for more than nineteen years, until
over-confidence led to it being allowed to fall
into ruins, as I myself saw in 1560.[2]

1.   BAHIA Bahia is situated at 12° 50'S: contemporary sources gave 13° 0' and
13° 20' (López de Velasco 1971, 288; Soares de Souza 1851, 117), so Andrada's 15°
may be a copying error or misprint.   In 1584 Bahia was estimated to have a
population of some 15,000, of whom 3,000 were Portuguese and the remainder
Christian Indians and black slaves (Cardim 1978, 175).   Note that Andrada uses
the term **'la Bahia'** which enables him to switch (confusingly) between the two
meanings, that of the bay and that of the city.

2.   BAHIA FORTRESS "Although the mouth of the bay is some twenty-five miles
wide, access is reduced to two channels, one on either side of the Island of
Itaparica.   ...   The passage for deep-water vessels is some five miles wide
between Itaparica and the promontory on the eastern extremity of the bay.   In
colonial times, ... sandbanks reduced the width of this channel to some two
miles" (Russell-Wood 1968, 43).   Andrada is later more specific about the
proposed fortification.   'On San Antonio Point a strongpoint should be
constructed, or rather the one which fell down should be rebuilt, then no enemy
fleet will enter because ... it would be in the centre of the range of cannon
firing from that point on the shore ... because the entry is obstructed with
sand, and the island there narrows it' (f44v).   The sandbanks may have been such
in the sixteenth century that the channel was nearer the shore, but Andrada
probably over-estimates the power of the proposed fort.   The earliest formal
Portuguese settlement at Bahia was in 1537 but serious fortifications were only
built in 1549-1551 (Varnhagen 1959, 1:241).   A 1587 description of the town
referred to the "channel of Santo António", two leagues across but with one
league of rocky shallows, and to artillery on Padrão Point, in order "to defend
the mouth of the channel against pirate ships, should they attack the city".   But
it continued with a view of the situation probably more realistic than that of
Andrada.   "From there the guns can do no more damage to the ships than to put
them off their course and prevent them reaching the port at first approach, for
the channel is very wide and ships can pass without the artillery harming them"
(Soares de Souza 1851, chaps.XIII,XVII, pp.125,128).   For the decay of the
fortifications, see note 9 below.   In 1592, Abreu de Brito called for the
reconstruction of Santo António Fort and the building of another fort on a "ledge
[of rocks]" lying in the mouth of the channel and dry at high-tide (Abreu de
Brito 1931, 85-6).

[The wreck of the 'São Paulo' off Sumatra - other disasters caused by the lack of a refuge or refitting port in West Africa]

To save the ship 'San Pablo' and those aboard, in passage to the East Indies we made port at Bahia, to winter there, for want of being able to water at Sierra Leone. **/f.25v/** This wintering was the reason why, after we left in October and doubled the Cape of Good Hope, we went so far astray that, by sailing outside the island of San Laurencio [Madagascar], we overshot India and reached Tapobrana, the island of Sumatra, where we were wrecked. Of the 840 persons aboard, thirteen of us survived and no more.[3]

3.   'SAN PABLO' WRECKED The 'São Paulo', commanded by Ruy Melo da Camara, sailed in April with the 1560 fleet, but after being becalmed off Guinea, in mid August had to seek port at Bahia in Brazil (the previous year it had been driven back to Lisbon) (Fonseca 1926, 366; Paez 1937, 62; Boxer 1968, 66-7). Bahia was not a regular port of call for India ships and during the sixteenth century only 24 made port there (De Matos 1988, 161). The **Misericordia** (municipal almshouse) at Bahia made a collection for the sick aboard the vessel (Russell-Wood 1968, 86). A stay of six weeks at Bahia coincided with the return of governor Mem de Sá from his successful attack on the French settlement in Rio de Janeiro, and "over a hundred men" left the ship to go on an exploring journey to the interior (but a few new passengers also joined the ship at Bahia). In early October, the ship left for India. After passing the Cape of Good Hope it took the course to the East of Madagascar, but in high seas eventually ran aground on an islet off Sumatra. A large party of survivors reached the mainland, and after suffering losses from an attack by local Muslims, reached safety. A popular account of this episode was published in 1565 and later incorporated into the **História Trágico-Marítima** (Boxer 1968, 4-12,56-107). According to other sources, pilots at Bahia had advised that the ship could leave in October provided that it headed for Sumatra and then sailed back to India on the February monsoon: it actually sailed in September but passed the Cape of Good Hope "too late" and had to take the outer course around Madagascar (Couto 1778, dec.7, liv.9, cap.5, 336; cap.16, 422-8; Salvador 1965, liv.3, cap.9 - this source contradicts the popular account by stating that the governor arrived back at Bahia in July). If the report of the pilots' advice is correct, Andrada is wrong about the ship's 'erroneous course'. He is certainly wrong about the numbers involved in the shipwreck: a few died after the ship struck but 330 or 340 reached the shore, of whom probably about 100 died later, so the final survivors must have numbered over 200 (Frazão de Vasconcelos 1948; Duffy 1955, 129,160; Boxer 1968, 78,88,102). Despite Andrada's categorical use of the first person plural, it must be doubted whether he was a participant in the shipwreck. While he refers several times to his later life in Brazil, he makes no reference to ever having lived in Asia, and no personal comment on any part of that continent. Hence it is likely that in fact he left the 'São Paulo' at Bahia, and that his knowledge of the Sumatra episode came from the 1565 publication. Moreover, an account of the shipwreck stated that one of the two Jesuits aboard served as **cura** (priest with pastoral responsibility) because the ship did not carry a **clérigo** (regular priest or chaplain) (Gomes de Brito, 2:27) - which suggests that the **clérigo** Andrada was not aboard. It is difficult to understand why Andrada should lie - or at the very least, word his statements so carelessly as to give a false impression. Perhaps he had been telling the story of the shipwreck for decades and could not now retract. His figure for the number of persons aboard the ship when wrecked, 840, is wrong, but is not inconceivable as a total if it instead represents the number who embarked at Lisbon, Portuguese vessels often being vastly overcrowded (Boxer 1959, 17). The 1565 account states that, when off Guinea, at one stage 350 were ill out of "over 500 people in the ship"; but it is not clear whether 'over 500' was the number still alive by that stage, or the number embarking at Lisbon (ibid., 64). Allowing for high mortality and for the "over a hundred" who disembarked at Bahia, Andrada's figure of 840 could perhaps have been reduced to the estimated number of 350-360 (330-340 survivors, plus twenty drowned) by the time the ship struck.

By such passages and roundabout courses, the
famous Manoel de Sosa was lost.[4]   And in 1562
Diego Lopez de Mezquita was lost.[5]   And while
your Majesty was in Lisbon, Captain Gaspar de
Brito was lost.[6]   And in 1588 Captain Diego
Dazambuja was lost in Angola (because he failed
to seek refuge at the island of St Helena when
on his way from India to Portugal); and when he
was conveying the goods from Angola (**la hazienda de Angola**) (where the ship was disabled by
worm-damage **/f.26/** in the latitude of the
Ialophos), the corsair, Antonio de Silva from
La Rochelle, robbed and plundered the goods.[7]
All these losses happened to Spain because Your
Majesty has not fortified the sea and its fine
waterways, those mentioned above and those to
which we shall hereafter refer.

4. MANOEL DE SOSA It is uncertain which 'famous Manoel de Sosa' is meant. Mentioned by Camoens in the **Lusíadas** of 1572 (and the subject of an epic by a minor poet published in 1594) was the death of D.Manuel de Sousa Sepulveda and his wife, after shipwreck on the coast of eastern Africa in 1552: an account of the shipweck was published at an uncertain date, possibly before Andrada wrote (Duffy 1955, pp/8-9). This was indeed a famous episode, yet it is difficult to see that 'roundabout courses' were involved during this return voyage from India. A possible but less likely alternative is the Manuel de Souza who commanded the 'Santo António' on the 1519 India fleet: in the Indian Ocean the ship lost touch with the other vessels and after leaving Mozambique ran out of food, which with other difficulties caused the death of the captain and "all his men - **uma miserabilissima tragedia**" (Paez 1937, 32). The episode bears some relationship to the voyage of the 'São Paulo', in that the ship was lost while travelling to India, but is probably too early for Andrada. An even less likely alternative is the shipwreck and death of Manuel de Sousa Coutinho, the returning governor of India, in February 1592 (Fonseca 1926, 423; Boxer 1959, 54). This occurred on the Garajos Shoals, to the East of Madagascar, and the passage of the 'São Paulo' was through this region; but the notice almost certainly reached Iberia too late for Andrada's composition.

5. DIEGO LOPEZ DE MEZQUITA Diogo Lopes de Lima, alias de Mesquita, commanded the 'Graça' in the 1563 fleet, but in February 1564 the ship was driven on to the Maldive Islands (Paez 1937, 64).

6. GASPAR DE BRITO King Philip was in Lisbon from 29 June 1581 to 11 February 1583 (Serro 1979, 20,23). Gaspar de Brito do Rio, posted to Ormuz, travelled in the 1582 India fleet on the 'Santo Luiz', which was forced to winter on the African coast and was then wrecked off Quelimane: the survivors had various adventures in the Zambesi region and Gaspar de Brito died from fever at Mozambique (Couto 1778, dec.10, pt.1, liv.3, cap.8, 324,326-7; Axelson 1973, 218, citing a manuscript account).

7. DIEGO DAZAMBUJA According to Couto, Diogo de Azambuja, after a distinguished military career in the East, returned in a ship which because of its leaky condition was lost in Angola, but he and the cargo were saved (Couto 1778, dec.10, pt.1, liv.8, cap.16, 373). Andrada's reference seems garbled, since Angola is nowhere near 'the latitude of the Ialophos'. If Andrada is correct, the ship was lost off Angola because of worm-damage causing leaks, and then later, when Diogo de Azambuja was proceeding from Angola with the goods, he was attacked as stated. However, **'La hazienda de Angola'** might mean the **hazienda real** (Portuguese **fazenda real**) or Treasury revenue from Angola. António da Silva has been mentioned earlier (f.8v).

[The English attack on Bahia in 1588 - the need for new fortifications, lest the English seize the city]

Returning to the discussion of the fortification of Bahia, I point out that, because it is not secure as it should be, in 1588 the English entered it with two ships and burned the entire fleet, which was anchored inside the bar and was laden with riches. And all the people of the city, religious and secular, ignominiously fled, because the city had no bastion, no towers, and not even the former earthworks (**cavas**), although it had once been a very strong place, as I observed in 1560.[8] This must be because the governors were neglectful /f.26v/ in times of peace.[9] They did not raise militia, although they were surrounded by wealth, as was the case at the time the city was conquered. An impregnable fort, under whose guns many ships could shelter, could be built in Bahia.

8. ENGLISH ATTACK ON BAHIA In April 1587 (not 1588), two English vessels commanded by Robert Withrington entered the roadstead of Bahia, seized a number of ships lying there, and spent a month in the bay. According to the English account, the captured ships had already unloaded and therefore no 'riches' were gained. An attack on the town was abandoned because of the growing resistance of the local Portuguese and their Indian allies (Hakluyt 1589, 798-801). Andrada's reference seems unduly critical of the Portuguese situation and the townspeople's response. Writing in 1592, Abreu de Brito also spoke of the weakness of the defences of Bahia and the afflictions imposed on the town in "the time of Your Majesty" by corsairs and Lutherites, but was not more specific about the latter (Abreu de Brito 1931, 85).

9. FORTIFICATION NEGLECTED A local writer noted in 1587 that the walls of the city had "crumbled to the ground because they were of mud and never repaired; as far as is known, either the governors were careless, or the city spread out beyond the walls. ... [Because of] the disorder of this city, the King should order it to be walled and fortified" (Soares de Souza 1851, chaps. VII, XIV, pp.118,125). Andrada repeats his call for fortification on f.44v.

Magellan Strait on a Portuguese map of c.1575, with an imaginary continent to the South (f.1v, passim)

The site [of the city] is similar [to the area]
from the Almada, facing Lisbon, to as far as
Cabo del Spichel.   Its boundaries are very
wide.[10]   I shall not discuss its wealth in
detail, in order not to deviate from my purpose
in this tract; and also because I shall deal
with it at greater length in a book I am writing, in the service of God, about the fourfold
division of the universe, which is intended to
encourage many religious to decide to go out to
preach the Gospel, once they have been persuaded by the many arguments I will present to them
for this.[11]   I must state here that **la Bahia**
['the bay'] and inlet extends nineteen leagues
northwards and in the middle is ten leagues
across.[12] /f.27/ The danger is great that Bahia
might be seized by those who oppose us, should
they decide to form a settlement there for the
purpose of entering Peru by way of Magellan
Strait.   For, indeed, sailing from this port
they could leave for Magellan Strait in
September and would reach it, going at a leis-
urely pace, in fifteen days with a favourable
wind; and if they were to leave in November,
they would have an even better voyage.   Once
clear of the strait they would carry out in
Peru whatever they wished in safety.

10.   EXTENT OF LA BAHIA The distance between the Almada, a locality on the South bank of the River Tagus, and Cabo de Espichel, the NW point of Baia de Setúbal, is nearly 30 km. This is less than the distance Andrada later states for the length of the bay; therefore he must be indicating the extreme boundaries of the city, although not of course the size of its built-up area.

11.   A BOOK I AM WRITING This work does not appear to have been published and perhaps it was never completed.

12.   THE BAY For a contemporary map of Bahia and the bay, see Varnhagen 1959, 2: opposite p.18. A league being about 5.5 km, and the actual length of the bay being about 50 km, Andrada exaggerates grossly by giving the length as 19 leagues (105 km); and the maximum width is similarly exaggerated.

Off Paraíba - a Portuguese ship attacks a French vessel, 1548 - note the Pitiguare Indians (ff.5v-6,31v)

[The renegades flee Iberian decline]

Although there are as many opinions [on the point] as there are speakers, I state the following. The intentions of the Lutherites are carefully concealed from men who are not [after all] soldiers, and in ignorance a number of pilots and navigators have gone over to England, not knowing what [the English] are determined to do against Your Majesty in one year or another. And they have begun to marry **/f.27v/** Lutherite women, behaving like men who have lost confidence in any remedy and like men without a country. They have gained a relish for the ill deeds they continue to commit at sea, and for converting the hearts of many of those whom they capture daily from the ships of Spain. To prevent this, it is necessary that Your Majesty command his vassals to close the doors of Janus, and take up the arms of faith and justice, in order to defend their country, so that by obeying Your Majesty they may extend God's religion.

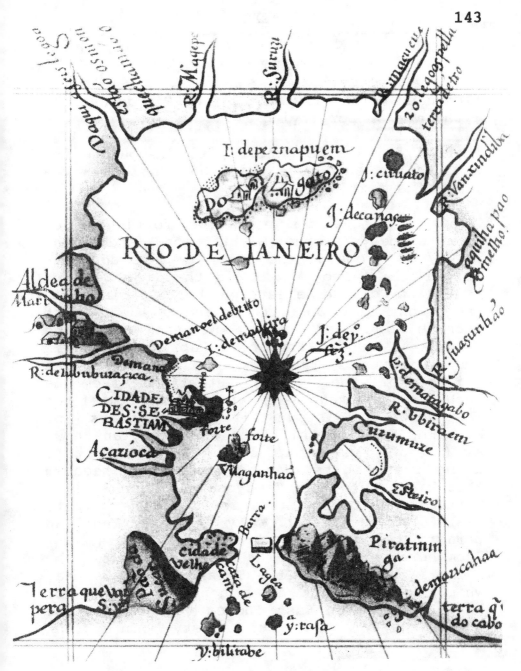

Rio de Janeiro c.1570 - note the 'lagea' and the
site of 'Villegaignon Fort' (ff.6,28-28v)

CHAPTER 10

[The need to fortify the city of Río de Janeiro
- the aim of fortifying it]

[Fortifying Rio de Janeiro, to discourage the
English and encourage the local Indians - the
site of a fort]

So far we have discussed the fortifying of
three places, Ialopho, Sierra Leona, and Bahia.
/f.28/ As regards the system we are advocat-
ing, it is [also] advisable that the City of
Sebastian (**ciudad Sebastiana**) be fortified.[1] It
stands on Rio de Janeiro, on the mainland coast
running North and South, down from Bahia and
exactly under the Tropic of Capricorn, and in
the Kingdom of the Tamoyos, who are great
friends of the French Lutherites from La
Rochelle.[2] Whereas Bahia and the Kingdom of the
Tupinambas are distant thirty-five degrees from
Magellan Strait, this City of Sebastian known
as Rio de Janeiro is the most coveted port
among those ports of the ocean sea, because
this kingdom [of the Tamoyos] has been [a sup-
port] for the Lutherites for more than twenty
years, and because the city is nearer Magellan
Strait, being thirty-three degrees distant.[3]
From here, sailing by the East-West route, the
Lutherites make for the Island of St Helena,
which is important as a general refuge for
those sailing on East Indies voyages and for
the /f.28v/ trade of Your Majesty.[4] On account

1.   CIUDAD SEBASTIANA For the 'City of (St) Sebastian', see note 1 to Chapter 3.

2.   TAMOYOS For the Tamoyo, see note 18 to Chapter 2; and for the Tamoyo and the French in the 1550s and 1560s, the Portuguese Jesuit attempt to win over a section of the Tamoyo, and the final Portuguese campaign against the Tamoyo of the 1570s and 1580s which led to the retreat of the remnants of the latter into the interior, see Soares de Souza 1851, chap.LVIII; Julien 1948, chap.IV.

3.   LATITUDES The correct latitudes South are as follows: Bahia 12° 50', Rio de Janeiro 22° 54' (thus almost 'exactly under the Tropic of Capricorn'), Magellan Strait 52° 30' (as generally recognised in Andrada's day, López de Velasco 1971, 277).   Therefore the distance between Bahia and the Strait is nearly forty degrees and between Rio de Janeiro and the Strait almost thirty degrees - an advantage for Rio de Janeiro so much greater than the one by Andrada's calculation that perhaps a misprint is involved.   'Tupinamba' was the name given by the Portuguese and French to the Amerindian people(s) around Bahia.

4.   ST HELENA For St Helena, see note 1 to Chapter 13.

From the **História Trágico-Marítima**

of these advantages, the Tamayos of that kingdom are favourably disposed towards the French,
so that they have become their subjects and
always help them against the Portuguese in
their continual wars; and if this city is not
fortified, it will have few **pueblos** (native
communi-ities) on its side. The English will
[then] gain the city by land and by sea.[5]   But,
whatever their strength, they will not do this
if Your Majesty commands that an impressive and
powerful strongpoint be constructed on the rock
at the mouth of the channel. At neap tide and
at low tide this rock emerges well above the
sea, and at spring tide it is completely covered; and therefore no enemies coming by sea
would have to be feared, for the channel is
narrow, only half a gunshot wide, and any
[ships] preparing to enter could be sent to the
bottom.[6] But if the city is not fortified, and
those who oppose us were to seize it, as /f.29/
they design to do, then they would gain the
island of St Helena, and in consequence all of
Brazil and Peru. For they know very well that
by winning this city they would also win
Cartagena in the New Kingdom [of Granada].[7]

5. FEAR OF THE ENGLISH   The fear that the English would gain Brazil, in particular by obtaining Amerindian allies, was not confined among the Portuguese to Andrada; but it was in the event exaggerated. Factors contributing to the fear were the long-term French alliance with several of the Amerindian peoples of Brazil, the spasmodic alliance in the 1570s and 1580s of Drake and his English successors with the **cimarrones** (run-away slaves) of Central America (leading to momentary fears of a general slave uprising in Spanish America), and two English naval assaults on Brazil in the 1580s - the battle of the Fenton expedition with Spanish ships at São Vicente in 1583, and the attack on Bahia of 1587 noted by Andrada earlier (f.28) (Madox 1976, 34-8). (Andrada wrote before Lancaster's 1595 assault on Pernambuco: Hakluyt 1598, 3:709-715). Had Andrada seen Hakluyt's 1589 volumes, he would have noted the publicising in English of a rutter of Brazil, although also of documentation of attempts to develope peaceful trading with Brazil - attempts, however, not necessarily regarded as peaceful by the Portuguese (Hakluyt 1589, 638-642,803-6). Moreover, as early as 1579-1580 Hakluyt had privately recommended the seizure of the "Iland of St Vincent", to back up the seizure of Magellan Strait (Taylor 1935, 141).

6. FORTIFICATION OF RIO DE JANEIRO   When Andrada repeats this recommendation, he refers to the rock as an 'islet', and adds that the city itself is well enough fortified (f.45). In 1587, Soares de Sousa pointed out that the battery of guns on a headland below the city covered the port but not the entrance channel. However, the entrance to the bay, half a league wide between two heights (one the famous 'Sugarloaf'), has "in the middle, created by Nature, a ledge of rocks (**lagea**), 50 fathoms long and 25 wide, on which could be built a fort, at little expense, which would be one of the best in the world, and would defend the river against all comers, for the channel is only a musket-shot away from the **lagea**, and ships entering are forced to pass within hail of it". Guns there would cover as far as the heights, which are too steep for counter-artillery (Soares de Souza 1851, chaps. 49,51, pp.81,83). In 1585, the Spanish admiral, Santa Cruz, also noted a **baxa** ('flats') in the entry suitable for a fort, on which he feared Drake might land guns to command the port (Hakluyt 1598, 3:531). For a contemporary map of these dispositions, showing the entrance and naming the **lagea**, see p.143 above; and for a modern description of the deepwater channel and the **'Laje'**, see Varnhagen 1959, 1: 323, n.1. Thus Andrada's proposal was sensible but not original.

7. THE ENGLISH STRATEGY   Andrada's wider and wilder notions of strategy now appear. The line of thought seems to be that (a) the English conquest of Rio de Janeiro would be followed by the occupation of St Helena, (b) hence Iberian control of the South Atlantic would be lost, (c) hence the English would conquer not only Brazil but also Peru, presumably by means of their unrestricted access to Magellan Strait, following Drake's example. Even less watertight logically is the final reference to Cartagena. It is not at all obvious that the loss of Rio de Janeiro would have entailed the loss of Cartagena, but perhaps Andrada

[How this fortifying would destroy the Lutherites]

I state, and may God be my witness - it being He who guides my tongue - that the Lutherites and their commanders are disposed to retain for all time and to settle for their security such maritime localities, because they love life on the ocean and the wealth it brings. This I can most exactly demonstrate to the point of con- clusiveness, as I will do should Your Majesty so command me. Were Your Majesty to fortify these various districts, the perils which threaten us as time advances would not cont- inue, and the sufferings of the kingdoms and provinces of Your Majesty would cease. The hardships which the Spaniards experience, the losses, robberies and **/f.29v/** assaults, all these would be switched to the Lutherites. For the Lutherites would perish in the midst of the seas and being only flesh and blood would sick- en in the Tropics, for it is clear that if there was no refuge for them in the ports men- tioned above they would gradually exhaust them- selves. Once they see that Your Majesty is awakened [to the threat], they will become dis- illusioned. And, please God, inasmuch as they sail wantonly against the Church, so the Spaniards will be spirited to proceed against them, seeing that Your Majesty's cause is just and your royal heart is in the hands of God. I so much long for those forts to be built, because their provision and effective operation would aid us, and indeed would lift our spirits and make us imitate our ancestors in supporting our country without fail, and, trusting God, in the service of Your Majesty. **/f.30/**

means that the loss of Peru, the assumed consequence of the loss of Rio de
Janeiro, would end the trade to and from Peru which passed, via the Isthmus,
through Cartagena, and hence would ruin that port. However, part of this was
common Spanish thinking. In 1585, Santa Cruz feared lest Drake gain in turn Rio
de Janeiro, São Vicente, Magellan Strait, and Ciudad de los Reyes or Lima
(Hakluyt 1598, 3:531).

Off Rio de Janeiro - a French ship attacks a Portuguese
ship (twice), 1554 - note the Tupinamba Indians (ff.6,28)

CHAPTER 11

[Santa Catarina Island - the English threat in Africa - the need to fortify the island - the need for new convoys and for more scientific knowledge of ocean conditions]

[The Lutherites at Santa Catarina Island]

Below Rio de Janeiro and the City of Sebastian, to the South, is an island called Santa Catalina. It is near the land and coast of Cananea and beyond the kingdom of Brazil, and is about fifteen degrees from Magellan Strait.[1] Here the Lutherites flock with so much skill in navigation that it is a thing to wonder at, although they are assisted by our mariners [and the] ports mentioned above.[2]

1.   SANTA CATALINA ISLAND In the sixteenth century, the precise boundary between the Portuguese and the Spanish domains on the Atlantic coast of South America, as laid down in the 1494 Treaty of Tordesillas, was uncertain, partly because of the contemporary inability to measure longitude exactly. "According to one of King Philip's cosmographers, there were no less than 54 ways to interpret the Tordesillas line" (Teixeira da Mota 1973; Goodman 1988, 53-65). In practice, since the Spaniards were chiefly interested in the Andean regions on the Pacific side of the continent and the Portuguese chiefly in the settler colonies of Bahia and Pernambuco on the Atlantic side, the coast between São Vicente and the River Plate estuary was a grey area, not very actively disputed by either party (López de Velasco 1971, 286-7; Soares de Souza 1851, chap.LXXIV, p.110; Haring 1947, 99). This coast was explored by the Portuguese before 1550 but not occupied. The Spaniards regarded it as a stepping stone towards River Plate and the interior. Several Spanish naval expeditions used Santa Catarina Island as a base; while Cabeza de Vaca in 1542 pioneered an overland route to Asunción which began on the mainland coast opposite the island. Andrada tactfully places the island 'beyond the kingdom of Brazil', that is, outside the official Portuguese domain. Santa Catarina Island lies at 27° 41' S, therefore some twenty-five degrees from Magellan Strait, not fifteen. For a contemporary description of the island, see Soares de Souza 1851, chap.LXVII, p.103; and for a contemporary chart of the island, see p.153 below.

2.   LUTHERITES FLOCK The 'Lutherites' are most probably the English, since after the 1560s the French operated only in northern Brazil. In 1580, an English trader anchored at Santa Catarina Island, and in 1582 the Fenton voyage anchored in a bay to the South of the island, but otherwise I cannot trace any evidence that English ships had made use of the island or its immediate vicinity by 1590. However, if Andrada's reference is to a wider area, in 1582 one Fenton vessel was wrecked in River Plate, in 1586 the Cumberland expedition visited the river, and in 1590 an English vessel attempted Magellan Strait - as became known to the Spaniards (Hakluyt 1589, 642,659,673,795-6; Hakluyt 1598, 3:562,839). In 1585 and 1587 a Spanish official writing from Buenos Aires warned about the threat to the coast between Cananéia and Río de la Plata if the English or the French established themselves on Santa Catarina Island, citing Fenton's visit to the river, and he asked that a fortress be built at Buenos Aires (Levillier 1915, 371,383-4,414).

[The Lutherites in western Africa]

They are so skilled that they depart from
England for [? **read** and] France, and no matter
how many days they spend at sea roaming about
in Spanish waters they arrive in twenty days at
Ialopho. There they refresh themselves, and
from there make their way along the whole of
Guinea, from port to port, [that is,] to
Gambia, Santo Domingo, **/f.30v/** Rio Grande,
Sierra Leona, Rio de las Gallinas, Bahia de los
Cestos, Mina, Axem, the islands of Príncipe and
São Tomé, Angola and Manicongo. And from
there, laden with gold, ambergris and other
riches of the Orient, they return from a
passage to the Equator.[3] Some of them carry on
trading and loading their ships as if they were
absolute lords, while they are defaming the
Christians by giving out arms. Others turn
themselves into heathens like the Blacks and
Indians, observing their rites, their bacchan-
alia, and their wicked customs, to the great
offence of God. Living like heathens they
change themselves into such.

3. GUINEA PORTS The list of localities along the western coast of Africa from Cape Verde to the Congo ('Manicongo', a common variant) and Angola, is in order from West to East, except that Axem should be immediately before Mina, and Manicongo before Angola. Only Congo and Angola are South of the Equator. It is unlikely that Andrada, from his base in the Cape Verde Islands, had ever visited any part of the coast East of Sierra Leone.

Santa Catarina Island, Brazil, as charted during the English visit of 1582 (f.30)

[Santa Catarina Island controls the River Plate and routes to the interior and Peru]

All this [occurs] because Santa Catalina Island is next to the mouth of Rio Grande, by which the Portuguese daily make an entry to Las Charcas del Peru,[4] more than 200 leagues on from this river.[5] And from Peru many come to Brazil [this way]. **/f.31/**

4. OVERLAND ROUTE TO LAS CHARCAS For an earlier reference, see f.7v and note 7 to Chapter 3. An overland route between the coast of southern (modern) Brazil and the River Paraná, the principal river feeding into River Plate, was opened up before 1550. This provided a shorter route to Peru, via Asunción in Paraguay, alternative to the longer route via the Plate estuary, the lower Paraná and Asunción. The shorter overland route was inaugurated for large-scale European travel by the Spaniard, Cabeza de Vaca, in 1542, but as he had assistance from a Portuguese guide, it appears to have been used previously by parties of Portuguese, as well as by Amerindians (Varnhagen 1959, 1:95,136). In mid-century the Paraná river system was extensively explored by the Spaniards, largely in the search for minerals (Levillier 1915, passim); and in 1554 "a small herd of European cattle was driven all the way from the coast to Asunción" (Parry/Keith 1984, 247). Andrada has earlier referred to this route for the interior (p.7v), and he now claims that Portuguese 'daily' use it - his information probably relates to the period of his own experience in Brazil, in the 1560s. It was in fact the Spaniards who regularly used the whole length of the route, although only occasionally because of its difficulties and dangers. However, it is clear that, from the 1530s and the establishment of an interior settlement at Piratinga, later São Paulo de Piratinga, individual Portuguese adventurers penetrated into the **sertão** (hinterland) from the São Vicente area, and some of these forerunners of the **bandeirantes** used the first section of the route (Varnhagen 1959, 1:136; Teixeira da Mota 1968, 10-12). For the 'Rio Grande', see the next note.

5. RIO GRANDE Earlier Andrada has stated that Santa Catarina Island is 'next' to River Plate (f.7v) (similarly, governor Tomé de Sousa reported in the 1550s that Asunción and São Vicente were "very close": Malheiro Dias 1924, 3:366). Now Andrada says that the island is 'next' to 'Rio Grande', while later he appears to say that the island is only distant from the mouth of this river 'a day and night' (f.45v). Which waterway was his 'Rio Grande' ?

'Big River' is a very common Iberian river-name, hence, for instance, two small waterways near São Vicente were at one time each known locally as 'Rio Grande' (Staden 1874, iv,lii). (It may even be relevant that a 1587 source described 'Rio dos Patos' as **"muito grande"**: Soares de Souza 1951, chap. LXVII, p.103.) A Spanish source of 1557 spoke of "a river called the Ygay, or Rio Grande, which emerges on the coast of Santa Catalina" (Levillier 1915, 224). Moreover, a tributary of the Paraná, the Iguaçu, which undoubtedly formed part of the interior portion of the overland route, has a Tupi name which means 'big water', hence the Spaniards called it 'Rio Grande' (López de Velasco 1971, 285); while the full Tupi name of the Paraná itself, Parana Uaçu, means 'big river' (not 'little sea' as Andrada suggests), and was originally applied even to the River Plate estuary. At the present point in the text, as in an earlier reference to 'Rio Grande', Andrada mentions a distance of 'more than 200 leagues' (f.7v). The earlier reference is capable of being read as indicating that 'Rio Grande' was a river navigable for some 200 leagues (700 km), and if this were correct, then it would rule out any river other than the Plate/Paraná itself. However, later in the present paragraph the Rio Grande is said to provide a route which 'emerges at the mouth of the Parana', thus ruling out the identity of the Rio Grande with the Paraná. Although Andrada fails to make it clear whether the

Here in this district, when I was on the mainland, on the coast of Cananea, I spoke with an Araucanian captain, who had come there as a captive in the hands of the Carijos, who belong to the kingdom of Río de la Plata.[6] This kingdom lies immediately below the island at 35°, on the same parallel as the Cape of Good Hope, at a distance of fifteen degrees, more or less, from Magellan Strait, as can be seen in the **Cosmographia.**[7] Since Brazil extends in a North/South direction from the Equator, the island lines up NE/SW with Magellan Strait. A healthy and fertile land, it is flat like Andalusia. Towards the West there are more than 200 leagues of pine trees, from which ships like those of Holland and Zeeland could be built. Also there is much gold there.[8]

passage by Rio Grande to Rio Paraná is an all-water route or a route partly (or largely) over land, provided that we assume that he had a reasonable knowledge of the local geography, he must have meant to indicate the latter. (Some contemporaries, however, believed in an all-water route between the Brazilian coast and the Paraná. "The settlers in the captaincy of São Vicente claim that they have been told by the Indians that the São Francisco River is a branch of the Para[ná]": Soares de Souza 1951, chap.LXV, p.101.) Despite the fact that maps produced by Fernão Vaz Dourado between 1568 and 1580 showed more than one waterway linking the coast South of Santa Catarina Island and the Paraná-Uruguay (PMC 1960, 3:plates 253,321), we probably need not consider the possibility that Andrada's 'Rio Grande' represented a river on the coast far to the South, such as the Rio Grande do Sul (alias Rio Grande de São Pedro), which was known as 'Rio Grande' at least by the early seventeenth century (Oliveira Freitas 1975, 239,264). It seems more likely that Andrada was describing the actual route to the interior from the coast (and not a route he had invented from a poor knowledge of the geography), that his 'Rio Grande' was a river close to Santa Catarina Island (hence a short river), and that the route only began with the Rio Grande and thereafter proceeded into the interior overland (although making use of some rivers on the other side of the watershed). The present point in the text supports this interpretation, and the translation of the earlier reference (f.7v), which is more ambiguous, has been shaped to fit. Andrada's 'Rio Grande' was probably not the tiny Rio Masiambu.

6.   AN ARAUCANIAN IN CANANEA The "coast of Cananea" (Cananéia), as described by Soares de Souza 1851, chap.LXV, pp.101-2, lay midway between São Vicente (modern Santos) and Santa Catarina Island. Andrada may have been on this coast in the 1560s while serving as a missionary in Brazil; and since the Portuguese from São Vicente occasionally visited the coast to the South to trade (Archivo Colonial 1916, 156), it is just possible that Andrada had visited Santa Catarina Island (and hence his phrase - 'when I was on the mainland'). The Amerindian people known to sixteenth-century Europeans as Carijos occupied the coast of southern (modern) Brazil between Cananéia (27° 59' S) and the Rio dos Patos (Soares de Souza 1951, chaps.LXV-LXVII, pp.102-4). Andrada describes the Carijo as belonging to 'the kingdom of Río de la Plata', but this is misleading, inasmuch as another Amerindian people, the Tapuia, occupied the coast between Rio dos Patos and the Plate estuary (ibid., chaps.LXIX-LXXII, pp.105-7). The Araucanian Amerindians lived in southern Chile, where they resisted the Spanish advance for a considerable period (giving rise to the Spanish epic poem, **La Araucana** by Alonso de Ercilla, published 1569-1589, which Andrada may have read). Possibly this Araucanian was a former Spanish captive who had been transported eastwards to Las Charcas and from there escaped further eastwards into the hands of the Carijo.

7.   RÍO DE LA PLATA River Plate does indeed lie at 35° 0' S - seventeen degrees from Magellan Strait, not fifteen - but the Cape of Good Hope lies at 32° 0' S.

8.   LIKE ANDALUSIA Santa Catarina Island is not all 'flat' and the coast opposite is hilly, but further South the coast and interior are "al a plaine land, and very low" (Hakluyt 1598, 3:278). In the 1580s, the island was "covered

Once this island is fortified, **/f.31v/** it will be possible to go from it to Río de la Plata by this river, emerging at the mouth of another river which enters Río de la Plata about thirty leagues upstream, a river called the Parana, which means 'little sea'. Copper is found in infinite quantity all along this river. And it comes down from the interior part of Las Charcas and Santa Cruz de la Sierra.[9]

with thick forest", but to the South the coast comprised only grasslands "and without woods" (Hakluyt 1598, 3:788; Soares de Souza 1951, chap.LXVII, p.103). The Englishman, Roger Barlow, who sailed with the Cabot expedition and spent some months on the island in 1526-1527, described "grete plentie of tymber, goodlie trees and of grete length"; and Cabot used the timber to build a ship (Barlow 1932, xxxv-xxxviii,150). Compared with those further North, the coasts near the island were said to be "like Spain" in climate, fertility, vegetation and appearance (ibid., chaps.LXII-LXIX, pp.98-105). Andrada repeats earlier Portuguese references to gold (and silver - hence 'Río de la Plata') in the hinterland of this coast (Teixeira da Mota 1968, 10,102). But the gold was probably that of far-away Peru rather than that of the Brazilian interior, which had not yet been discovered.

9. COPPER Santa Cruz de la Sierra (Bolivia) had an earlier site, said to be marked by ruins near San José de Chiquitos (Parry/Keith 1984, 437). For copper in Río de la Plata provinces, see López de Velasco 1971, 282; and for Spain's search for copper, to make bronze cannon, see Goodman 1988, 110-117. Andrada's syntax and punctuation are such that what 'comes down' from the interior may be either Río de la Plata or the copper, but is probably the former.

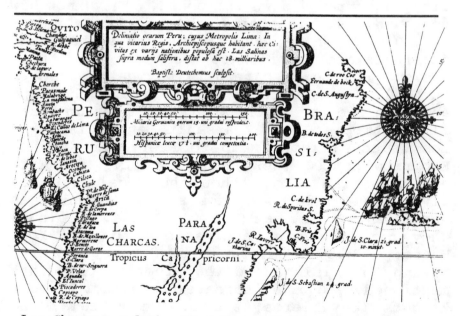

Las Charcas and the Paraná, as shown on a Dutch map
of 1598 (ff.7v,30v,31v)

[The Lutherites threaten from River Plate to
the northern coast of Brazil]

Over that crossroads the Lutherites now cast
their net. For they block Río de la Plata, and
threaten St Helena, Brazil, and Peru, via the
mouth of that river and Magellan Strait; and
thus, as I have indicated, the Lutherites plan
and make their navigations to the rivers and
ports of the Orient.[10] They also cross the
Equator above Paranapuca [Pernambuco], which is
the Province of New Lusitania, and from there
they visit the city called Filipina [Philip's
City] and travel down the coast. They know how
to round, even in storms, Cabo de Santo Agustino, /f.32/ where many fleets and ships bound
for India and Brazil have been lost with their
crews. But being carefully navigated to capture the winds, [their ships] round the cape
and then rob the strongpoints and prey on Brazilian shipping. They assault Bahia city, and
Los Isleos [Ilhéus], up to Puerto Seguro and
Espiritu Santo, [next] the city of Cabo Frio
and Sebastian City, [then the localities of]
Biriquioca, Tañaem, Santos and S. Vicente, as
far as this point, at Santa Catalina.[11] [Thus]
they direct their machinations against Your
Majesty. But you may be assured that, by fortifying this island and the other strongpoints
mentioned, you will increase the number of your
knights (**cavalleros**) and create vassals; and
you will weigh heavily on all those opposed to
Your Majesty and make yourself feared.

10.   LUTHERITES IN THE ORIENT The only 'Lutherites' who by 1590 had voyaged to the East by Magellan Strait were English, the voyages being those of Drake in 1577-1580 and Cavendish in 1586-1588.   A 1590 English voyage entered the Strait but failed to pass through (Hakluyt 1598, 3:839). By inference, at this point Andrada acknowledges the English circumnavigations.

11.   CIUDAD FILIPINA A 1590 document spoke of "Pernambuco da Nova Luzitania" (Malheiro Dias 1924, 3:287). For **Cidada Filipina**, see note 16 to Chapter 2. The localities named, from Cape St Augustine to Santa Catarina Island, represent a southwards movement down the Brazilian coast, except for 'Tañaem', presumably Itanhaém, which lies a little to the South of the locality represented by 'Biriquioca', Santos and São Vicente.   There was no 'city' at Cabo Frio. Elsewhere Andrada refers to 'Pernambuco', yet here he uses a variant of the original Amerindian form, 'Paranapuca' ("Paranabuca", Aires de Casal 1817, 2:128) - why ?

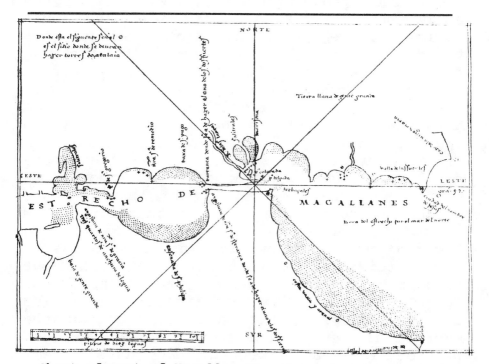

Chart of part of Magellan Strait, made by Sarmiento de Gamboa, 1583 (ff.22v-23)

[The re-routing and the loss of ships demand
their travelling in convoy]

I affirm, **nemine discrepante** (no-one can
dispute it), that in England, and in all of the
North (**Norvegia**), the Lutherites say among
themselves that Spain lacks arms, people and
seamen, as they judge entirely by the appearance /**f.32v**/ of what they have seen on the
ocean in the period from 1580 up to the present
day. They prognosticate on the basis of the
small number of ships sailing on the India
voyage that reach the Island of St Helena compared with the number that used to do this, and
to a certain extent they are correct.[12] For it
is not right that Your Majesty's fleets should
have to seek out circuitous routes and new
horizons in order to navigate directly to
Spain. Instead, they should follow the
straightforward route in convoy, as the nature
of the sea demands and as good and experienced
pilots do. I detest the contrivances of the
merchants and say this. I beg that fortresses
be built, for [our] merchants have enriched
England and France by ordering their ships to
sail outside the proper season, singly and out
of convoy, which has led to total disaster for
Spain. Assuming that fortification is carried
out, the ships of the East and those of the
West /**f.33**/ will neither be lost nor seized,
provided they sail in convoy, as I have stated.

12.   AVOIDING ST HELENA The danger to Portuguese ships of being attacked by English vessels at or near St Helena led to royal instructions being given in 1592 to the effect that no fleets returning from India were to touch at the island (Duffy 1955, 98).   Andrada's proposals for St Helena suggest that he was unaware of these instructions and therefore probably writing before they were issued.   (However, the instructions were not maintained: in 1596 an India ship stopped at the island and waited three days for the rest of the fleet, as so ordered by its instructions; and it picked up a man left there the previous year by two Portuguese vessels: Vaz Monteiro 1974, 150,156-7).

A Portuguese fleet at St Helena, probably in the 1580s
(1v, passim)

[Scientific knowledge required in order to direct ships along the best sea routes - the abstract knowledge of the Ancients modified by modern practical experience]

I declare that, as is obvious from the evidence, the shipping routes of the area from the Tropic of Cancer to Peru, to Nombre de Dios, and to Mexico and its coasts, and [also] those of the area from Sierra Leona to São Tomé and Angola, suffer very many losses of ships caused by the lack of security on the part of the fleets and ports.[13] And since those routes are directed through East-West latitudes, it necessarily requires knowledge and experience of the course of the winds and currents, and of the rising and setting of the sun. Going from Spain to India, and from Spain to the Indies, one traverses all the climes of the rotund and spherical world, a world which is regulated by the stars in their natural course, a course from which they cannot deviate or withdraw. The [present] direction [of these sea routes] has been laid down **/f.33v/** by much study of the Ancients and the experience of sailing from Pole to Pole, as carried out by various individuals who have themselves sailed these routes, in despite of all the science of Ptolemy, of Purbach and his followers, and of Euclid, since most of these [writers] based what they wrote [only] on what they knew in the abstract, not on [actual] navigation and [practical] cosmography, of which truly they had no experience.[14]

13.   SHIP LOSSES   The routes indicated are those to the Caribbean, and thence either to the Isthmus for the Peru connection or to Mexico, and those to the Guinea coast.   More broadly, Andrada is referring to the central zone of the Atlantic, through which passed the ships of the Spanish **Carrera de Indias** and the Portuguese **Carreira da Índia.**

14.   KNOWLEDGE AND EXPERIENCE   In a rather confused passage, Andrada dismisses those, both Ancients and Moderns, who have only theoretical cosmographical knowledge, Ptolemy, Euclid, 'Purbach and his followers'.   Georg von Peuerbach laid the foundations for spherical trigonometry, by establishing an observatory at Nuremberg in 1471 and compiling astronomical tables for the period 1475-1506 (Bagrow 1966, 275).

A Portuguese vessel under attack by English and
Dutch ships c.1600

[The cosmic structure and the need for understanding of it by navigators]

Without doubt the Sphere divides into two parts, the Ethereal and the Elemental, and Elemental Science differs very markedly from Supreme Science. Since Astrology and Astronomy are prognostic sciences, I am not dealing with these, for they have no role in fortification. But I state that only certain matters aid navigation, and good pilots take satisfaction in [understanding] these points, which are the following: the position of the fixed northern stars, the /f.34/ circumference of the Zodiac; the stars of the Southern Cross; the South wind that indicates the pole of the second hemisphere; the quarters of the moon and its course; the tides and winds. This includes how to calculate [position] in terms of the regions of the globe, of which there are twelve, distributed according to the twelve supreme planets; and the dozen signs [of the Zodiac] that influence the seven inferior planets, and hence provide the continual motion by virtue of which Nature and the secondary causes bring forward their active and passive powers.[15] And all this is what should be taught in Your Majesty's universities and maritime towns, because Spain is wanting in the art [of navigation] and in the practice of it.[16]

15.   KNOWLEDGE FOR NAVIGATION   Andrada's summary of current cosmographical knowledge is "very crude, reasonably comprehensive, but does not draw from any one author in the form it which it appears" (p.c. Ursula Lamb, 18.4.1988).

16.   UNIVERSITIES   Although sixteenth-century Iberia had a relatively large number of universities by contemporary standards, the university courses did not extend to technical studies involving applied science, and even astronomy and mathematics were rarely studied.   However, King Philip was sympathetic to such studies and in 1583 organised for young nobles a court academy whose curriculum included architecture, gunnery and fortification, hydraulics, cosmography and navigation (Kagan 1974, 38,163).

'Achim', the Islamic state in Sumatra, as imagined by a Dutchman, 1603 (f.6v)

CHAPTER 12

[The strategy of King Manuel - better ship's officers]

[Ill effects of the abandonment of Socotra]

Only because fortification and the knowledge of navigation are closely connected **/f.34v/** do I advise Your Majesty that it is necessary to have what I say carried out. It is necessary in order to preserve your kingdoms, estates, and riches, and in order to protect the system of shipping which was ordained by King D. Manoel of Portugal, grandfather of Your Majesty, to whose vigour and spirit is due the honour of the discoveries and conquests in far parts of the globe - parts he discovered, conquered and fortified. So he had the island of Zocotorá fortified at the mouth of the Red Sea in the East, and if it had not been deserted later but retained until after Aden, the capital of the Arabias, had been gained, the Turk would not have enjoyed life or repose there as he now does; for with the riches brought to him there from Your Majesty's India, he defends himself against the Persians, who are called Sophies, and he assaults only Christians.[1]

1.   ZOCOTORA Socotra, an island off the southern coast of Arabia, with some of its population Christian but previously under Islamic rule, was conquered by the Portuguese in 1507. A fort was built, but in 1511 the Portuguese withdrew (the native population remaining, it was not strictly 'deserted'), the island being considered too isolated for effective control. Neverthless Portuguese ships and missionaries continued to visit the island, at least until it passed under Turkish control (Pereira da Costa 1973; Serrão 1980, 114). The Portuguese originally hoped to occupy Aden too, their aim being to block the Red Sea, in order to stop the trade conveyed in Islamic shipping between the Indian Ocean and that sea; but a 1513 Portuguese attempt to seize Aden failed. In later decades some Portuguese argued that the re-occupation of Socotra and further attempts on Aden were necessary to prevent the advance of the Ottoman Turks down the Red Sea and into South Arabia, and hence the entrance of Turkish warships into the Indian Ocean. In fact, Turkish expansion in this direction may have been partly in response to what was seen as a Christian irruption into an Islamic sphere - perhaps even as a threat to the Holy Cities of Mecca and Medina. Having conquered Syria in 1516, Egypt and most of Arabia in 1517, and Iraq in 1524, the Turks in 1538 captured Aden and promptly sent a fleet against the Portuguese in India. Although thereafter the Turks were less active in the Indian Ocean, fear of them forming an aggressive alliance with Islamic polities in India and Southeast Asia persisted in Portuguese circles up to Andrada's day (Boxer 1969a). However, the Turks also engaged in incessant wars with Shiite Persia throughout the century, and this inter-Islamic struggle helped to check their advance, as the Portuguese noted with relief. The Iberian attitude to 'the Turk' was of course shaped by a confrontation which was even fiercer in Europe than it was in Asia - King Philip's resources were expended as much in holding off the Turk in the Mediterranean as they were in containing heresy in northern Europe.

[Better use and training of ship's officers]

But to return to the subject of fortification. /f.35/ Your Majesty should command that, in the **Casas de Contratación** of your kingdoms, a register be kept listing the mariners and pilots of each province and kingdom, so that at the time of a fleet sailing, the register is examined and individuals drawn from it by name are equipped to sail and load their ships, as is already the case in Portugal. For greed has completely destroyed the correct ordering of things. The pilots of the East Indies, the second pilots, the masters, and the second mates, are very many, but only ten or twelve of them have the benefit of their offices, because [only] these men have the money to give to those who fit out the ships - as used to be the case with the pilots of the West, the Islands, and the North, [who had money] as if they were **colegiales** of the military order and members of the royal household. For formerly the office of pilot had to be [regarded] among Spaniards as it is [today] among the English and French, as far as was possible, on account of the loyalty /f.35v/ and courage pilots need to possess, and on account of their having to behave differently from the ordinary sort of men who decline to fight and who surrender to the enemy.[2]

2. PILOTS MISTREATED Lack of sufficient pilots, and to a lesser extent of other ship's officers, and the inadequacies of the existing pilots and officers, were constant themes in government and mercantile circles in Spain and Portugal during the later sixteenth century (Boxer 1959, 11-15; Chaunu 1955, 3: 104,513 and passim). But the considerable expansion of the Iberian shipping fleets, the high mortality of seamen, and the wastage when seamen stayed in either Indies, made the shortages inevitable; while the criticisms relating to incompetence were often exaggerated, given the technical difficulties of contemporary long-distance voyaging. Andrada appears to be making at first two points. In Spain unregistered pilots were employed (and Andrada claimed to have personally worked in conjunction with the **Casa de Contratación** at Seville), whereas in Portugal corruption prevented full use being made of the existing pilots (a point repeated in Chapter 14). Certainly the dearth of pilots made it difficult at Seville to enforce any regulations, and by the 1580s many 'unexamined' pilots were being employed, some from Portugal, some from other Spanish ports, many of the latter lacking the clearance for overseas routes. Andrada makes the further point that seamen were no longer appreciated - "contempt for sailors and their profession was a characteristic of contemporary Spain and Portugal" (Boxer 1959, 11). Andrada argues that pilots were more highly regarded in England and France, a slightly doubtful assertion., The distinction between the pilots of the East and those of the West, Islands and North is probably one between Portuguese and Spanish pilots; but the whole of this passage is difficult to make sense of. Andrada seems to be complaining that the pilots have insufficient remuneration to pay the necessary bribes to the fitters! Be that as it may, his general complaint relates to the insufficient standing of pilots. The puzzling reference to **'colegiales** of the military order' may indicate the privileged students of the three colleges of the military orders at Salamanca, entrance to which was limited to sons of knights of the orders (Kagan 1974, 66-67,154). If so, the further reference to the royal household may hint at the existence of King's College at Alcalá, entrance to which was limited to sons of servants in the royal palace (ibid., 67).

In order that certain gentlemen in whose hands this **aviso** may fall shall not laugh at it, I say in my defence that Solomon was a pilot, as were Ptolemy, Charles V, Don Manoel, Don Juan of Austria, Alonso de Alburquerque, Don Vasco da Gama, Marco Antonio, Andrea Doria, the Marques de Santa Cruz, and Pedro Melendez, besides innumerable other excellent persons whom I will not mention, for brevity's sake.[3]   I add only this.   Let it be commanded that those who follow the profession of navigation should have a knowledge of mechanics and of how ships and all other vessels are built, a knowledge of how to protect themselves at sea and on land, a knowledge of how to make gunpowder and how to be a gunner.[4]   And those who crave honours, decorations (**habitos**) and rewards (**encomiendas**) need to know these things in order /f.36/ to fight more resolutely against the enemy.[5]   And by following this system, and even better ones that may be established, they will succeed in commanding the world with due firmness, as will the Crown of Your Majesty.

3. FAMOUS PILOTS An odd list. Apart from Portuguese and Spanish naval commanders - Albuquerque, da Gama, Santa Cruz, Menéndez - and the commanders on the Christian side at the momentous naval battle of Lepanto in 1571 - Don John of Austria (King Philip's half-brother) and Gian Andrea Doria (Philip's captain-general of the sea, but possibly confused by Andrada with his more distinguished father, Andrea Doria) - Andrada extends the title of 'pilot' to two monarchs who backed Iberian exploration, Charles V and King Manuel (King Philip's grandfathers). He then adds individuals of earlier times. Ptolemy is presumably included on the strength of his having been a cosmographer and cartographer. Marco Antonio is, however, probably not the Roman commander who sailed to Egypt, ruled the East, fought the decisive naval battle of Actium - and lost it. Instead, Andrada is more likely naming Marco Antonio Colonna, commander of the papal vessels at the battle of Lepanto - hence an associate of Doria who is actually mentioned next. King Solomon made "a navy of ships" to send to Ophir, putting on them "seamen that had knowledge of the sea" (2 Chronicles 9:18; 1 Kings 9:26-28); and his proverbs included - "There be three things which are too much for me: the way of an eagle in the air, the way of a ship in the midst of the sea, and the way of a man with a maid" (Proverbs, 30:18-19). Spanish writers on navigation in the the earlier sixteenth century (e.g., Martin Cortés, Pedro de Medina) regularly cited Solomon as the author of the view that sailing out of sight of land was difficult (Goodman 1988, 73).

4. NAUTICAL TRAINING A system of formal study of nautical science, partly for the purpose of training, examining and licencing pilots, was instituted in Spain during the first half of the sixteenth century (Goodman 1988, 73-80). The Spanish system was sufficiently impressive in theory for Hakluyt to publish an account of "the examination of the masters and pilots which saile in the Fleets of Spaine", supplied to him in 1586 by a Spanish pilot (Hakluyt 1598, 3:866-8). In Portugal, a corresponding system probably had its origins in the fifteenth century but appears to have been formalised more slowly in the next century than was the system in Spain. In 1592, more or less as Andrada was writing, a very formal examination for pilots and ship's officers was introduced in Portugal (Teixeira da Mota 1969; Albuquerque 1985). Andrada appears to want these systems to be extended to more than training in navigation, and in fact the 1592 Portuguese regulations required ship's officers to be examined regarding the construction of vessels and modes of defending them from attack (Teixeira da Mota 1969, 44). Andrada was clearly contributing to a current Iberian discussion about the operation and reform of the system of training seamen, a discussion fuelled by the fact that (as stated above in note 2) the system was much less than fully effective in practice - King Philip in 1586 ordered a reform of the Spanish system of examining pilots (Goodman 1988, 77). Andrada continues his remarks about navigators and their training in Chapter 14. In 1592, Abreu de Brito similarly discussed the disastrous loss of skilled navigators caused by the lack of encouragement and "privilege"; he called for the setting up of three "schools of the art of navigation ... [and] military tactics at sea", at Seville, in the Algarve, and at Lisbon; and he detailed the necessary curriculum. But, unlike Andrada, he proposed as trainees "sons of the poor" as well as sons of nobles (Abreu de Brito 1931, 88-91).

5. HONOURS FOR PILOTS The idea of encouraging good pilots by awarding some

CHAPTER 13

[St Helena - a proposal for settlement - ships that miss St Helena]

[The French and St Helena]

In order to complete this fortification of the ocean sea, I state that it would be fitting for Your Majesty, for reasons that I have already given, to have this island of St Helena settled, since, according to all that has been said in the preceding chapters, this is the most important point on the route to India.[1]

of them honours such as the Habit of Santiago or minor grades of nobility was part of a current discussion regarding the wider use of such honours, previously reserved in the main for military men. At a much earlier date it had been suggested that they might be given to Indies entrepreneurs (p.c. Ursula Lamb), and in the 1590s a bishop recommended that the Habit of Christ should be awarded to converted African kings (Brásio 1964, 390).

1.   ST HELENA   Andrada has referred many times previously to the island of St Helena, stressing its importance 'as a general refuge for those sailing on East Indies voyages' (f.28), the disasters caused when Portuguese ships failed to reach the island (ff.18,25v,37v), the threat of Lutherite seizure of the island (ff.5,6v,7v,29,31v), and the decline in the number of Portuguese vessels now calling there, because of fear of Lutherite attacks in the seas around the island (f.32v). The island was indeed a most important point of refuge and recovery for Portuguese vessels returning from the East. "St Helena serves, on the passage from one world to another, as a resting place to portable Europe, and it has always been a hospitable inn, maintained by divine clemency in the middle of immense seas for the Catholic fleets of the East" (Gracian, an early sevententh-century Spanish writer, quoted in Duffy 1955, 97; cf. De Matos 1988, 163). Similarly, a 1591 source which rapturised about the island's fruitfulness called it "a true miracle of nature ... placed there by divine providence" (Lopes/Pigafetta 1965, 13,15). Although St Helena was normally uninhabited (apart from two hermits, and sometimes two or three recuperating sick or abandoned miscreants), the Portuguese erected a number of buildings, in order to provide shelter for crews of ships calling there: English visitors in 1588 noted a church and some 30-40 empty houses (Hakluyt 1589, 812; 1598, 3:823; Lopes/Pigafetta 1965, 15; De Matos 1988, 166-8). Presumably it was these buildings that Andrada had in mind when he spoke of the enemy proposing to 'raze by fire this island' (f.5). He goes into more details about the proposed settlement later (ff.45v-46). In 1592 Abreu de Brito argued against those who proposed to settle St Helena, partly on the curious grounds that since the island was divinely provided it should be left to be defended by divine providence, and partly because he advocated settling instead Ascension Island - so that it could act as a port of call for ships travelling between Angola and Brazil, and also for ships returning from India and seeking a safer point than St Helena (Abreu de Brito 1931, 37-38,87). It is curious that, whereas Abreu de Brito argued against advocates of settling St Helena - e.g., Andrada - Andrada himself refers, a few sentences later, to 'the opinion [against settling St Helena] of many persons of sound judgement' - e.g., Abreu de Brito. It is unlikely, however, that either had seen the other's writings, and more likely that their references testify to a current general discussion about the role of St Helena among Iberian arm-chair strategists (for an undated Spanish '**consulta**' arguing that it was necessary to fortify the island, see De Matos 1988, 163). In the late 1580s, when a knowledgable Portuguese was asked why the island had not been fortified, despite the recent threatening oceanic out-thrusts of Drake and Cavendish, he replied that the reason was the impossibility of bringing building materials from Europe to such a far distant locality (Lopes/Pigafetta 1965, p.16).

Even that does not say all, for when the
fortress of Rio de Janeiro was won from the
Lutherites, in the year given above in Chapter
3, **/f.36v/** and the governor of Brazil was Mundo
de Saa, among the libraries we captured that
were burned, because they belonged to the college of Calvin they had there, were a thousand
papers [evidencing their plans].[2]   And there
were many Frenchmen who confessed and stated
that all that force and the extensive support
were there for a single purpose, which was to
settle St Helena, leaving no doubt that what
they had in mind was to enter [the Indian Ocean
by] the Cape of Good Hope and ruin India.[3]

2. FRENCH PLANS For the 1560 capture by the Portuguese of the main French base in the Rio de Janeiro, see f.6-6v and note 1 to Chapter 3. ("Mundo de Saa" is an odd version of 'Mem de Sá', probably a slip.) The French settlers in the colony included many Protestants, some of whom had been recruited by Calvin himself, apparently on request from the leader of the colony, Villegaignon. But Villegaignon later recovered his Catholicism and turned against the Protestants, savagely persecuting them and driving some of them back to France. After Villegaignon also returned to France in 1559, there may have been a "Protestant counter-revolution" (Julien 1948, 210). Yet Andrada's reference to a 'college of Calvin' in the leaderless, divided and dispersing colony of 1560 probably overstates the Protestant influence. The Jesuits in Brazil strongly backed the assault on the French and were therefore understandably anxious to make the campaign a religious issue. Their distinguished representative, Father José de Anchieta, denounced the colony as a hotbed of heresy, claiming that, when the base was conquered, "a great number" of heretical books were discovered (ibid., 194-200,210). Andrada, who only reached Bahia after the base had fallen, may conceivably have seen French books and papers that were brought from Rio de Janeiro to Bahia to be burned, but it is more likely that he is merely repeating a Jesuit story. Again, he may have encountered French prisoners on this occasion, but given his very recent arrival it is perhaps unlikely that he was in a position to either see or talk to them. If he did actually speak to the prisoners, there must have been a problem of communication, since elsewhere he says that he communicated with Lutherites in either Latin or Tupi (f.24). (This implies that he had no French, and also that none of them had Spanish or Portuguese, the latter admittedly being difficult to believe.) Andrada cannot have known Tupi on arrival in Brazil in 1560, so could only have communicated in Latin, which would limit contacts. On balance, it is most likely that he is merely repeating what local Portuguese circles believed to have been revealed by the French under interrogation.

3. ST HELENA THREATENED Was there in fact a real threat to the Portuguese use of St Helena ? Certainly from the late 1580s English and Dutch vessels lurked there, or in its vicinity, in order to attack the weakened Portuguese fleets, with the result that in 1592 the crown ordered ships returning from the East to avoid the island (Duffy 1955, 98). As for settlement there, the French had first visited St Helena in 1530, and since French ships operated in the South Atlantic between the 1540s and the 1580s, along the coasts of both Brazil and Guinea, it is not inconceivable that passing thought was at one time given to forming a base on St Helena, perhaps particularly during the ambitious marauding expeditions of the 1560s (Julien 1948, 264,323). But there is no evidence of a serious French intention to settle St Helena, either in the 1560s or later, and Andrada's assertion that French prisoners in Brazil had revealed this intention may represent merely an officially-inspired rumour. On the other hand, the English, even although their first visit to St Helena seems to have been only in 1588, did consider seizing the island. In 1582, Edward Fenton, the leader of an English expedition that had set out with the intention of going to the East, spoke of St Helena as "wholly without inhabitants, a place, moreover, suitable and convenient for a settlement, where having constructed walls we could establish a colony and there await the return of the Portuguese, who laden with spices come to this place to water in the month of May" (Madox 1976,

[Proposals to settle St Helena, and defend the Iberian coast, by extending the military Orders]

I can well see that, in accordance with the opinion of many persons of sound judgement, it will be said that the island of St Helena being very small, there cannot be a settlement there. To this I will reply that, however many fortresses there are, the most suitable place for the investment, every four years, of some fifty Commanders of the Orders of Christ, Avis, and Santiago, is, after Malta, the island of St Helena.[4] The Order and the settlers would be [selected] in accordance with Your Majesty's choice, since it is necessary that the only participants are /f.37/ men of pure blood and true gentlemen, being friends of Your Majesty whom I recognise. And if King D. Sebastian had been permitted to carry out this idea of mine and to found [an establishment] at Sagres, the strongpoint taken by Francis Drake, he would have founded there a monastery of the Knights of [the Order of] Christ, in imitation of the Residence at Malta, so that, from this seminary, would be provided commanders of galleys, galleons, **naus** (general ships), and fortresses. It would have been excellent to have had this house of religious on the coast of the Algarve, for since the Spanish kingdoms were gained by arms and knightly skills, it would be in keeping that they should be sustained and supported by force of arms.[5]

32-3,181-2,185,264,268,314). Fenton proposed the seizure of St Helena during the weeks his expedition was in refuge at Sierra Leone; the proposal was not pursued and the expedition next sailed to a port near Santa Catarina Island in Brazil. (Coincidentally or otherwise, St Helena, Sierra Leone and Santa Catarina Island were three out of the five South Atlantic strategic locations which a few years later Andrada recommended should be fortified to forestall the English.) In 1587, an English memorandum, apparently inspired if not dictated by Drake and Hawkins, called for a voyage "to ruin the Spaniards" which would include a visit to St Helena "in order to rob the Portuguese fleets coming from Calicut ... as the Portuguese are tired with their long voyage they may easily be robbed" (CSP Spanish, 1587-1603, 20-22). Further evidence of English interest in St Helena is provided by Hakluyt's 1589 publication of a brief account of the island (Hakluyt 1589, 222). In the late 1580s an Italian correctly indicated that the threat to St Helena was from the English (Lopes/Pigafetta 1965, p.16). Thus Andrada's anxiety in 1590 had some justification, although he misrepresented the threat by dating it from the 1560s and by relating it mainly to the French.

4. MALTA Malta was regarded as the frontline base of Christendom in the Mediterranean. The knights of the Order of St John of Jerusalem moved their headquarters to Malta after the conquest of Rhodes by the Turks in 1522, and in 1565, with Spanish help, they beat off a Turkish attack on Malta.

5. MILITARY ORDERS The three Portuguese military orders were by 1590 no longer active in crusade, but instead formed an award-system that enabled the crown to dispense honours and privileges, with little or no relationship to military prowess or enterprise. Attempts in the 1570s to require the knights of all three orders to go to war, on land or sea, when so required, were of limited avail; while the number of comenda (grants of honours with attached revenues) was continually increased (Almeida 1930, 2:215). In 1593 King Philip gave thought to reforming the orders (Serrão 1979, 292-3), so Andrada is contributing to a current discussion. But the future of the orders had also been discussed under King Sebastiao - partly in relation to the frontline against Islam in Morocco and Malta, and partly in relation to a proposal from the king to defend the Algarve against attacks from the sea by establishing a residence of the Order of Christ at Cape St Vincent (Brásio 1964, 116; Serrão 1980, 72-3). Andrada is clearly alluding to this earlier proposal (Sagres is near Cape St Vincent), which he links to his St Helena proposal, and I think that what he is saying (in a very obscure paragraph whose translation is uncertain) is that the earlier scheme, made in the same spirit as his own, would have been adequate in the 1570s, but now that enemies range further afield a scheme for establishing knights on St Helena is necessary. In 1592, Abreu de Brito also called for an establishment of knights on the Algarve coast (at Cape St Vincent or at Sagres), but preferably manned by the "Knights of Malta", whose ships would then defend the coast (Abreu de Brito 1931, 4,92). Andrada appears to be suggesting that he should be associated with the monarch in these schemes, but this seems so implausible that it must be suspected that this section of the text is garbled.

[Directions for ships that miss St Helena]

The port on the island of St Helena is perilous
to enter unless it is firmly in our hands for
that voyage. And if the ships fall short they
cannot return to the island that year with that
same motion of the sea. They can only re-route
themselves to Angola, and they remain powerless
/f.37v/ to do other than seek a remedy by leaving on an East-West course. On this course,
they are overwhelmed and lost, like the ship
'Flamenca' in the year 1556 which sank while on
it.[6] The same has happened to many other ships
coming from India which, because they did not
make the island of St. Helena, roamed along the
coast of Brazil in difficulty, this being
against the prevailing winds, and eventually
were wrecked in remote places, without escape,
because the motions of the sea were confronted,
as it has been said they can be. But when
ships are re-routed because they cannot make St
Helena, they should sail NW and reach Brazil at
the Bay of San Salvador, at 13° of latitude, and
enter the bar at South-North. There is no
doubt that the best time to reach there, in
order to travel from there to Portugal in
safety, is in April, May, June and July. If
they do not make the Island of St Helena, it
would be better **/f.38/** to go to Bahia in
Brazil, and not to go to Angola, where no ship
can go in safety.[7] Also safety is possible
westwards from Brazil or in the Indies, as was
demonstrated by Bernardin Ribero, commander of
the **Carrera de la India** in the year 1590,
saving himself [this way].[8]

6. 'FLAMENCA' For the loss of the 'Flamenga', see note 7 to Chapter 8.

7. BAHIA AS A REFUGE Luanda in Angola lies NE of St Helena, and somewhat further North than Bahia, which lies almost due West. By bearing too far to the West with the winds after passing the Cape of Good Hope, vessels returning from India were liable to miss St Helena. In this case it was better to head for Bahia than for the nearer Luanda, since when they proceeded from Luanda the winds would carry them across the Atlantic to the more dangerous coasts of North Brazil. (For occasional instances of India ships reaching Angola, see De Matos 1988, 161.) For Bahia, see note 17 to Chapter 2 and note 1 to Chapter 9. Andrada is correct: the entrance to the bay is from the South, and the prevailing winds in the South Atlantic suited sailing ships returning to Europe between April and July (Soares de Souza 1851, 117; López de Velasco 1971, 284).

8. 1590 VOYAGE For this voyage, see note 10 to Chapter 6.

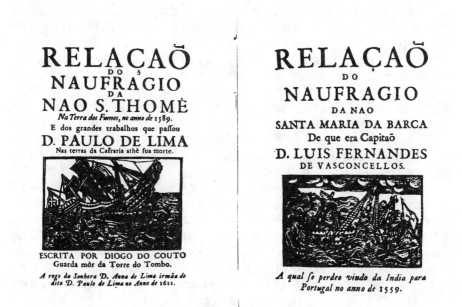

D. Paulo de Lima (f.6v) - his shipwreck and death,1589:
D. Luis' (f.22) - his first marine disaster, 1552

CHAPTER 14

[Grievances of seamen - the ill consequences]

[Seamen and a levy paid to the Jesuits]

In order that Your Majesty may feel secure, the
fortification of the sea having been effected,
it is very necessary that, at Lisbon, Your
Majesty should free those sailors and seamen
who travel to the East from the taxes and levies they pay to the Theatines, the religious
who are said to belong to the Society of Jesus,
which Your Majesty should not allow. /f.38v/
They pay this because King D.Sebastian gave
[these religious] a licence, that from each
seaman they should receive, in his India House,
as many ducats as the boxes each carried. This
was not the policy of King D.Manoel, grandfather of Your Majesty, who, in order to retain
many seamen, granted as a dispensation to each
man sailing to the Indies that he could carry
[back] one box of spices without paying any
duty on it. In times past, as long as [being
employed on] the sea was free [of charge] in
Your Majesty's navigation in the **Carrera**, there
were more than five thousand mariners, but
today there is not one, for ever since [King
Sebastian's decree] they have all regarded this
as a grievance. The reason why they had to pay
this tribute to the Theatines must have been
because the religious were building the church
of San Roque in Lisbon and sought charitable
support from the king, in the form of this levy
out of his royal estate. /f.39/ And although
the church is now completed, they still make
and receive the levy.[1]

1. JESUIT LEVY The religious mentioned were the Jesuits. The Theatines were a different religious order, but in Iberia they were often confused with the Jesuits - c.1590 a Spanish Jesuit referred to "the Theatines (as they call us in this Babel)" (Brodrick 1947, 3; Kamen 1985, 82). The Lisbon Jesuits built their major church of Sao Roque between 1565 and 1575 (Serrão 1980, 400). But Andrada appears to be complaining about a 1574 royal grant to the Jesuits by which they received in perpetuity, as an **obra pia** (work of piety), 50,000 **reis** from each quintal of pepper reaching Lisbon and 100 **reis** from each quintal of other spices, the money to go towards the maintenance of their College of Santo Antão - not towards the church, as Andrada thought (Rodrigues 1931, 1/1:468-70; 2/1:216-8). Such levies applied not only to the royal revenue but also to individual imports. Seamen on the **Carreira da Índia** were allowed to bring home 'liberty chests' containing their personal purchases of certain spices and other goods, an ordinary sailor being allowed one liberty chest. On the goods in these chests they paid reduced or no duties, but a sum for **obras pias** was levied (Boxer 1959, 18,278).

RELAÇAõ

DA MUY NOTAVEL PERDA
DO
GALEAõ GRANDE S. JOAõ

Em que se contaõ os grandes trabalhos, e lastimosas cousas que acontecèraõ

AO CAPITAõ
MANOEL DE SOUSA
SEPULVEDA,

E O LAMENTAVEL FIM, QUE ELLE,
e sua mulher, e filhos, e toda a mais gente
houveraõ na Terra do Natal, onde se perdè-
raõ a 24. de Junho de 1552.

The shipwreck of 'Manuel de Sosa', 1552 (f.25v)

[Good ship's officers discouraged and incom-
petent ones engaged - hence shipping losses]

Another reason [for discontent] is that the
provisioners and those who fit out the ships
sell the posts of the pilots, and anything else
pertaining to seamen, to whoever will give the
most money. From all this arises a sense of
injustice, because the ships are not provided
with good officers, and [instead] take on useless men, who do not know how to control the
rudder or understand the rhumbs of the compass.
This is why all the ships are lost, or the
English capture them, or they return without
having made their voyage. This last occurrence
happened to four ships commanded by Mathias de
Alburquerque in the year 1590, all of which returned to port, with great loss and the denial
of profit to Your Majesty's Treasury.[2] If the
cause of these disasters and losses is not generally understood, the remedy will not be
adopted, which is fortification, /f.39v/ since
only this could correct such evils.

2.   ABORTED VOYAGE For this voyage, see note 10 to Chapter 6. Since the episode had occurred only a short time before Andrada wrote about it, his view that corruption and incompetence were to blame for the return of the ships was probably a wide-spread view, although not necessarily a fair one. Andrada might have noted that the fleet left "out of due season" (Boxer 1959, 7).

The town of Praia in the Cape Verde Islands, 1585
(Introduction, note 16)

Thus it is that the captains who used to go on this marine service were worthy gentlemen (**generosos hidalgos**), but nowadays on the pretext of undertaking trade with India, the entrepreneurs appoint captains who have little experience, and some are of humble birth.[3] These are the men who reduce the King's income by their abortive voyages, and one of them let Your Majesty's ship, the 'San Felipe', be captured by Drake, entire and undamaged, in the year 1587.[4] In the year Your Majesty was in Lisbon, another pilot returned to port with the Malacca galleon - and together with the 'San Pablo', the Malacca galleon was also lost off Sumatra in 1560.[5] From this record of disasters derive many evils; and from this lack of system [in navigation] over these many years innumerable shipwrecks have occurred in those [oceanic] parts, without anyone advising /f.40/ Your Majesty or anyone endeavouring to propose remedies for such regular evils affecting the family and estate of Your Majesty.

3. SOCIAL EVILS As distinct from the pilots who were experienced seamen, the captains of sixteenth-century vessels in the **Carreira da Índia** were normally "blue-blooded fidalgos", landsmen with limited experience at sea (Boxer 1959, 27). Andrada's complaint that some pilots were inexperienced and some captains not gentlemen no doubt represented popular reaction to mounting ship losses but was superficial.

4. 'SAN FELIPE' CAPTURED Drake took the 'São Felipe' in the Azores. According to an English account, it was taken "without any great resistance", and its capture "the Portugals tooke for an evil signe, because the ship bare the Kinges owne name" (Hakluyt 1598, 2/2:123). Andrada's degree of disgust was matched in extent by the English degree of self-congratulation - "the taking of this Cara[c]k wrought two extraordinary effects in England: first, that it taught others, that Caracks were no such bugs but that they might be taken ... and secondly in acquainting the English Nation more generally with the particularities of the exceeding riches and wealth of the East Indies" (ibid.; see also Hakluyt 1589, 'To the Reader').

5. MALACCA GALLEONS For the 1582 Malacca galleon, see note 1 to Chapter 8; and for the 1560 wreck of the 'São Paulo', see note 3 to Chapter 9. I have not traced the 1560 wreck of a Malacca galleon.

CHAPTER 15

[The damage done by renegades - conclusions]

[Disaffected seamen flee the country]

It would be right, then, for Your Majesty to order that instruction in navigation be provided, and right that what Your Majesty commands should be carried out with enthusiasm. Again, seamen should be favoured in some way, as they are now very downtrodden and poor. Affected by the unreasonable treatment they receive, they flee to England and France, and [our] navigation is ruined, which is the most necessary thing Your Majesty must sustain and regulate, because it is obvious that without naval force and careful counsel Spain can neither maintain /f.40v/ itself nor dominate and defeat the Lutherites.

[Four renegades, especially Bayão]

I advise Your Majesty that, because of these difficulties, many evils have been generated in Portugal. In the time of your uncle, King D. Enrique, who did not care to favour navigation as far as Mina was concerned, four pirates rebelled against him and gave instruction to the Lutherites, and I am about to mention their names in sequence.[1] The son of the blind man from the Algarve went to La Rochelle, and in one year there were captured and taken to France, to La Rochelle alone, 25 ships laden with riches, as well as what was taken from Mina.[2]

1. MINA SHIPPING NOT FAVOURED King-Cardinal D. Henrique's sister, D. Isabel, was the mother of King Philip. The events subsequently mentioned indicate that Andrada is carelessly referring not only to the period when Cardinal D. Henrique was king (1578-1580) but also to the earlier period when he was regent (1562-1568), during the minority of King Sebastião - and even at times to the period between. As regent, D. Henrique attempted to reform the crown monopoly of the Mina gold trade, and at one stage introduced stricter regulations for its conduct which alienated some of the seamen engaged in it (Vogt 1979, 119-120). In 1567, the French ambassador in Lisbon commented in terms similar to those of Andrada. "The Portuguese greatly blame the Cardinal for having driven to desperation a number of Portuguese who had long and faithfully served their king, by poorly recompensing them at this time, as a result of which they have become instigators of the French and their captains and pilots, to the damage of other Portuguese" (Bourdon 1954, 7).

2. SON OF THE BLIND MAN The reference to 'the blind man from the Algarve' almost certainly indicates Francisco Dias, nicknamed Mimosa ('darling'), a native of Faro in the Algarve, who by the 1550s had removed to France, where he was later naturalized, and who lived at Le Havre with his family. In the 1560s, he piloted French ships to Guinea and the Caribbean, and participated in the French attack on Madeira (see note 5 below). He was pursued diplomatically by the Iberian authorities, and when French protection gave way was executed in 1569. In diplomatic correspondence he was described as "the one-eyed Portuguese pilot", and he had a son who in 1568 was also termed a pirate (Bourdon 1954, 88-89,96,105). The year in which the Portuguese suffered severe depredations, supposedly from the activities of the son of Francisco Dias, is difficult to identify; but given that the father died in 1569, it is unlikely to have been earlier than 1570. Even the reference to Mina is difficult to date. In 1582, the Portuguese governor of Mina allowed a French fleet to trade there and gold was taken back to France (Vogt 1979, 131). But if **'de la mina'** means 'belonging to Mina', Andrada may be alluding to the capture of a Portuguese caravel from Mina carrying gold, by the French from La Rochelle, in 1575 (ibid., 123; Gray 1965, items 18,19,22). Neither date, however, falls within 'the time of your uncle'.

Pedro Bayão went to England, where the queen made him her admiral, and he gave instruction to Francis Drake, an infernal being, as has been clearly seen. I do not know whether I dare to tell what I myself saw after /**f.41**/ he [Bayão] was captured in Guinea - where I was serving as provisor and vicar-general for King D.Sebastian. I saw this great pirate taking the sun, which was obscured and hidden behind clouds, when the astrolabe was no use to him at midday, by using his Jacobs-staff (**ballestilla**) - the one [afterwards] I had in my study for a long time - **graduada doctrina** (calculated learning).[3] Doubtless he would venture to aff-irm that Ptolemy had not studied this, since he deals with the East-West position (**altura**). And this [instrument] is an addition to the mariner's astrolabe, which I also possessed, and I [? **read** he] took the sun according to the East-West rule, four hours after midday, which is the greatest achievement of that art, a subtle and delicate art provided by nature in order to inform the sailor, and one worthy of being made known throughout the world.[4]

3.   BAYÃO   Bartolomeu (not Pedro) Bayão, a Portuguese pilot, was in England in 1570-1571, and during his stay offered his services to the Spaniards as well as to the English (but to Hawkins, not to Drake) (Andrews 1982, 70-1). Apparently he had fled from Portugal some years earlier (perhaps indeed in 'the time of your uncle'), since in 1565 he had commanded an English ship trading in Guinea; while in 1570 he escaped from prison in Spain after being charged with illegal trading in the Caribbean.   His Atlantic experience may have been considerable: he seems to have offered to pilot the English to Magellan Strait and he was reported to have fought an African ruler in Sierra Leone (Almada 1984, chap.18/12; Williamson 1927, 99; Rumeu de Armas 1945, 1:593-7).   Andrada's reference to Bayão's instruction of Drake may be a general derogatory assertion, or it may indicate that, although he never specifies it, Andrada was aware that in 1572 Drake participated in the joint French and English raid on Nombre de Dios.   But in the same year Bayao was captured by the Portuguese, as Andrada states.   He had been trading in the Ilhetas, near Cacheu in Guinea, and was taken to Santiago in the Cape Verde Islands in June 1572 and there sentenced to execution in August 1572 (Donelha 1977, 337).   When, where and how Andrada came into personal contact with Bayão he does not explain, nor is it easy to work out. Since as far as we know Andrada was not in Guinea before 1572, he cannot have encountered Bayão on any earlier occasion when the latter was in Guinea.   Andrada must therefore have met Bayao after the former reached the Cape Verde Islands in mid December 1572.   (For details of Andrada's arrival in the islands, see note 8 to Chapter 8; and for his career there, see the Introduction and its notes 15-17.)   Andrada claims that he had witnessed Bayão 'taking the sun', and that he subsequently acquired Bayão's nautical instruments (according to the sentence of execution all Bayão's possessions were confiscated).   We must therefore suppose that Andrada visited Bayão in his Santiago prison and had him demonstrate his skill in the courtyard.   Our only information about the trial of Bayão comes from a Spanish document, a certificate of exculpation on behalf of a Canary Islands captain who had become associated with Bayao's activities, had then given information to the Portuguese authorities in the Cape Verde Islands, and had presumably attended the trial (Rumeu de Armas 1945, 1: 594-7, notes 126,128). This certificate, dated 11 August, after citing the case against Bayão, states that "the governor immediately carried out execution (**luego despacho esecucion**)". But if Bayão was executed before 11 August, how can Andrada have met him in December ? Either Andrada made up the whole story of meeting Bayão (it does seem unlikely that a new arrival would be allowed instant access to an important prisoner - unless Andrada went as confessor), or else the certificate is not entirely accurate.   It is just possible, although perhaps not very likely, that what the governor did "immediately" was to give sentence and order its "execution", but that the killing of the prisoner was delayed for some months, perhaps while information was sought from him.   The only shred of evidence in support of this theory is that the certificate does not give an actual date of execution.   Andrada's curious introduction to this episode ('I do not know whether I dare to tell') may perhaps indicate a precautionary willingness to concede, if challenged, that he has misremembered.

(It is just possible that Bayão was the inspiration for a verse in the epic **Argentina** by Martín del Barco Centenera.   Barco Centenera, who travelled on the Zárate expedition (and is a major source for it), who reported Andrada's arrival

The other pirate was Manoel Caldera, or rather Francisco Caldera, who **/f.41v/** left La Rochelle with a very powerful fleet and went to the Island of Madeira, a Catholic island, which he attacked with fire and sword, profaning the churches, and leaving with loot amounting to more than two **cuentos** of gold.[5] As well as this man, there went over [to the enemy] Pedreanes de Sea, a native of the Island of Tercera, where he committed terrible assaults and robberies, in company with the Lutherite Ribaos and Sorias.[6]

in the Cape Verde Islands, who must have heard of the Bayão episode and learned that the renegade was working for the English, and who is not known to have visited the islands subsequently, wrote of Santiago Island as follows.

> El sitio es apacible y deleytoso,
> La gente muy lucida y muy galana,
> Por el Ingles cossario y bellicoso,
> En ronda suele andar cada mañana.

(The place is peaceful and delightful, the people very gay and very gallant, (but) on account of the piratical and warlike Englishman, they regularly patrol every morning.)

Was this a dim recollection of the islanders' fear of Bayão, the English agent, in 1572 ? Barco Centenera's episode was only published in 1602 (although perhaps composed in part much earlier), so the verse may instead only indicate a knowledge of later English assaults. I am indebted to Professor Frank Pierce of Sheffield for his comment on this point.)

4.   NAUTICAL INSTRUMENTS As a means of obtaining latitude, the astrolabe could be used for taking the height of the sun only at midday. For sighting the sun before and after midday with the Jacobs-staff, see Waters 1958. For both instruments, see the illustration on p.207 below.

5.   FRENCH ATTACK ON MADEIRA In October 1566, a French expedition under Peyrot de Monluc, sailing from Bordeaux (not La Rochelle), captured and looted the town of Funchal on the island of Madeira. The main pilot was Gaspar (neither Manoel nor Francisco) Caldeira, allegedly a native of Tangier, at one time an attendant on Cardinal D. Henrique, and a Guinea pilot. Caldeira later acted as a double (or treble) agent in dealings with France, England and even Spain, but was caught by the Portuguese and executed in 1568 (Santarem 1843, 393; Julien 1948, 265; Bourdon 1954, 5-56; Serrão 1980, 3:62). This episode did fall within the regency of Cardinal D. Henrique.

6.   LUTHERITES The reference to 'the Ribaos and Sorias' indicates the Frenchmen, Jean Ribault (see note 4 to Chapter 4) and Jacques de Sores (see note 4 to Chapter 8). Could 'Pedreanes de Sea' be Pedro Eanes, a Portuguese seaman known as 'The Frenchman', who flourished c.1520 (Serrão 1980, 167)?

[Other depredations of the Lutherites and their renegade allies]

All this, without taking into account the deplorable expedition of the famous Pié de Palo, an admiral of the Lutherites, who came and sacked the Island of La Palma; and, after him, his followers sacked Gomera, where they burned in the market-place the statue and image of glorious St Francis, and after profaning the churches, left laden with riches.[7]   On St Matthew's day [24 February], 1587, the Island of Cuervo was reduced to ashes, as were Florida and Fayal.[8]   Furthermore, innumerable other losses have been caused [by these Lutherites], for instance, at Cadiz, to the armada of the Duke of Medina /f.42/ in the Flanders Channel, and in the assault on Lisbon, Peniche, Sagres and Cascales; and what they are bringing about today can be seen with one's own eyes.[9]   The Lutherites do it with the help of [our] sailors, captains and pilots, who have gone over to the other side, driven away by bad government and lack of favour rather than by hatred of Your Majesty.

7.   FRENCH ATTACK ON THE CANARIES   In July 1553, François le Clerc (known as 'Jambe de Bois' or 'Pié de Palo', i.e. 'Timberleg'), in command of a French fleet, and after a campaign in the Caribbean, attacked, looted and burned the town of Santa Cruz on La Palma Island in the Canaries.   In 1570 and 1571 there were French attacks on Gomera (Rumeu de Armas 1945, 1:149-157,522,552).

8.   ATTACKS ON THE AZORES   The named islands in the Azores were subject to regular landings and attacks by the English.   In 1589 an expedition seized the town of Fayal on Flores Island (Andrada's 'Florida'), and it was reported that the town of Santa Cruz on Flores had been "burned about two years before by certaine English ships of war" (Hakluyt 1598, 2/2:156-158).

9.   ENGLISH ASSAULTS   The references are to Drake's attack on Spanish shipping at Cadiz and subsequent capture of Sagres in 1587, to what the British call the 'Spanish Armada' campaign of 1588, and to the largely unsuccessful English assault on Lisbon in 1589, when only the localities on the seaward side that Andrada mentions were occupied.

From the **História Trágico-Marítima**

[Improving navigation, fortification, and Catholic zeal]

In concluding my advice to Your Majesty, I repeat the celebrated words of the Blessed St Gregory, **"minus iacula feriunt quae previdentur"** ["a blow foreseen hurts less"], that is, "great remedies must be applied to great evils". Your Majesty should favour your labourers and seamen, by a system which, further to this, I shall give if I am commanded. For the fortification I have spoken about must be organized and carried out by experienced seamen who know the Sphere, the sea, and the terrestrial orientation, as I have stated in previous chapters, **/f.42v/** through science and experience, and not in the astract, which is no use at all. I add only this: that it would be good if hearts throughout Your Majesty's kingdoms, hearts of the seculars and the religious alike, were awakened and filled with zeal for the Holy Catholic Faith, inasmuch as, in respect of so eternal a goal, God has said - **"non veni pacem mit[t]ere in terris sed gladium"** ("I came not to send peace [on earth] but a sword", Matthew 10.34). All the fortification mentioned above is summed up in the following short epitome.

Philip, the First of Portugal, the Second of Spain

E P I T O M E

[The first fortification, to be built at Bezeguiche]

The first thing that has to be done is to fortify the port of the Ialopho king, which lies at 15° North of the Equator; it is near Your Majesty's fortress, the castle of Arguin. This fortification should be built on a secure and rocky islet which is at the mouth /f.43/ of the entry to the port, and there should be constructed a strongpoint on the islet, and the city should be built on the headland of the mainland. With security provided by the fortification on the islet and the city on the mainland, there would be no [enemy] fleet which could enter the port, because any ship seeking an entry would have to pass within gunshot of either the city or the islet, and would be sent to the bottom.[1]

1. BEZEGUICHE For this port, see ff.2v-3. The details of the fortification of the port now given repeat those on f.11-11v. The distance between Cape Verde and Arguin is actually some 700 km.

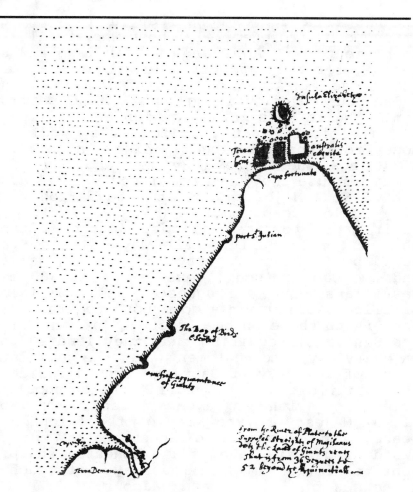

Sketch map made in 1578 during Drake's circumnavigation, with the earliest correct representation of the southern tip of America, i.e., without a continent further South (ff.9v-10,31v)

The people who are needed for this fortification

The people needed to construct the city and the strongpoint are precisely those who are already to be found on the islands of Santiago and San Felipe, for they are all soldiers and sailors, and these men from the island would so much value Your Majesty giving them **/f.43v/** permission to build this fortification and to live in it as citizens that I believe they would pay money for [the privilege]. Also, in this land of Guinea there are many men who have fled there because they have committed illegal acts, but if Your Majesty were able to pardon them, they would accept pardon and give a fifth of their goods towards the cost of the fortress that is to be built.[2] The way to help Spain would be for Your Majesty to send one galleon and two **çabras** (small vessels), with 300 men, Castilians and Portuguese, and sufficient artillery, all under a governor, together with letters to those on the island[s] of San Felipe and Santiago, requiring that they lend support in every way, and that men under the administration of the city of Santiago should reside in the fortification.[3] The fortification should be solemnized with an embassy sent from Your **/f.44/** Majesty to the King of the Ialophos in peace, and this should announce to him the award of certain favours and honours, and present to him in a magnanimous way gifts such as harnesses for horses, and weapons.[4]

2.   PROPOSED SETTLERS Andrada goes into more details about the proposed settlers than he did earlier, where he limited them to 'adventurous and enterprising people, all mariners', from Santiago Island (f.11). He now terms them 'all soldiers and sailors', and adds Fogo Island (neighbouring Santiago Island), for which he uses the alternative name 'São Filipe'. He further proposes as settlers the **lançados** ('runaway' adventurers) on the mainland, a suggestion he made elsewhere (ff.20v-21). For the **lançados**, see note 8 to Chapter 4 and note 13 to Chapter 7.

3.   CASTILIANS Andrada tactfully calls for a joint Spanish-Portuguese expedition.

4.   KING OF THE IALOPHOS For the 'King of the Ialophos', see f.2v and note 1 to Chapter 1. Having criticised the Lutherites for giving weapons to the heathen (f.5), even to these particular Africans (f.3v), Andrada now proposes that the Portuguese give weapons to the Ialophos.

A Catholic church on the Portuguese island of
Annobom, attacked by 'heretic Lutherites', the
Dutch - 1601

The second fortification, to be built in Sierra Leona

In order to fortify this **sierra**, the same procedure as that in Ialopho should be followed, except that it would not be necessary to appoint an ambassador because the people are savages who do not understand such courtesies. The fortification should be established in Tagarin or Mitombo, which are two similar rivers, one as good as the other, and there should be a fortress at the point of the mainland. For these fortresses, stone, lime and wood in large quantities can be provided by the lands mentioned.[5] /f.44v/

The third fortification, [to be built at Bahia] in Brazil

When a strongpoint has been constructed on San Antonio Point, or rather the one which fell down has been rebuilt, then no [enemy] fleet or single ship will enter the Bahia de Todos Santos, because it could only do so by passing through [a channel] where they would be in the centre of the range of cannon firing from that point on the shore. This is because the entry is obstructed with sand, and the island there narrows it. Twenty men would be sufficient for this fort. From this headland to the city of San Salvador is half a league, and it is necessary that the city be ordered to be walled, to make it impregnable. It would be even more secure if Your Majesty were to command that no governor should be there for more than three years.[6] /f.45/

5. SIERRA LEONE FORTIFICATION For the rivers, see note 6 to Chapter 7. The references to 'savages' (instead of 'idolaters') and to the material for a fort are new, but the locality is the same as in f.18v.

6. BAHIA FORTIFICATION Andrada enlarges on his earlier reference to fortifying Bahia (f.25) - see notes 2 and 9 to Chapter 9. He earlier said that the city had neglected its defences and that the governors had been careless (f.26-26v), hence his recommendations now.

RELAÇAŌ
DA 5
VIAGEM, E NAUFRAGIO
DA
NAO S. PAULO
Que foy para a India no anno de 1560.
De que era Capitaŏ
RUY DE MELLO DA CAMERA,
Meſtre Joaŏ Luis, e Piloto Antonio Dias.

ESCRITA
POR HENRIQUE DIAS,
Criado do S. D. Antonio Prior do Crato.

'The voyage and shipwreck of the "São Paulo", 1560'
(ff.19v-20,25-25v)

The fourth fortification, [to be built at Rio de Janeiro] in Brazil

In order to prevent entry by any adversary into the port of the City of Sebastian, it is necessary that the city erect a strongpoint on an islet which lies in the middle of the bar, the city itself being at present well enough fortified.[7] Still, the more people Your Majesty sends to Guinea and Brazil, the more useful this will be, for the land [in both places] is large and rich, but lacking in people to cultivate it, to settle it, and defend it, [yet] Spain is over-populated.[8]

The fifth fortification, [to be built] on the Island of Santa Catalina

For the Island of Santa Catalina, Your Majesty might /**f.45v**/ find people and send them to the governor of Brazil, so that he can train them and give them experience, in order that they may settle that island, which is empty. There is plenty of water, stone and wood, and within a day and night they can get assistance, and food and drink, from the mainland, from the mouth of the Rio Grande, the access route from Peru to Brazil. Once this island is settled the Río de la Plata will also be settled, and the latter settlement has been the desire of Spain for very many years, as well as [settlement in] the famous Magellan Strait.[9]

7. RIO DE JANEIRO FORTIFICATION This summarises what Andrada said on f.28v, but he now concedes that the city is otherwise 'well enough fortified' - for details of the fortification, see Soares de Souza 1851, chap.LI, p.83.

8. SURPLUS PEOPLE Andrada introduces the view that Iberia is over-populated, hence settlers can and should be sent to Guinea and Brazil.

9. SANTA CATALINA ISLAND FORTIFICATION This enlarges on the reference to fortifying the island in f.31-31v. See note 1 to Chapter 11; and for the reference to Rio Grande, see notes 4 and 5 to Chapter 11.

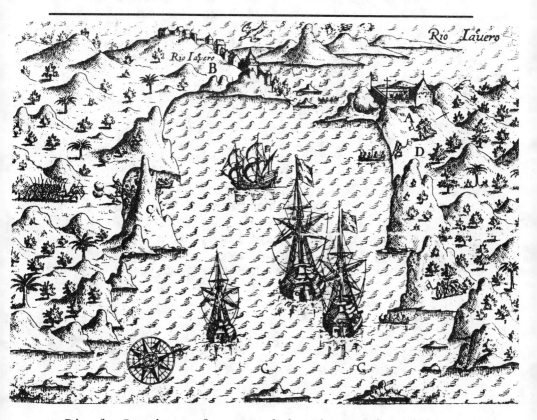

Rio de Janeiro under attack by the Dutch, 1599 - a
fanciful depiction (f.28-28v)

The sixth fortification [is to be on St Helena]

The sixth fortification should be constructed on the Island of St Helena. A bulwark should be built at the point where the turn is made into the port, and it should be manned by twenty or thirty men **/f.46/** who would live there for three years at a time. They could maintain themselves without doing harm to the island, which would serve only as a fortress. The island has an infinite number of goats, and numberless fruits, together with soft fresh water and good and healthy air. Provisions and merchandise could be shipped to and from the island to the Island of Santa Catalina, San Vicente, the City of Sebastian, and all of Brazil. Also, if Your Majesty pleases, they could round the Cape of Good Hope and go to Mozambique. It would be advisable that Your Majesty order that the captain who resides at St Helena should be a member of the **Casa de la India Oriental** (Board of Trade for the East Indies) as are other captains, and entitled to send three ships annually for commerce and trade to the whole of the coast from the Cape of Good Hope to Angola, and to the entire sea-coasts of Angola and Mozambique, and to Brazil.[10]

Then all would be well for the stability of SPAIN and the CROWN of YOUR MAJESTY.

10.   ST HELENA FORTIFICATION   Andrada considerably enlarges on his previous reference to St Helena, which related to settling the island (ff.36-37).   See notes 1 and 3 to Chapter 13.   But he now limits his proposal to one of a permanent fortification, involving a rota of soldiers.   The suggestion that the island become an entrepôt for South Atlantic trade, with a resident government representative, was unrealistic.

Seamen using a cross-staff to measure lunar distances and an astrolabe to determine the altitude of the sun (f.41) - the scene represents a Portuguese vessel sailing to Brazil, 1547

SPANISH TEXT

in facsimile

[pp.211-257]

NSTRVCION
QVE A V. MAGE-
stad se da, para mandar fortificar el mar Oceano, y defenderse de todos los contrarios Piratas, ansi Franceses, como Ingleses, en todas las nauegaciones de su Real Corona, dentro de los Tropiccos.

(:.)

OFRECELA DON
Felipe de Albornoz. Compuesta
y ordenada por su maestro en
la Mathematica, el Licen-
ciado Manoel de Andra-
da Castel Blanco, Ca-
pellan de Vuestra
Magestad.

(.:.)

PRIMERAMEN
te, es de confiderar
que todo el mar O-
ceano naucgable, es
de V. Mageftad, à
todos los quatro vié
tos, y feñorca legiti
tos, y feñorca legiti
mamente todo los Reynos y conqui-
ftas, fiendo defenfor de la Fê, por la
qual caufa los paganos Inglefes, y
Francefes le contrarian y roban en
todo el mar Occano, en todas fus nauegaciones, anfi de Oriente, como de
Poniente, haziendofe ricos y pode-
rofos, para fuftentar guerras contra
la Yglefia Catolica, y Corona de
V. Mageftad. Para defenfa de lo
qual, apunto todos los remedios que
abaxo fe diran, que fon facados Ma-
thematicamente, por la dimencion
del Mundo, del Quadripartito del

A 2   Acce:)

DISCVRSO D
toda efta inftrucion, que es de
la importancia del faber nauegar, y proceder contra
los Luteranos.

DR WILLIAMS'S LIBRARY
RED CROSS STREET
LONDON

3

montorio, la qual Ciudad llamá los Portuguefes Caboverde, que defcubrio porfu perfona propia el Infante de Portugal dó Enrrique, año. 1472. primer nauegante, y defcubridor de todas las Islas adiacentes hazia Poniente, que fon San Felipe, Santiago, San Nicolas, San Anton, Santa Lucia, San Bicente, la Isla de la Sal, la de Mayo, la Isla Braua, y las Islas de Caboverde.

¶ Capitulo. II.

N BEZEGVI-che, cabeça del Reyno de los Ialophos, eftá vna Bayay Enfenada muy grande, capaz y hermofa, que anclaran en ella cien nauios de alto bordo y

Acceço, y Receço del Sol, y mouimiento de las aguas, que naturalmente tiene fus raros y varios efetos.

¶ Capitulo Primero.

N QVINZE grados de altura de la parte del Norte, en la contracofta de Africa, eftá vn Reyno llamado del Ialopho, que en fu propio nombre fe llama Gudumel, que quiere dezir, tanto como Granduque, el qual es muy poderofo y rico, mas faltale para fu defenfa artilleria y nauegacion, aunque tiene muchos exercitos de acauallo: y en la mifma altura precifa eftá Bezeguiche, Ciudad donde affifte fu corte, que finifica en fu lengua la grande Enfenada, ò Promontorio,

mas; y de remo mas de duzientos,
con todas fus barcas y baxeles, y es
tan breue y buena efta derrota y nã
uegacion, que fe va en treze dias á
ella, como yo lo tengo efperimenta
do, auiendo falido de Lisboa, y aqui
hazen puerto y fu efcala, los Luteranos de la Rochela, de Bordeos, Abra-
degracia, y de toda la Bretaña, y
mas Epiratas, de la Prouincia de la
Galia y fu nauegació, fin q̃ nadie fe
lo impida: y llcuá para Francia mucho, Oro, Anbar, Marfil, Coram-
bre, varias y preciofas Algalias en
gran cantidad, dexando en abundã-
cia muchos inftrumentos belicos á
los Ialophos, que vá admitiendo la
Secta de Mahoma, como fon lanças,
crifes, efpadas, alfanges, adargas, y
todo lo prohiuido por la Bula de la
Cena, y aqui hazẽ aguada, proueyé-
dofe

dofe de baftimentos. Y defte puerto
fe diuiden en flotas, vnos para la cofta de la Burburuata, donde en cauo
de la Hacha, compran con los Efpa-
ñoles Oro y Argenteria, y mas riquezas, como fon Efmeraldas, y muchas Cornerinas, y eftos fon los que
faquean la cofta, y mar de Cartagena, y nombre de Dios. Para defenfa
de lo qual V. M. trae algunas Galeras, las quales de gufanos fe gaftan
y hazen gaftos exceffiuos, y fin prouecho, por no poder pelear en mar braua, contra nauios de altobordo, q̃ alli
van por difcurfo de todo el año: por
que los tales Epiratas con monçió de
Abril, y Norueftes, Flacos, van à efte
falto y robo de la Equinocial. Y defpues de deuaftar, y faquear, fe bucluẽ
con los vientos Sudueftes y Ponien-
tes, figuiendo en todo la orden naui-

A 4   gatoria,

gatoria,que guardada los sustenta en la mar. Deste dicho puerto se diuidé otros cosarios para las Islas de Poniéte,como son la Trinidad,la Margarita,Santa Marta, Santo Domingo, y la Habana,otros á puerto Rico, Bera cruz y honduras,que es la nauegació de Mexico,todo esto nauegan y roban.Otros se parten al Sur,y saqueando toda la costa de Guinea,es á saber la casa de contratacion de V. Magestad , que está en el Rio de Santo Domingo. Y ni mas ni menos roban al Rio grande , que es Rio de los Bujatras , y de alli van a la sierra Leona , discurriendo por toda la costa de la niña , que estando dentro de la Equinocial rey grados de altura,corresponde en el sitio del Orbe,por las latitudines, y longitudines de la Cosmographia,a la contra costa

de Argel, y Fez, y á su Mcrediano,há fallegar a la Isla del Principe, y Santo Tome,haziendo grandes robos y males, hinchendo de Armas estos incognitos Reynos,armando a los infieles,de que resultan grauissimas perdidas á V. Magestad.Otros nauegan hazia Angola , Congo, y a la Isla de Santa Elena,y hazen en ella agua da desde Setiébre,hasta Março,có las monciones que traé reguladas, para entrar y salir en la Torrida,ò Equinocial,á donde han intentado a quemar a la dicha Isla:loqual, si Dios no los vuiera cegado lo vuierá hecho:y si la vuierá poblado, como lo há querido hazer,dende el año de.1550. edad corriente,hasta la presente de .1590. fuera para ruyna de todo el Oriente: porque los Moros de Arabia,y Móbaça,y los de la Isla Zocotorá , y la

fuerte

fuerte y populofa ciudad de Aden, en la boca y entrada del mar Bermejo, fe cófedederarian có los Inglefes, y dandoles puerto paffarian al cabo de Buena efperança, con mas facilidad que paffan el de Magallanes, y à tal mal no auria reparo, y ayudarfehia el Turco de la ocafion, y la India fe leuantaria, como lo quifieron hazer en tiempo del Virey don Luys, cercando a la cabeça Goa. Otros difcurren y llegan al mar de Pernambuco en el Brafil al Poniente, doblada tambien la Equinocial, donde eftá la ciudad Filipina, que V. Mageftad aora poffee, ganada de Franccefes, y contratan en toda la cofta del Brafil, llegando a la famofa ciudad y cabeça del Reyno, que fe dize la Bahia de todos Santos, ciudad de San Saluador, que correfponde en la mifma altura, y en

el

el Paralelo de la ciudad de los Reyes del Peru, y à Sáta Marta, y al Cuzco, y baxan Norte Sur por la latitud, fembrando armas por el Reyno de los Pitiguares, y Reyno de los Tupinambas, y à los Tupinaquins, y Tamoyos, hafta la cofta de la Cananea, llegando al Tropico de Capricornio, y aguadas del Rio de la plata, y eftrecho de Magallanes.

¶ *Capitulo. III.*

ASE DE ADVERtir, que en efte fitio, à donde aora eftá efta ciudad Sebaftiana fundada, eftuuo el fuerte Caftillo, que tenia de prefidio con ochocientos, y mil hombres Francefes Luteranos, Mofeur de Vide Galá, maeftre maestre de campo general del Rey de Francia (cuyo maestre de campo fue vn sobrino suyo deste Moseur, q era caballero del habito de Rodas) de cuya mano año de 59. lo ganò la señora Reyna doña Catalina de santa memoria, tia de V. Magestad, con mucha artilleria gruesa, y mucha munición, ganando juntamente la Isla de la Palma, con mucho nombre de los Portugueses, siendo Capitan general de la mar, Bartolome de Bascócelos, religioso del habito de Auis. Y el año de 1587. Don Pablo de Lima caballero Portuges, en la India de V. Magestad Oriental, destruyò y subuertio la fortaleça del Emperador de Dachen, de la Imperial Isla Tapobrana, que dé la mesma edad, que los Franceses armauan á poblar la Isla de Santa Elena, poblarò y for-

tificaron

tificaron en las haldas del Reyno de Sion, que es el perturbador de la nauegacion de la China, en el estrecho del cabo de Sabaô, vna ciudad, donde le ganò por guerra y batalla Naual, muchas galeras y baxeles, y en tierra á fuera, matarmas de 30 U. hombres Moros y Turcos; y les ganò mas de 30 U. arcabuzes, y cinco ò seys mil pieças de artilleria gruessa, y abrassô los fuertes, y subuertio la ciudad, desde el fundamento. Y toda esta maquina, que los Luteranos hizieron en el mar Oceano de Poniente, de tantos años á esta parte, la conuinauan los Moros en la India Oriental, con pensamiento de se apoderar del Oceano, contra V. Magestad, poblando y fortificando los mas peligrosos, è importantes, dos puertos que ay en el, como es la dicha Isla de

de Santa Elenã, en Ocidente, y alcã
bo de Sabaõ en Oriente, y de todo
efto refulsò, que los Luteranos, vien-
dofe defarraygados de la Florida, y
del Rio de Parayba, y Rio de Enero, paffan la Equinocial, y baxan del
Brafil al Rio de los Patos, y a la Isla de Santa Catalina, que eftà junto al Rio de la Plata, y Reyno de
los Carijos, robando toda la cofta y nauegacion del Cabofrio, Biriquioca, San Bicente, amenaçando perturbar las Charcas del Peru,
que en aquel puerto tiene entrada
por el Rio grande, Rio de agua dulce
que fe nauega por la tierra adentro,
mas de duzientas leguas, y aquife pro
uen de fus aguadas y baftimentos,
para paffar el eftrecho de Magallanes
y naucgan el mar Oceano del Peru,
de la contracofta del Brafil, fe buel-

uen

uen por el mifmo eftrecho, reparan-
do fus nauios por los puertos arriua
dichos: y quien dize que toman otra
derrota por la parte del Norte, y Baca
llaos, ô tierra del Labrador, y Cortes
Reales, no fabe la Efphera, ni la di-
menfion de los Cofmographos, ni
à nauegado, y yo hare la demo-
ftracion todas las vezes que fe me
mande. Y aduierto que la dilacion en
efto podra dañar mucho, y la breue-
dad aprouechar, y vefe, que quando
falen de Inglaterra ciento y mas naues, algunas vezes en el año, no fabe-
mos donde fe defparecen, es la caufa,
que difcurren faliendo de Anglia para toda la cofta de España, y Iflas de
Canaria y Madera, Larache del eftrecho, cabo de Aguer, dãdo armas a los
Africanos, hafta entrar en el Tropicco
de Cácro, y cofta de Arguin, y entrar

en el

en el puerto señalado del Ialopho, q es pecho, y puede ser amparo del Oceano indico Español, y Oriental de Ethiopia, y Poniente del Brasil y Magallanes, y principio de las mas fuerças que V. Magestad tiene, para reparo de su Corona. Y rehechos los Luteranos en este puerto del Ialopho, salieron a combatir año de 1567 aquel antiguo castillo de Arguin su vezino, y le ganaron, y lleuaron toda su artilleria, y en el año de ochenta, vn Portugues natural de la Isla de Madeyra, que se llamaua Cabeças, nauegò, saliendo de las Terceras, con orden del tirano Manoel de Silua, hermano de Antonio de Silua Epirata (que se casò y biue en la Rochela) entrò en la Isla de Santiago de Cabo verde antigua, Catolica y memorable, y la saqueo, y arruynò, y abrasò, dando principio a ello

t ello alguna clerigo, o clerigos, y feglares que fueron a la mar, o tierra, rescatando con los Lueranos en tal razon; crimen que hasta aora no se castigò, ni purihcò, de quienes eran, como se hizo en los de la Tercera. Y claro es, que no acontecieran estos robos, ni otros inumerables en toda la costa de Guinea, de nauios y hazienda, ni estarian perdidas las Almadranas de Arguin de V. Magestad, de tantos años a esta parte.

¶ Capitulo. IIII.

SOBRE TO-
da la verdad destos
sucessos, podemos
afirmar, que los Lu-
teranos andan pujan
tes por la mar, por ser muy diestros

B en

en la arte nauegatoria, y sacan las alturas de los Reynos, Prouincias y lugares precisas, y nauegan sin error en algun cierto modo, sin recebir perdidas, en comparació de las nuestras. Y con la arte Matematica Francisco Draques, vino à ser tan perfeto nauegante, y tan perfeto cosario, que en el año de.76.y.77. estãdo yo siruiendo a V. Magestad en las Islas de Cabo verde, peleamos con el y su armada, y lo hizimos apartar de la tierra, yendo el con siete galeones, robando y destruyendo los nauegantes de España, como fue por toda la mar, hasta el estrecho de Magallanes, passolo, y robo en el mar del Sur, muchos talentos de Oro, por hallar las naues del mar Oceano del Sur, sin orden de guerra, y sin artilleria. Este fue el primer viage que el hizo, despues q̃ se hizo

Epirata.

Epirata: En este año lleuò en su armada, mucha artilleria y gente noble, para fortificarse en las Prouincias remotas, lo que dexò de hazer mudando consejo, despues que se vido las naues cargadas de Oro: y boluiose por el mismo estrecho nauegando hazia la parte del Norte, auiendose auenturado à nauegar en el segundo Emispherio, mouido de interes, riyédose de Ioan Ribao famoso cosario, que auia fortificadose en la Florida, que es costa del Reyno de Mexico, tierra esteril enpantanada: y porq̃ alli lo vé cio el buen Capitá Peromelendez, general de los Galcones de V. Magestad en la carrera de Indias, y lo destruyò el año de.69. Y porque los Luteranos acaben de perder el desseo q̃ tienen de poblar, è inhabitar los Reynos, y descubrimientos de V. Magestad,

A 2

ſtad, es de mucha importãcia que ſe
fortifique y gane eſte puerto y aguada de los Ialophos. Y porque es capaz
de ſuſtentar las armadas de V. M.
que alli aportá, q̃ por el puerto ſer tal,
el Señor Rey Don Manuel, Rey de
Portugal, dio licẽcia al generaliſimo
Alfonſo de Alburquerque, yẽdo por
general de ſu flota para la India Oriẽ
tal: que ſi conforme al eſtatuto naue-
gatorio, a caſo no pudieſſe paſſar la
Equinocial por dia de S. Iuan, auien
do ſalido de Lisboa en el mes de Mar
ço, q̃ alli ſe rehizieſſe, por no perder
viage lo q̃ el hizo, como grande Pilo
to que era: y de mas de ſetenta años
a eſta edad preſente, tratan los nauc-
gantes Portugueſes cõ eſte Rey la lo
pho en ſu comercio, y ſiẽpre ha deſſea
do q̃ ſe fortifique ſu tierra, y ſea poblada de Criſtianos: porq̃ como los

mora-

moradores de las Islas de Cabo verde
ſon oriũdos de aquel Reyno, ellos ſe
aman y auezinan, y quieren mucho.
Y fortificandoſe eſte puerto con el
de la Sierra Leona (como abaxo ſe di
rá) creceran las rentas de Guinea à
V. Mageſtad mas de cinquenta quen
tos, y lo que lleuan los Luteranos, ſerá
mejor que venga a Eſpaña: y quãto a
la fortificacion deſte puerto, ſe poder
hazer, ſerá coſa facil, porque la Isla de
Santiago tiene mucha gente vẽturera
esforçada y toda nauegante, deſta coſa
de lançar los luteranos de ſus cõfines.
Y haſſe de auertir, que eſta tal fortificacion ſe ha de hazer en el lugar q̃ dire.
En la boca deſta enſenada, eſta vna Is
leta apeñaſcada, en la qual haziendo
V. M. vn Baluarte fuerte con ſu preſi
dio, no ſerá poſſible q̃ ſe puede entrar
el puerto por ningun contrario, ſin q̃
de

DE la Isleta los echen al hondo, y ni mas ni menos de la punta de la tierra firme los echaran al hondo, que ferá de la ciudad q̃ V.M. mandará leuantar y fundar en fu fitio inexpugnable: porque eftando alli la ciudad, por la parte del mar es fuerte, y por dedentro queda la enfenada, que la haze mas fuerte. Y por parte del Norte, la Ifleta es tan fuerte y cerrada, que no puede ningun nauio acometer la entrada, de fuerte que haga fu difinio, por fer peña afpera. Y fortificandoffe efte puerto, ganará V. Mageftad, los moradores por amigos y vafallos, y las animas, con el Batifmo que les mã dará predicar, que lo admité al Euangelio: porque todo el Reyno del Ialopho, aunque fon vifitados de los Mahometanos, fon tan gentiles, que no tienen Alcoran, ni Mezquita, folo

es

Es verdad q̃ el Rey es Moro, y algunos hidalgos con el, ya hazen Zalema, mas con todo piden pan, y no ay quié les deftribuya la palabra deDios, á falta de fortificacion. Y porque tardá áles y r á predicar, vienen los Africanos Caçizes allá á corromperlos, con noticias de la falfa Seta: que fi de aca fueffen religiofos (amparados defta fortaleza) que les enfeñaffen la Fè, creo que fe Baptizaran, y conuertiran todos. Y teniendo V. Mageftad en fu amiftad efte Rey Ialopho (como por razon aurá de fer) amigo, ferá de gran prouecho á vueftra Mageftad, por los tratos y contratos de toda Etiopia, y mar: porque efte Rey feñorea toda la tierra de Africa por lo interior, hafta el confin de Marruecos. Y por la otra parte, que es hazia Oriente a los confines del Reyno de Tremecen, y

B 4   por

por la marina señorea el Rey Berbeá
fin, y al famoso Rio çanagá, que diuide a la banda del Norte los montes
claros, y Reyno del Fulo Barbaro, y
del grande Tumbucutum de Exipto,
que es ciudad famosa, tiene el comercio del Schyo a la parte Austral, en lo
interior de Africa, tierras llenas de
Oro, Marfil, Ambar, y caualleria de
Elefantes, Leones, y de muchos Vni-
cornios, y tierra sana, que goza la influencia de buen Cielo, q es el Tropico de Cancro en el paralelo de Persia,
Mesopotamia, y Mexico. Desta forta
leza del Ialopho, puede V. Magestad
procurar tener comercio con todos e-
ssos Reyes gentiles, para juntamente
estoruarles los Tesoros que lleuan de
Tumbucutum á Argel para el gran
Turco, y rescatarschá, y saluarse há mi
llares de Cristianos captiuos del Ma-
rrucco,

rrucco, Fez, y Argel, huyendo por la
Tierra firme, con las Caphilas de los
Barbaros: y por razones que daré, y
demostracion, afirmo. Que este puerto en Ocidente si fuesse poblado, que
seria remedio de España, y confusion
de los Lusitanos, si Dios fuesse serui-
do, que V. Magestad tuuiesse ganada
la ciudad de Adem en Oriente, que
está en la entrada del mar bermejo,
será Señor del Mundo, sobre los
Cesares, Alexandros, Darios, Mo-
gores, Sophios, y Turcos, porque
esta es su entrada por la Equinocial en la India, y estos puertos
comprehenden en si el Orbe, y
dan por sus sitios y esperanças, que
por España se sustentará la Iglesia
Catolica, y se augmentará con vida y braço de Vuestra Magestad,
siguiendo las pisadas de sus Santos

B 5   Cato-

po los faltará otro. Responderemos q̃
que el mar Occeano es grande; y tiene
por Geometria, Corpospherica, E-
quidiftante, por lineas paralelas, que
es la Equinocial, que lo diuide en dos
mitades al mundo, como lo dize Ptolomeo, y Ariftotiles, y todos, y yo q̃
lo nauegé, y tiene dos tropicos, y dos
circules, y tiene quatro meridianos, q̃
por efta Quadripartita, vienen a fer
realmente doze partes iguales, cor-
refpondientes a los doze fenos y plan-
tas del Cielo por cuya influencia fon
mouidas las aguas del mar, y el fluxo
y refluxo de las mareas que fe mue-
uen, crecen y menguan, fubliuadas y
mouidas de la fuerça de los fiete Planetas inferiores al regimiêto del Sol,
que como animofo, con fu calidad
procreante, haze produzir la tierra,
emuiandole fus Inuiernos, Veranos,
Otoños

Catolicos padres y aguelos Carlo Quinto, y al Rey Don Manuel,
aguelo de V. Mageftad de inmortal
memoria: para que ceffen tantos males, robos y heregias, aprouechando
V. Mageftad a fus Reynos y vafallos,
y crecera la Iglefia Catolica; pues nõ
caben predicadores por los Colegios
de Efpaña, fin confiderar, que el fin de
fus habitos, reditos y rentas, es predicar el Euangelio, y no fofernar el ta-
lento, con tanta rifa de los Luteranos
peruerfos.

¶ Capitulo. V.

SI POR CON-
trariedad dixeren a
V. Mageftad, que
quitando efte puerto
a los Luteranos, que
no

Paradoxo, y breue compendio de la fortificacion, tan necessaria a la Iglesia Catolica, de suerte que bastara fortificar solamente los puertos principales, para que dellos se amparen todos los inferiores, y queden las nauegaciones mas breues, y de facil nauegar vendran los Christianos a no temer el auenturarse y ra buscar la vida, y entre predicar el Euangelio, enrriquecerse a si, y a su patria, como lo hizo el inmortal capitã de V. Magestad, Alõso de Alburquerque, y don Vasco de Gama, que se señalaron entre los hõbres del mundo, en nauegar y descubrir, y conquistando sujetaron a V. Magestad tantos imperios, tantos Reynos, para que V. Magestad los mande cultiuar, como verdadero padre de las familias de nuestro Capitolio Romano, y de la viña del Señor: mandan-

Otoños, y Estios, los quales tiempos en el Orbe hazen las mónciones a quatuor ventis, que son Septentrion, el Lausto, y el Oriente, y Poniente, que comprehenden en su medio, debazo del Zodiaco, la Esphera Elemental, que es el mar Oceano, exalador de los vientos, que son tantos, quantos son los grados de la Longitud, y Latitud de la Zona, ò del Zodiaco, que vienẽ a ser por dotrina de Ptolomeo, trecientos y sesenta grados, por desuario de los quales vientos y exalaciones, los hombres nauegan en vno y otro Emispherio, no quando ellos quieren, sino quando es moncion, y los que ca nauegamos contra moncion, ò los que en los Antipodas contra ella nauegan se pierdẽ, si no tienẽ mucha arte, y puertos donde se reparar y faluas, que es el fin que yo señalo en este

Parado-

miſmas reſiduas tierra, y coſta de Guinea.

¶Capitulo. VI

S LA SIERRA
Leona muy rica de
Oro,tanto y mas que
todo el diſtrito del Pe
ru. Eſtá eſta Sierra
Leona,en altura de ſeys grados de la
Equinocial para el Norte,es fertiliſſi
ma de gente negra,abundoſa de todo
lo neceſſario al ſer humano, tiene
Oro, Criſtal, Açucar, palo de Braſil,
Ambar, Eleſantes, Buſanos, Leones,
Tigres, Gazelas, Venados, Pimienta,
mejor q̃ la de la India,q̃ ſe llama Mã-
tibilia. Tiene eſta ſierra grandiſſimas
riberas de agua dulce,donde ſe halla
Oro en cantidad,de las quales vna es
muy,

mãdando muy deveras hazer las Mã
tematicas naucgatorias, en todas ſus
ciudades y puertos maritimos:'porq̃
es la Matematica ciẽcia,de direcció y
demoſtracion,con la qual el ſoldado
ve, y eſcoge,y naucgãdo: pelea por
ſu ley, Rey y patria,y juntamente yrã
el terror ſobre nueſtros aduerſarios.
Y Dios viendo nueſtra diſpoſicion,
fauorecera a la cauſa de V. Mageſtad,
pues es defenſor de ſu Igleſia Catolica: para ſuſtento de cuyos hijos, y
Baptizados pueblos en Oriente y Po
niẽte,entregò a V. Mageſtad la naue
gacion de todo el Orbe, y aſsi como
por tantas razones conuiene ſea poblado el puerto del Ialopho, con todo el ſecreto poſſible de los aduerſarios, es juſto,mande V. Mageſtad tras
el,'poblar y fortificar la ſierra Leona; Reyno del _ Zapi, que eſtá en la
miſma

muy celebrada, que se dize Tagarin,
donde las naues grandes de la India
de Portugal hazen aguada, y se baste
cen de todo lo necessario muy ligera
mente, y aqui se vienen de contino a
rehazer los Inglefes y Francefes, para
destruyr el Oceano, como queda dicho, y aqui roban el comercio de V.
Magestad, de la nauegacion de Cabo verde, y todo el mar, como en el
año de.1577. la entrò vna armada
de Rochelenfes para la ganar, y el
Rey don Sebastian, que Dios perdone, mandò vna armada de galeras y
todas naues, a desarraygarlos, por el
Capitan Antonio Vello Tinoco, que
antes de vencer esta batalla fue ven-
cedor de otra que estaua anclada den
tro en el Reyno y puerto de los Ialofos, y los nauios de los Luteranos erã
muchos y muy llenos de municion,

armas

armas y mercaderias. Y de la misma
fuerte el año de.1570. corrientes, el
Capitan Melchior Montero con sus
galeras, disparatò y vencio otra arma
dade Luteranos en el puerto del Ialopho, que dista de la sierra Leona, ha
zia el Norte, nueue grados Norte y
Sur, a diez y siete leguas y media por
grado. De suerte, que de contino, y a-
ora mas que en otro tienpo, los Lute
ranos tienen adquiridos a su compañia muchos marineros, y Capitanes
Españoles, contrarios al seruicio y le
yes de V. Magestad, y esta Inglaterra
llena de esperanças, para perturbar la
paz Cristiana, fauorecida de los a-
parcialados de don Antonio, Prior
de Crato que fue. Y si V. Magestad
no proueyere su nauegacion con di-
ligencia y buena orden, que Dios nos
ayudara a poner en fortificar y po-

C   blar,

de treinta quentos de Oro, en la arribada de las quatro naues, que arribaron del año de 1590. de la conserua y viage del Virey Mathias de Alburquerque, y la derrota que lleuò el mismo año Bernardino Ribero general, en auer derrotado de la Isla de Santa Elena, por toda la Equinocial, hasta las Españolas, y Francisco Giraldes gouernador del Brasil, que partiendo de Lisboa en el año de ochēta y ocho, anduuo dos años debaxo del Tropico de Cancro, destruyēdo la flota sin remedio, por falta de no tomar puerto en el Ialopho, o sierra Leona. Y si estos dos Reynos se fortificaren, luego en el mismo Guine se poblaran suauemente otros puertos, de que aqui no trato por euitar prolixidad, como aura de ser Santo Domingo, donde está la contratacion de V. Mage-

C 2   stad

blar, temo que en breues dias, como los Lueranos son muy nauegadores que hagan algun falto dañoso a España, sino se da remedio a tan eminētes peligros, que acaezca lo que vino a ser despues que yo auise de muchas cosas semejantes a don Cristoual de Mora, que sera testigo de que notifiqué lo que aora, y de lo porq̄ no se hizo, para que aora con bibeza se de remedio a males futuros, tomando por exēplo de lo que digo, la grande perdida de las naues de la carrera de la India, que desde que la India es descubierta hasta aora, vn año por otro han arriuado de ochenta años a esta parte, mas de cien naues, entre arriuadas y naufragadas, con notabilisima perdida de gente, y el lucrocesante de la hazienda de los Lusitanos, y tesoro de V. Magestad, que deuen ser mas
de

ftad, y el Reyno de los Buyafras en el poderoso Rio grande, de cuyos dos puertos oy dia se lleuan a las Indias de Poniente, todos los esclauos que sacan el Oro de las minas.

¶ *Capitulo. VII.*

PVES AVEMOS mostrado las razones de poder fortificar la sierra Leona tras el lalopho, bien es declaremos el modo de como se puede poblar y fortificar a poca costa de V. Magestad esta entrada en la mar. En esta playa ay vna punta de tierra, q es alta, y casi está toda aislada y cercada de agua, y puedese aislar facilmente, es este vn sitio hermoso, donde se puede de fundar vna de las mas populosas ciuda-

ciudades del mundo ; porque demas de procrear esta tierra de Guinea, y Zape todo lo que cria España, de todo el minero de tierra, se saca Oro finissimo. Esta sierra Leona es la que el señor Rey don Sebastian tenia dada a don Antonio prior de Crato, para la poblar, y segun tégo oydo a todos los nauegantes estando yo en Guinea, dezian que conuenia que en fortificandola, se intitulase, Duque, o Rey de la sierra Leona, y afirmo, que quien fuere señor della tendra mejor Reyno que el de Fez, y aunque el de Marruecos, porque en tierra firme tiene mas de cien leguas de longitud, q es el districto de la mina de Portugal, y por lo interior de la latitud sube diez y siete grados, y confina con el Rey de Nubia, y Libia la arenosa, debaxo del Meridiano de Fez, y a la parte Oriental.

C 3.

perder en la Bahia del Brasil, y al o-
tro año en Samatra. Y demas desto,
tendra la mina, que es el castillo de
san Iorge de V. Magestad, defensa
en su distrito, y seran echados. desta
costa los Epiratas que hazen escalas
en el Rio de los Ceitos, y en la Bahia
de las Gallinas, donde rescatan los
Luteranos, con sal, oro puro, y lo
lleuan sin remedio : y desta fortificacion nacen muchos bienes, y el mayor es, que puede venir todo el tesoro
de la mina, para quien V. Magestad
cada año haze vna sola armada, puede venir en dos, o tres fragatas lige-
ras, sin costa ni peligro, de la mina a la
sierra Leona; y dende alli al Ialopho,
y de alli en flota con todos los nauios
de Caboverde, y contrato de Guinea a España, para no ser dellos toma-
dos de Epiratas, como los cogen cada

C 4   dia

tal, llega al Rey de Mandinga, por o-
tra nombre çumba, que es Rey, cuya muger y Reyna tiene el gouierno,
y es conquistadora destas tierras, y da
habito a sus capitanes, q es vna chya
de grana, colgada en el pecho, que es
noucidad descubierta entre Barbaros,
y esta pretende de la sierra Leona, por
las riquezas de Oro que le lleuan sus
conquistadores. Y boluiendo a la for
tificacion desta sierra y puerto, entran
en la mar dos caudalosos Rios, vno se
dize Tagarin, y el otro Mitombo, en
esta aguada hizicró en tiempo del S.
Rey dó Iuan tercero aguada muchas
vezes, naues dela India, q es capaz de
dar reparo a quantas armadas alli lle-
garen, quando no pudieren doblar la
quinocial, para no perder viage. Y si
mi Capitan Ruy demelo, y cndonos
para la India aqui llegára, y se rchizie
ra, no nos fueramos a naufragar y

dia por venir ſolos, y fuera de cami-
no, como los tienen robados de abiſi-
nio de la Rochela. Y aora los Ingleſes,
lo que por todas vias ſe eſforçará ſi ſe
fortifica la ſierra Leona, y ſe hará fa-
cilmente ſin guerra, y el Zape y ta-
lopho quieren la amiſtad de los Luſi-
tanos de V. Mageſtad, porque en eſta
ſierra Leona andan muchos hóbres
huydos de la juſticia por caſos crimi-
nales, que no deſcan, ſino que V. Mageſtad los perdone, y cóſienta poblar
la ſierra: y eſtos hazen en ſu tiempo
la carga a los Epiratas, y contratan có
ellos Oro, Marfil, Ambar, Pimienta y
mas coſas. Y cóſideradó yo en la verdad delos naufragios nŕos, y robos pa
decidos, propuſe por deſcargo de mi
cóciécia darle eſtos auiſos a V. Mageſtad, afirmando, que ſolos los hóbres
retirados en eſta Guinea, ſeran los pobladores

bladores deſtas ciudades, que ſon in-
cartados y valientes y nauegantes, y ſerá mucha la merced que V. Mageſtad
hará a ellos, y a Dios mas ſeruicio, re-
duzirlos no ſolaméte a ſu gracia, mas
a la de Dios, que como no tiené Igleſia, los vnos ſiendo ſeglares baptizan
los hijos vnos a los otros, y las barre-
ganas, y cometen mil delitos: y vuo
hombre Eſpañol que con los Ethio-
pas llegò à comer en ſus guerras carne humana. Y los naturales deſta ſierra ſon Idolatras de poco juyzio, ſin
direction, ſolo ſiguen al Sol, y la Luna, y conuiertenſe el dia que les pre-
dican el Euangelio. Su arma es arco,
y flecha, tienen minas por poſſeſsió,
ſon hombres que ſacan hierro de las
ſierras, ſon herreros, carpinteros, y pla-
teros: y eſtos deſta ſierra ſi tuuieſſen
induſtria de fundir artilleria, ſerian

C 5   con pa-

-comparados a los Malabares de la India, que fon nauegantes, y en toda la
tierra ay montañas . de mil generos
de arboledas, y naranjales brauos , y
naturales cañaucrales de açucar.

¶ Capitulo. VIII.

L Año que V. Ma-
geftad eftaua en Por-
tugal, yendo para la
India, arribo defta fie-
rra Leona , el galeon
de Malaca , andando naufragando
ocho mefes, y pudiera fin daño, fi fe
reparara en efta fierra Leona, y radc-
lante, y no arriuar, como arriuo, año
de mil y quinientos y cincuenta : el
goucrnador del Brafil fuego del Có
de de Linares, y afsino fe vuiera perdido Luis de Alter de Andrada con
fu

fu naue en la cofta del Brafil, fin efca-
par quatro hombres, ni don Luis hijo
del Arçobifpo don Heroado no fe
perdiera, ni don Diego de Mendoça
con fiete naues que llebaua de Seuilla , por mandado del feñor Carlo
Quinto prepotentifsimo Empetador
padre de V. Mageftad, que pafsó por
la fierra Leona, y fue a perderfe a la
ifla de Santo Tome, ni Iaime Rafchin
con otra tanta flota tras el fobredi-
cho capitan , no fe perdiera fobre el
Rio de la plata, ni la naue Flamenca,
que venia de la India Oriental, no fe
deshiziera alli en Santo Tome, defpues que no pudo doblar al cabo de
las Palmas, junto a la fierra Leona. Y
es de ponderar, que defpues que Iaime Rafchin fe perdio con fus ocho
naues, vna vez boluio en Scuilla a
hazer otra flota, y fiendo fegundaria-
mente

mente contrastado de las monçiones junto al Ialopho se saluara, y de alli no teniendo puerto, fue a la Isla de Santiago, donde toda la géte se le murio fin quedar hombre ninguno. Y tras estos Capitanes año de. 1572. crio V. Magestad a Iuan Ortiz de çarate Vizcayno por Adelantado del Rio de la plata, y me llebaua por su Vicario general, en respeto que le aprefte en Seuilla en la cafa dela contrataciõ de V. Magestad, los pilotos y marineros, y fuymos nauegando hasta Caboverde, donde el dicho Adelantado mudo consejo, y fue a parar con sus deshordenes a la isla de santa Catalina, debaxo del Tropico de Capricornio, que fue causa de no poblar al dessado Rio de la plata. Y resultò de su mal viage, no hazer el capitá Dicgo Flores su efeto, ni poblar el estrecho

cho de Magallanes, quando por partir contra moncion de Sanlucar, y auise a don Cristoual en Portugal, que no yua bien encaminado el Capitan Flores, y que se perderia, que se detuuiesse la armada hasta la moncion, y no vuo efeto, ni se poblaran aquellas partes tan longincas, y que estan en los nuestros Antipodas, sino vuiere saberse nauegar, y sino partieren las naues con moncion, pues fuera y dentro de los Tropicos, los Elementos en este mundo obedecen al Cielo estrellado, y la nauegacion es tanto peligrosa y ardua, quanto es el vso della violento, que al fin entrando los hombres en el mar, salen desu centro, por lo que es menester faber nauegar, so pena que se perderan todos los que no fupieren lo que conuiene en la arte de nauegar : y V. Ma-

dad de Dios dotrina a muchos;Lute-
ranos, que fe conuirtieron, por fa-
berlos yo facramentar en medio destas guerras, a vnos por la lengua de
Indios que ellosfabian, a otros en lé-
gua latina, y afsi alcance redoblando
mis vigilias con el eftudio y arte;Ma-
tematica que la nauigatoria, que es
buena a los atreuidos, para feruir a
V. Mageftad en el exemplo de San
Pablo, que naufrago tres vezes por
aumentar la Fé de nueftro feñor Iefu
Chrifto : qui non venit mitere pacé
in terris fed gladium, por lo que es
jufto que V. Mageftad mánde fortificar la Equinocial con todas las ve-
ras, porque Moros, Etiopios, Turcos,
Francefes, Inglefes, fe defengañen, q
fino, ellos no tiené menos propofito,
que poblar y robar los Reynos Equi-
nociales de V. Mageftad, y dizenque
fe

V. Mageftad por feruicio de Dios
me deue dar crédito a loq efcriuo, por
que me halle cafi en todas eftas cofas,
y no las fé de abftraéto, fino de ciécia,
y expiriéncia, que de treynta y vn a-
ños a efta parte he vifto, nauegando
todo el mar Oceano con todos eftos
Capitanes, Gouernadores, y Genera
les figuientes. Con Iorge de Lima, y
con don Iorge Tubara, en las Terceras; con PeroMelendez, con Iuã Or-
tiz; con Eftatio de Saa, con Antonio Vello Tinoco, con don Pedro Leitaõ, afuera o-
tros, y eftos de altobordo: y en galc-
ras, con Fernádaluarez, có Bernabe
de Sofa, có Diego Lopez de Sequeira: y los nueue años predique el Euan
gelio en fu propia lengua a los Brafi-
les, y defpues en Guinea otros cinco.
En lasquales prouincias por la bon-
dad

y rica. Es la Bahia mejor puerto, que quantos ay en la Equinocial, y está en quinze grados de altura de la equinocial para el Sur: tiene a la entrada de la barra vna Isleta que la daña, de fuerte, que siendo su entrada de tres leguas de ancho, no puedē ningunos nauios de-alrobordo entrar en este puerto, sin passar à tiro de cañon, de vna fortaleça que hizo el señor Rey don Iuan año de .1540. en la punta de la Tierra firme, conque se defendio de los Luteranos de Francia, por mas de.19.años, hasta que de confiança la dexaron caer y aruynar, como yo mismo la vi, en el año de.1560. yendo para la India Oriental, donde aportamos à Inuernar, a falta de no auer podido hazer aguada en la sierra Leona, a saluamiento de la naue de San Pablo y gente. Y fue esta Inuer-

D   nada

se han de perpetuar, respondiendo à quien les pregūta d' porque causa andan en guerras ilicitas, que nuestro padre Adan que murio fin testamento, y que el mundo es de todos; y no de los Españoles: y no es la causa desta su pertinacia y latrocinio, fino estar en oy dia estos puertos de la mar, sin fortaleça, ni Iglesia, ni religion.

¶ *Capitulo. IX.*

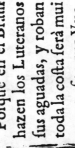

Porque en el Brasil hazen los Luteranos sus aguadas, y roban toda la costa será mui a proposito que Vuestra Magestad fortifique los lugares mas importantes y mas suficientes a defesar la mar, como son, la Bahia de todos Santos, ciudad muy populosa y rica

nada ā caula,que deſpues qūando parā
mos en Octubre,doblādo el cabo do
Buena eſperança , fuymos tan erra-
dos,que nauegando por deſucra dela
Iſla de San Laurencio, paſſamos por
la India haſta llegar a la Tapobrana,
Iſla de Samatra,donde nos perdimos,
y de aquella gente,que eramos ochocientos y quarenta hombres, queda-
mos biuos treze,y no mas. Y por e-
ſtos paſſos y rodeos ſe perdio el Manoel de Soſa famoſo.Y año de. 1562
ſe perdio Diego Lopez de Mezquita. Y eſtando V. Mageſtad en
Lisboa,ſe perdio el Capitan Gaſpar
de Brito. y̅ el año de. 1588.ſe perdio
en Angola(por no auerſe reparado en
la Iſla de Santa Elena,viniendo de la
India para Portugal)el Capitan Diego Dazambuja : el qual trayendo la
hazienda de Angola (donde ſe deſ-
hizo

hizo la nauecoñ el guſano en la altura de los Ialophos) el coſario Antonio de Silua de la Rochela,la robò y
ſaqueo.Y todas eſtas perdidas acaecé
à Eſpaña,por no tener V. Mageſtad
fortificada la mar,y ſus tan hermoſas
aguas arriba dichas, y las que vamos
declarando.Y boluiendo a hablar en
la fortificacion de la Bahia, digo,
Que por no eſtar fuerte como conuiene,los Ingleſes con dos nauios,en
el año de.1588.la entraron , y toda
la flota que eſtaua dentro de la barra
cargada de riquezas la quemaron, y
fueſſe huyendo toda la gente de la
ciudad,religioſos y ſeglares afrento-
ſamente,por no auer en ella baluarte
ni torres,ni las Cauas antiguas, auien
do ella ſido muy fuerte , como yo
la vide año de.1560.y eſto deue de
ſer,porq̃ ſe deſcuydaron los governa-

D 2   dores

ne diez de Diametro, y es mucho el peligro en que está, de ser tomada por los contrarios, si quisieren poblar para el efeto, de entrar al Peru por Magallanes: por razon, que si nauegando deste puerto, partieren hazia el estrecho de Magallanes en Setiembre : llegarán al estrecho en quinze dias cantando, que es moncion, y si partieren en Nouiembre mejor yrá, y euocado el estrecho, hará enel Perulo que quisieren a su saluo: y puesto q̃ las opiniones son tantas, quãtas las cabeças, digo: que las intenciones de los Luteranos son muy ocultas a los hombres que estan fuera de la milicia, y no sabiendo el numero de los Pilotos, y de los nauegantes que se há passado en Inglaterra, ni lo que determinan hazer contra V. Magestad vn año, ó otro, y han empeçado a casarse

D 3   con

dores en el tiempo de la paz, y no se dauan a la milicia, llenos de riqueza, como quando la conquistaron. Puedese hazer en la Bahia vna fortaleça inexpunable, debaxo dla artilleria, de la qual se ampararan muchas naues: el sitio es el mismo dela Almada, que está frontero de Lisboa, hasta el cabo del Spichel : sus comarcas son muy grandes. No trato de sus riquezas por particular, por no salir de mi intento en este compendio, y tambié porque lo tratare muy difusamente en vn libro que hago de la Quadripartita del vniuerso, por seruir a Dios, y mouer a muchos religiosos a que quieran yr a predicar el Euangelio, persuadidos por muchas razones que para esse fin les traygo, no dexãdo de dezir que la Bahia y Ensenada sube hazia el Norte diez y nueue leguas, y el medio tiene

ne-

es que para lo que pretendemos en la misma orden, se fortifique la ciudad Sebastiana, que está en el Rio de Enero, abaxo de la Bahia, en la contina costa de Norte y Sur, debaxo de la precisa altura del Tropico de Capricornio en el Reyno de los Tamoyos, aniciísimos de los Franceses Luteranos de la Rochela. Y si la Bahia y Reyno de los Tupinambás, dista del estrecho d Magallanes 35 grados: esta ciudad Sebastiana, y nóbrado Rio de Enero, es el mas dessecado puerto, q quátos ay en el mar Occano: porque estuuo por ellos este Reyno mas de 20 años, y porque dista menos del estrecho de Magallanes, como son 33 grados, tienen alli por la nauegacion de Leste, Aueste, la importante Isla de Santa Elena, remedio total de los nauegantes de la India Oriental, y

D 4 contra-

có las Luteranas, como hombres del confiados de remedio, y que no tiené patria, y enfaborecados de los latrocinios que van haziendo por la mar, alterando los coraçones de muchos, de los que captiuan cada dia en los nauios de España. Para euitacion de lo qual, es menester q V. Magestad man de a sus vasallos cierré las puertas de Iano, y que tomen armas de Fè y justicia para defender su patria: y obedeciendo a V. Magestad, aumentar la ley de Dios.

¶ Capitulo. X.

PVES Auemos dicho destas tres fortificaciones, que son las del Ialopho, y sierra Leona, y Bahia. Bien

es

contrato de V. Magestad. Por estos prouechos los Tamoyos deste Reyno estan inclinados a los Frãceses, por que les fueron sujetos, y los ayudan siẽpre cõtra los Portugueses en sus continuas guerras, y si no se fortifica esta ciudad, tiene pocos pueblos de su parte. Los Ingleses por tierra y mar ganaran la ciudad, lo que no haran cõ ninguna fuerça, si en la piedra que esta en la boca de la barra, V. Magestad mandare fundar vn rico y fuerte baluarte, esta piedra de aguas muertas, y baxa mar de menguãte, descubre mucho sobre el agua, y de aguas biuas se cubre toda, y por mar a esta causa no se puedẽ temer aduersarios ningunos, porque la barra es estrecha, y a medio tiro de cañon, echaran al hondo a los que intentaren yr alli: y si no se fortifica, y los contrarios la ganaren como lo

lo dessean, luego ellos ganaran la Isla de Santa Elena, y por la consequẽcia todo el Brasil, y Peru: porq̃ muy bien saben ganando esta ciudad, juntamẽte ganar a Cartagena del nueuo Reyno. Y digo, y a Dios tomo por testigo (que es el que mi lengua guia) q̃ los Luteranos y sus caudillos estan puestos a todo tiempo biuir, y poblar lugares maritimos a su saluo, amando la vida y riquezas del Oceano : y esto mejor lo demostrare, que la demonstracion siempre concluye, como lo hare mandandomelo V. Magestad. Y fortificando V. Magestad estas partes, no yran adelante los peligros, que segun la reuolucion de los tiempos nos estan amenaçando, y cessaran de padecer las Prouincias y Reynos de V. Magestad: y los trabajos que los Españoles reciben, y perdidas, robos

A 5   y asal-

S T A mas abaxo del Rio Enero, y ciudad Sebastiana hazia el Sur, vna Isla, que se llama de Santa Catalina, esta junto a la tierra y costa de la Cananea, y a fuera del Reyno del Brasil, esta distante del estrecho de Magallanes como quinze grados, aqui se auezinan los Luteranos con tanta destreza de nauegar, que es admiracion, ayudandose de nuestros marineros y puertos arriba dichos, y tienen tal arte que de Anglia, a Francia salen, y los mas dias que nauegan en discurrir el mar de España, en veynte dias llegan al Ialopho, y alli refrescan, y de alli van por toda Guinea, de puerto en puerto, a Gambia, a Santo Domin-go,

Y assaltos, todos se conuertiran sobre los Luteranos, porque pereceran en medio de las aguas, y como son de carne enfermaran en la Equinocial, que sino tuuieren refugios en los puertos arriba dichos, esta claro que se consumiran poco a poco: y viendo que V. Magestad despierta, ellos se defensarán. Y pluguiera a Dios, que assi como ellos nauegan desenfrenados có tra la Iglesia, assi los Españoles tuuie ramos animo de proceder cótra ellos, pues la causa de V. Magestad es justa, y su Real coraçon está en manos de Dios. Desseo tanto se hagan las fortificaciones, pues la facilidad con buena orden nos ayuda: bien es leuantemos los animos a imitar nuestros antepassados, sustentado nuestra patria, fin recelo, confiando en Dios siruamos a V. Magestad.

¶ Capi-

go, Rio Grande, Sierra Leena, Rio de las Gallinas, Bahia dlos Cestos, Mina Axem, Islas del Principe, Santo To-me, Angola, Manicongo; y de alli se bucluen cargados de Oro, Ambar, y mas riquezas Orientales, a la yda pa-ra la Equinocial, y vnos quedan con-tratando, y haziendo cargas, como si fuessen señores absolutos, disfaman-do de los Cristianos, dandoles armas: otros se hazen Gentiles como los Ne-gros y Indios, guardando sus ritos su bacanalia, sus costumbres peruersas, con gran ofensa de Dios, y biuen co-mo los Gentiles, y se transforman en ellos: todo esto porque la Isla de San-ta Catalina está junto a la boca del Rio Grande, por donde los Portugue-ses entran cada dia a las charcas del Peru, por mas de duzientas leguas del Rio : y del Peru bienen muchos al

Brasil.

Brasil. Y aqui en esta parte, estando yo en la Tierrafirme, y costa de la Ca-nanea, hablé con vn Capitan Arauca-no, que vino alli captiuo, de mano de los Carijos, que son del Reyno del Rio de la Plata, que está luego abaxo desta Isla, en treynta y cinco grados, en el mismo paralelo del cabo de Bue-na esperança, distante quinze grados mas a menos, como por la Cosmogra-phia se verá el estrecho de Magalla-nes. Y corriendo el Brasil desde la E-quinocial Norte y Sur, corre esta Isla con el estrecho de Magallanes, Nor-deste y Sudueste: es tierra sana fertil, y tierra llana como Andaluzia, hazia Poniente tiene nas de duzientas le-guas de Pinares, de que se pueden ha-zer las naues, tales como las de Olan-da, y Gelanda, alli ay mucho Oro. Y: fortificandose esta Isla, della al Rio

de

portemporales,del qual yā muchas armadas y naues de la India,y Brasil y gente se han perdido , y ellos certeros en la moncion le doblan,robando las fortalezas y nauegacion brasilica,la Bahia ciudad, y los Isleos a Puerto seguro,al Espiritu Santo,la ciudad el Cabofrio,la ciudad Sebastiana,Biriquioca,y Tañaem ,Sátos, S. Vicente hasta alli en Santa Catalina,ordenar sus maquinas cótra V.M. Y sea V.Magestad cierto,que para se fortificar esta Isla,y las mas fuerças arriba dichas, acrecienta sus cavalleros,y cria vasallos , y oprime a todos sus cótrarios,y se haze temer,y afirmo q(nemine discrepante)en Anglia dizen,y en toda la Noruegia, entre Luteranos , que España no tiene armas,ni gente,ni nauegantes,juzgándolo todo por la aparencia de

de la Plata yran por este Rio,y van à salir a la boca de otro Rio, que entra treynta leguas dentro del Rio de la Plata,que se dize Parana, que quiere dezir mar pequeña,en todo el ay mucho Cobre infinito, y baxa de la parte interior de las Charcas,y de Santa Cruz de la sierra:y en esta encruçijada echan aora los Luteranos su red, porque tapan el Rio de la Plata,amenaçan a Santa Elena,y Brasil,y Peru por la entrada deste Rio y Magallanes,y assi hazen los Luteranos con sus disinios la nauegacion,por las riberas y puertos de Oriente,como dicho tengo, vienen tambien doblada la linea Equinocial sobre Paranapuca,que es la Prouincia de la nueua Lusitania,y visitá alli a la ciudad Filipitania,y van por la costa abaxo, y saben doblar el cabo de Santo Agustino, por

fi nauegan con orden, no fe verá per-
didos ni vencidos, como dicho tégo:
declarando, que lo que fe nauega del
Tropico de Cancro hasta el Peru, Nó
bre de Dios, y Mexico, y fus riberas: y
lo que defde la fierra Leona, hasta
Santo Tome, y Angola, hazen tantas
perdidas de los nauios, como fe ven
por euidencia, es por les faltar feguri-
dad de armada y puertos, y porq los
tales rumbos eftan direttos a la altura de Lefte Aufte, que neceffariamen
te requiere fabiduria y experiécia del
curfo de los vientos, y aguas, y del A-
ççoy Receço del Sol: pues de España a la India, y Indias, fe paffan todos
los Climas del mundo que es redon-
do y fpherico: y tiene fu obediencia
en manos de las Eftrellas, y fu natural
curfo, de que no pueden faltar, y re-
troceder. Cuya direttió fe ha facado

E   con

de lo que vieron en el Oceano, en tó
da la edad de ochenta, hasta el prefen
te dia, pronofticando fobre la flaque-
za de las naues de la India, que no lle
gan como folian a la Isla de Sáta Ele
na, y en cierta manera tienen razon:
porque no es jufto que las armadas de
V. Magestad busqué redobles, y nue
uos orizontes, para venir por fu naue
gacion recta a España, fino que ven-
gan fu via recta con orden de flota, co
mo la naturaleza del mar lo pide, y lo
fienten los buenos Pilotos expetrimé
tados. Y deteftando la inuencion de
mercaderes digo efto, y pido fortificacion, pues ellos han enriquecido a
Inglaterra y Francia, en mandar nauegar fus nauios fuera de tiempo, y
folos, fin orden de flota, que es total
perdicion de Efpaña. Y fupuefta la
fortificacion, los de Oriéte y Poniéte
fi

con mucha vigilia de los antiguos, y vso de nauegar al vno y otro Polo, como lo tiene aquel y aquellos, q por si han nauegado, no obstante toda la ciencia de Ptolomeo y Purbachio y sus sequaces, ni Euclides, que solo se fundaron en escreuir los mas dellos, en lo que sabian de Abstracto, y no de nauegacion y Cosmographia, que verdaderamente no lo han alcançado: porque sin falencia la Espherase diui de en dos, en Etherea, y en Elemental, y diuide la ciencia Elemental, de la suprema con mucha diferencia. Y pues la Astrologia, y Astronomia es ciencia que pronostica, no trato della, porque no sirue para la fortificacion, mas digo, que solo presta a la nauegatoria algunas cosas, de que se satisfazen los buenos Pilotos, y son. El puesto de las estrellas del Norte sijas. La circun-

circunferécia del Zodiaco, y las estrellas del cruzero del Sur, o Austro, q señalá el polo del segundo Emispherio. Los quartos de la Luna, y su curso. Las mareas y vientos. Y aquise incluye el saber sacar segun las regiones del Orbe, que son doze, distribuydas a los doze Planetas, que son supremos. Los doze Sinos, q influyen a los siete inferiores, y dan el contenido mouimiento: por virtud del qual la naturaleça, y las seguidas causas lle tan adelante sus potencias actiuas y passiuas. Y esto es lo q se deue de leer en las Vniuersidades, y lugares maritimos de V.M. porq carecé dela Arte, y de toda la platica en España.

¶Capitulo. XII.

Y SOLO porque es anexo a la fortificacion el saber nauegar,

auiso

auiso a V. Magestad q̃ le estan necessario el mandar hazer lo que digo, como el conseruar sus Reynos y sus estados, y sus riquezas, guardádo en todo la orden Nautica, q̃ el señor Rey don Manoel Rey de Portugal, aguelo de V.M. ordenò, a cuya fortaleça y espiritu se deue la honra de los descubrimiẽtos y cõquistas longincas del Orbe, q̃ yua descubriendo, conquistádo y fortificando. Y assi como el mãdó fortificar la Isla de Zocotorá, q̃ es la boca del mar Bermejo en Oriente, no la despoblaran despues, hasta q̃ se ganara Adem, q̃ es la cabeça de las Arabias, ni tuuiera el Turco vida ni reposo como tiene, q̃ con las riquezas que por alli le lleuá dela India de V.M. se defiende de los Perlas, q̃ llaman Sophio, ofende solamẽte a Cristianos. Mas boluiendo al proposito de la fortifica-

tificacion, mãde V.M. que se haga en las casas de su contratació de sus Reynos, vna matricula, q̃ contenga los marineros y Pilotos de cada Prouincia y Reynos, para que al tiempo de la nauegacion, desta matricula se saquen y sean nõbrados y proueydos para anauegar y lleuar sus nauios, como se hizo ya en Portugal, y la codicia destruyó toda la buena ordé. Los Pilotos de la India Oriental, y sotapilotos, maestros y cõtramaestros, son muchos, mas solos. 10. ó. 12. goza de los cargos, por que tiené dineros que dar a los armadores, assi auiã de estar los desPoniéte, los de las Islas, los del Nõrte, como si fuessen colegiales dela orden militar, y familiares de la Corõa que el officio de Piloto, auia de andar entre Españoles, como anda entre Ingleses y Frãceses, si se pudiesse por la lealtad,

E 3   que

q es menefter q tengá y ánimo, y no hóbres ordinarios q no pelean, y rin défe a los contrarios. Y para q defte a-uifo no fe criá algunos feñores (a cuya mano puede llegar efte auifo) digo luego por mi defenfa, que fue Piloto Salomó, Ptolonico, Carlo quinto, dó Manoci, don Iuá de Auftria, Alonfo de Alburquerque, don Vafco Daga-ma, Marco Antonio, Andrea Doria, el Marques de Sáta Cruz, y Pero Me-lendez, afuera de inumerables perfo-nas excelentiffimas, que dexo por eui-tar prolixidad. Solo digo, que fe de tal orden, que los que profeffaren nauc-gar, fepan fer Mechanicos, y hazer naues y todos baxeles, que fepan forti ficarfe en agua y tierra, y fepan fer poluoriftas, y fer artilleros, que lo há menefter faber los que quieren hóras y habitos y encomiendas, para muy

mejor

mejor fe córtaftar có los aduerfarios, y confeguiran con efta orden, y otras mejores que fe le pueden añadir, feñorear el mundo con firmeça deuida y Corona de V. Mageftad.

¶ Capitulo. XIII.

PARA Dar fin a efta fortificació dl mar Oceano, digo: que có-uiene a V. Mageftad por las razones que té go referido, fe ha de poblar la Isla de Santa Elena, q fobre todo lo declara-do en los precedétes capitulos, que es el mas inportante paffo que ay para la India, y mientras mas, no digo que conuiene a todos los prouechos, porq quando en el año fobre efcrito (en el capitulo tercero) fe ganó de los Lu-teranos la fortaleça del Rio de Enero

E 4   fien-

fiendo gouernador del Brafil Mũdo
de Saa, entre las librerias que alli ga-
namos q̃ fe quemaron, por fer del co-
legio de Caluino, q̃ alli tenian, auia
mil papeles, y vuo muchos Francefes
que confeffaron y dixeron, q̃ toda a-
quella fuerça y extenfas, no erá para
otro fin, fino para poblar a la Iſla de
S. Elena, no dudado auerfe de entrar
al cabo de Buena efperança, y arrui-
nar la India, y bien vco, qual pare-
cer de muchos juyzios diran, q̃ la Iſla
de S. Elena es muy pequeña, y q̃ no
puede alli auer població, a lo q̃ yo ref-
ponderc: q̃ es la mas abil para criar ca
da quatro años, cinquéta Comédado
res de los habitos de Chrifto, Auis, y
Santiago q̃ quátas fuerças ay defpues
de Malta, es la iſla de S. Elena. Y la or
den y pobladores fe dará, a gufto de
V. M. porq̃ ello es menefter q̃ entré

folo

folo hóbres limpios y mui caualleros
amigos de V.M. q̃ yo conozco: y fi
efte penfamiento mio lo dexaran exe
cutar al Rey dõ Sebaftiã, y fundar en
Sagres, q̃ es la fuerça q̃ Francifco Dra
quez tomò, alli queria hazer vn mone
fterio de caualleros de Chrifto, a la
imitació de la cafa de Malta, para q̃ de
aq̃l feminario fe proueyeffen los capi
tanes de galeras y galcones y naues,
y las fortaleças: y fuera harto bueno
auer efta cafa de religiofos en la cofta
del Algarue, para q̃ pues las Efpañas
fe ganaron por armas, è induftrias de
caualleria, bié feria q̃ por armas fe fue
fteffe y cóferuaffe. Es efta isla de S.
Elena difcriminofa de entrar, fino fe
afcrra el puerto de aq̃l viage, y fi def-
caen las naues, no pueden boluer aq̃l
año cõ aqlla monció a la Isla, fino dcr
rotar Angola, y q̃uedar impotentes

E ;   para

para se salir con remedio, por la altura
de Leste Sueste, en que se engoltan,
y se pierden, como hizo la naue Flamenca año de.56.que alli se perdio,
y otras muchas naues, que viniendo
de la India, no tomando la Isla de Sáta Elena, discurré por la costa del Bra
sil con tormenta, por ser contra moncion, y van a naufragar por partes remotas, sin remedio, porque se encuen
tran las monciones, como se ha dicho
podrian: pero viniendo derrotados,
quando no pudiessen tomar la Isla de
Santa Elena, nauegando al Norueste
y entrar en el Brasil, en la Bahia de S.
Saluador, a treze grados de altura, y
la barra entra Sul Norte, y no ay duda, sino que es tiempo bueno para la
entrar, el de Abril, Mayo, Iunio, y Iu-
lio, de aquella costa, para de alli venir
a Portugal a saluamento, y mejor seria

sia no tomando la Isla de Santa Elena, entrar en la Bahia, en el Brasil, que
no yr en Angola, donde ninguna naue se puede saluar, y en Poniente del
Brasil, o Indias, assi como se saluo Ber
nardin Ribero general de la carrera
de la India, año de.1590.

¶ Capitulo. XIIII.

P A R A que Vues-
tra Magestad se ase-
gure, hecha esta forti
ficacion en el mar, es
muy necessario que
en Lisboa abuelua V. Magestad a
los marineros y nauegantes que llegá
de Oriente, de los pechos e imposi-
ciones que pagan a los Teatinos, religiosos que se dizen de la Compañia
de Iesus, que no se lo deue V. Magestad,

ftad, porque el Rey don Sebastian les otorgò, que de cada vn nauegante re cibieffen tantos ducados en fu cafa de la India, quantos caxones traxeffen. Y efto no lo hizo el feñor Rey don Ma noel, aguelo de V. Mageftad, q para tener a muchos nauegantes concedio de merced, que cada vn hombre delos que nauegaffen la India, traxeffe vn caxon de drogas, fin pagar derechos. Auia en los tiempos paffados mien tras eftaua la mar franca en la nauega cion de V. Mageftad en la carrera, mas de cinco mil marineros, y aora no ay ninguno, porque totalmete def pues a ca fintieron efto por agrauio. Y porque les hazé pagar efte tributo a los Teatinos, q deue fer, que como ha zian la Iglefia de S. Roque en Lisboa, por modo de limofna pidieron a el Rey efte cenfo de fu hazienda Real.

Y aun-

Y aunque la Iglefia es acabada, toda via le lleuan y recauan: y porque tã bien los proueedores y armadores de las naues, venden los cargos de pilo tos, y todo lo que es oficio de Ma rineros aquel que mas dinero da. Y de aqui viene defta finjufticia, que no fe proucan las naues de oficiales bue nos, y lleuan hombres inutiles, que no faben tener el timon, ni faben los rumbos de la aguja, por lo que to das las naues fe pierden, o las lleuan los Inglefes, o arriban fin hazer fu via ge, como lo han hecho quatro naues, en el año de 1590. de la conferua de Mathias de Alburquerque, que todas arribaron con tan grande perdida, y lucro cefante de la hazienda de Vue ftra Mageftad. Y no fe entendiendo la caufa deftas ruynas y perdidas, no: fe dará remedio, que es la fornificació,

Pues

tã à V.Mageſtad,ni quiẽ procure dar remedio a males tan continos de la familia, y hazienda de V.Mageſtad.

¶ Capitulo XV.

VISTO ſerá pues, que V. Mageſtad mande proueer en que ſe lea la nauigatoria, y que ſe ponga por obra lo que V.Mageſtad manda, con mucho calor, y q̃ ſienta algun fauor la gente naueganta, que anda muy arropellada y pobre: y mouidos de muchas ſinrazones que ſe les hazen, huyen para Inglaterra, y Francia, y la nauegacion ſe pierde, que es la mas neceſſaria coſa que V.Mageſtad a meneſter procurar, y poner en orden, pues vemos q̃, ſin milicia naual, y prouido conoſcijo, no ſe puede ſuſtentar Eſpaña: mi, podra

pues ſolo con ella ſe puede remediar tantos males. Y pues es anſi, y los Capitanes que yuan en eſta nauegacion eran generoſos hidalgos, aora a color de eſtar arrendado el comercio de la India, los arrendadores ponen Capitanes que no tienen mucha experiencia, y algunos que ſon hijos de padres humildes, y dexan perder la hazienda con eſtas arribadas, y vno dexo lleuar la naue ſan Felipe de V. Mageſtad entera y ſana al Vrquez, año de 87. Y el año que V.Mageſtad eſtaua en Lisboa, arribo otro piloto con el galeon de Malaca, que con la naue ſan Pablo tambien ſe auia perdido en Samatra, año de 1560. Y deſte deſconcierto ſalen muchos males, y han ſuccedido por eſta deshorden inumerables naufragios de tantos años a eſta parte, ſin auer quiẽ dello aduiert

ta

podra oprimir, ni vencer a los Lutera
nos. Y a V. Mageftad, que de
ftos defconciertos nacieron a Portugal muchos males, en tiépo del Señor
Rey don Enrrique tio de V. Mageftad, que no queriendo fauorecer a la
uegacion fobre cafos de la mina, fe le
uantaró quatro cofarios, que dieron
dotrina a los Luteranos, cuyos nom-
bres yre poniendo fuccefsiuamente.
Fuefle el hijo del ciego del Algarue
para la Rochela, y vuo año que lleua
ron de prefa dentro a Francia, folo a
la Rochela, venticinco naues cargadas de riquezas, a fuera lo que lleuaró
de la mina. Y Pedro Bayaó fe fue á
Inglaterra, y la Reyna lo hizo general fuyo, y efte dexó fu dotrina a Fran
cifco Draques, tan infernal como fe:
ha bien vifto. Y no fe fi tenga atreui-
miento, para dezirlo (y yo vi) defpues,
que

que fe prendio en Guinea, donde yo
eftaua firuiendo de prouifor y vicario
general, por el feñor Rey don Seba-
ftian) efte gran Pirata tomar el Sol o-
culto y efcódido entre las nuues, quã
do no le feruia el Aftrolauio al medio
dia, vfando de vna fu balleftilla, que
yo tuue en mi eftudio mucho tiempo (graduada dotrina) y fin duda ofa-
ria afirmar no la auer hallado Ptolomeo, porque toca a la altura de Lefte
Aufte, y es adicion del Aftrolabio de
Mariño, que yo tambien tuue, y to
mé el Sol por la regla de Lefte Aufte,
a las quatro oras defpues de medio
dia, que es la mayor difpenfacion defta Arte, fi la naturaleça tiene por co-
municar a los marineros fotil y deli-
cada, y dina de fer notoria al mundo.
El otro cofario fue Manoel Caldera,
ò verdaderaméte Francifco, que de la

F   Roche-

Rochela falio con vna muy podero-
fa armada, y vino a la Isla de la Made-
ra(Catolica Isla)y la metio a fuego y
fangre, y profano los templos, y lle-
uo de faco mas de dos cuentos de oro.
Y tras efto fe paffó Pedreanes de Sea
natural de la Isla Tercera,donde hizo con los Ribaos Luteranos, y los
Sorias, eftraños afaltos y robos, a fuera no contar la infelice jornada que
hizo el famofo Pie de palo, general
de Luteranos,que vino a faquear la Is
la de la Palma, y tras el los Icquaces,
faquearon la Gomera, donde quema
ron en la plaça, la eftatua y imagen
del gloriofo San Francifco, y profana
dos los tẽplos, fe falieró ricos. Y en la
era de. 1 5 8 7. dia de San Mateo, fue
abrafada la Isla del Cueruo, y Florida
y Fayal, afuera innumerables otras per
didas que ban caufado, como fue la
de Cadiz, la Naual del Duque de Mc

diña en el canal de Flandes, y la entra
da de Lisboa, y Peniche, Sagres, y Caf
cales, y lo que caufan oy dia fe ve
por el ojo,que lo hazen por medios
de marineros, Pilotos y Capitanes, q̃
fe paffaron al contrario vando, con
ducidos de mal gouierno y disfauor,
mas que de odio, de V. Mageftad, ad-
uirtiendo a V. Mageftad concluyen
do, digo aquel celebrado dicho del
Bienauenturado San Gregorio. Minus iacula feriunt quæ preuidentur,
de fuerte que fon meneſter grandes
remedios a tan grandes males, y fauo
recer V. Mageftad a fus trabajadores
y nauegantes, por la orden que mas
deſto dare ſiendome mandado, pues
eſta fortificacion que relato, ha mene
ſter fer ordenada y exercitada por na
uegátes eſperimentados,q̃ ſepan la Eſ
phera, y mar, y fitio del Orbe,como tẽ
godcho en los capitulos precedétes

por ciencia y esperiencia, no in abstra
to, que no aproue cha nada, solo seria
bien que desperassen los coraçones
adormecidos por todos los Reynos
de V. Magestad, con celo de aumentar la Santa Fè Catolica de seglares y
religiosos : pues para tan Eterno fin
Dios dixo. Non veni pacem mittere
interris sed gladium. Toda la qual
fortificacion arriba dicha, se resume
en este breue Epitome.

EPITOME.

LO Primero que se ha de hazer,
es fortificar el puerto del Rey la-
lopho que dista de la Equinocial para el Norte quinze grados, esta junto
de la fortaleça de V. Magestad, del
castillo de Arguin, y esta fortificació se
ha de hazer en vna isleta que esta a la
boca

boca de la entrada del puerto fuerte y
peñascosa, y hase de hazer haziendo
en ella vn baluarte, y en la punta de la
tierra firme hazer la ciudad, de suerte,
que hecha la fortaleça en la isleta, y
ciudad en la punta de la tierra, no ay
armada que pueda entrar en el puerto, porque todo nauio q quisiere entrar a de passar a tiro de ballesta, ô de
la ciudad, ô de la isleta, y será echa-
do a fondo.

¶ La gente que à menester esta fortificacion.

LA Gente que es menester para
hazer la ciudad y baluarte, es la
misma gente que ay en la Isla de San
tiago, y san Felipe, porque son todos
soldados y marineros, y estiparan en
junto los de la Isla, darles V. Magestad

F 3

ftad licencia para hazer efta fortificacion y biuir en efta por ciudadanos, q creo lo comprarian a dinero. Y porq en la mifma tierra de Guinea andan retirados muchos por hechos que han cometido contra jufticia, puede Vueftra Mageftad perdonarlos, q lo acc taran ellos, y daran el quinto de fu hazienda, para el beneficio de la foraleça que fe hiziere. Y el modo del focorro de Efpaña, fera, mandar V. Mageftad vn galeon y dos çabras con trezientos hombres Caftellanos y Portuguefes con fu artilleria baftante, y con vn gouernador, con cartas para los de la Ifla de fan Felipe y Santiago que den para ello todo fauor, y fe hallen en la fortificacion los del regimiento de la ciudad de Santiago, foleniçando efta fortificacion, con vna embaxada que fe de de parte de Vue

ftra Mageftad al Rey de los Ialophos de paz, comunicandole algunas mercedes y honras, prefentandole algunas prefeas nuguinamente, jaezes de cauallo, y armas.

¶ Segunda fortificacion que fe ha de hazer en la Sierra Leona.

PARA fortificar efta fierra, fe ha de guardar la mifma orden que para el Ialopho, excepto que no ha menefter Embaxador, porque es gente barbara, que no mira cumplimientos. Y hafe de hazer efta fortificacion en Tagarin, o Mitombo, que fon dos Rios iguales, tan bueno el vno como el otro, haziendo en la punta de la Tierra firme vna fortaleça, que para eftas fortaleças, las mifmas tierras tienen piedra, cal y madera, en gran cantidad.

F 4   Ter-

45

¶ Tercera fortificacion del Brasil

EN la punta de San Antonio he-cho vn baluarte, o reedificando el que esta caydo, no entrará ningu-na armada ni bagel dentro de la Ba-hia de todos Santos, porque no pue-den passar sino a medio tiro de cañon de la punta desta tierra, por ser la en-trada de la barra ciega de arenas, y te-nerla Isla que la daña, y bastaran pa-ra la fortaleça a veynte hombres. Y de-sta punta de tierra hasta la ciudad de san Saluador ay media legua, y la ciu-dad es menester mandarla murar, por que quedará inexpunable, y mas in-expunable será si V. Magestad prouc-yere, que no esté hallan ningun Go-uernador mas de tres años:

Quarta

¶ Quarta fortificacion en el Brasil

PARA que no entren en el puerto de la ciudad Sebastian, ninguu contrario es menester en vna Isleta que tiene en medio de la barra hazer vn baluarte la ciudad, por aora basta-le la fortificacion que tiene. Y mien-tras V. Magestad mas gente embiare a Guinea y al Brasil, será demas pro-uecho, porque la tierra es larga y rica, y faltale gente para la cultibar, y po-blar y defender, lo que sobra en Espa-ña de gente perdida.

¶ Quinta fortificacion en la Isla de Santa Catalina.

PARA la Isla de Santa Catalina, puede V. Magestad mandar hazer

F 5   gente

gente, y embiarlos al gouernador del Brasil dirigida, que la trueque por la experimentada, para poblar la dicha Isla por estar desierta. Tiene mucha agua, piedra y madera, esta su sitio de tierra donde mañana y noche tienen socorro de Tierra firme, con comer y beuer en la boca del Rio grande, que por el se comunica el Peru con el Brasil. Y estando esta poblada, se poblara el Rio de la plata desseado de España ha tantos años, y este estrecho celebrado de Magallanes.

¶ Sexta fortificacion.

LAzer en la Isla de santa Elena, haziendo vn baluarte en la punta del callejon, en que se toma puerto, y poblarla con ycinte, o treinta hombres, formando

formado los moradores de tres a tres años, porque se puedan sustentar sin destruyr la Isla, por noscruirmasque defortaleça. Tiene esta Isla infinissimas cabras, y muchas frutas sinquãto, y linda agua dulce, buen cielo y sano, y desta Isla pueden yr y venir por mercacias, y su prouecho a la Isla S. Catalina, san Bicente, ciudad Sebastiana, y todo Brasil, y doblar al cabo de Buena esperança, a Moçanbique, si V. Magestad le parciere. Y será de importancia que V. Magestad ordene que el Capitan que residiere en Santa Elena, sea data de Vuestra Magestad en las de la casa de la India Oriental, como las demas Capitanias, y conceda Vuestra Magestad que pueda el tal Capitan embiar tres nabios cada año al comercio, y rescate a toda

toda la cofta, y cabo de Buena efperança, a Angola, y toda la nauegacion
entre los limites de Angola, y Mo-
çambique, y Brafil, y todo redundará
en bien de Efpaña y eftabilidad
de la Corona de Vue-
ftra Mageftad.

(.?.)

APPENDICES

and

BIBLIOGRAPHY

APPENDIX A : History of the tract and Acknowledgements

The copy of Andrada's tract in Dr Williams's Library, although noted in the Library's printed catalogues since 1727, appears to have gone unnoticed by historians and bibliographers until the 1970s. It was then noted by Dr A.M. García during a bibliographical survey of Hispanic material, and thus became known to historians in London. Around 1980 Professor C.R. Boxer drew it to the attention of Professor Ursula Lamb of the University of Arizona, in connection with her well-known studies of sixteenth-century Iberian cosmographical writings. Professor Lamb obtained a photocopy and did some initial work on the tract, in particular producing a draft translation; and in 1983 she read a paper on the tract to the Society for the History of Discoveries. The paper remains unpublished and she has allowed me to use material from it. Her intention being to produce an edition of both the tract and another contemporary work, she invited me to contribute notes on the section of the tract dealing with Guinea, and I prepared material. In 1986 ill-health led her to reduce her commitments and she eventually invited me to take over the editing of the Andrada tract. The extent of its West African content is such that I was persuaded, despite being inexpert in both Iberian and Latin-American history; and the present edition would undoubtedly have benefitted if Professor Lamb had been able to contribute more in these fields, as well as in the field of historical cosmography.

I have, however, had a good deal of assistance. The translation from the Spanish has been checked and revised several times. I am very much indebted to Miss Moira Johnson for line-by-line guidance; and equally to Miss Ann Mackenzie of the Department of Hispanic Studies, University of Liverpool, for a detailed early check on the translation, as well as for advice on a variety of Hispanic issues. Dr John Villiers and Professor J.S. Cummins kindly read through the text and annotation and indicated errors; and Professor D.B. Quinn did the same for the introduction. Dr A.M. García of the Department of Spanish and Latin-American Studies, University College, London, the rediscoverer of the tract, made useful suggestions as well as providing an Appendix. My greatest debt remains to Ursula Lamb, who encouraged me both to begin and to proceed, who supplied me with references and rare material as well as with the draft translation, and who has regularly commented on matters I have put to her. Responsibility for faults in the present translation and the editing rests, however, solely with me.

Finally, I am indebted to Mr John Creasey, Librarian of Dr Williams's Library, for allowing me easy access to the Andrada tract and answering queries about its history, for providing Professor Lamb and myself with photocopies of the text and end-leaves, and for giving me permission to publish a facsimile.

APPENDIX B : The translation - its treatment of the text and names

Andrada's text is divided into chapters, but these have no titles, not surprisingly, since no chapter limits itself to one consistent theme, the author's anxieties, schemes, historical examples and presentday references being jumbled up in chapter after chapter. Within each chapter there is no division into paragraphs, and the sentences are often very long, consisting of loosely related clauses, linked by flabby conjunctions, or by pronouns which (despite their gender in Spanish) can sometimes be related to more than one preceding noun, making the sense ambiguous. The general style (I am told) is not uncommon in Spanish writing of this kind in the later sixteenth century, but I find it crabbed and at times impenetrable.

The translation is presented in readable English, which cannot therefore be a total reflection of the argument, and scholars citing any part of it are recommended to check it first against the original text, here given in facsimile. The edition adds headings to chapters which indicate the main themes of each. Paragraphs are formed, and are given sub-headings indicating their content in more detail than the chapter heading. Long sentences are broken up into their constituent meaningful segments.

As the facsimile shows, the original text contains occasional misprints, but since the corrections are normally obvious it has not seemed necessary to draw attention to these. When words in Spanish are given, either the word or its proposed English translation is given in round brackets. Editorial insertions intended to assist the flow of a sentence, or to explain a specific term, are given in square brackets; but nouns inserted to replace pronouns (sometimes necessary because of the lack of gender-agreement in English) are inserted silently.

Some of the Spanish terms used by Andrada do not lend themselves to a consistent or word-for-word translation. **Navegación** is the procedure of making one's way by sea, either in general, or, more often, along a particular route, hence it can specifically refer to the route itself, or to the flow of ships along the route. **Fortificar** can simply mean to fortify a locality including an existing settlement, but it also has the more general meaning of establishing a fortified settlement and hence has a meaning close to 'to settle'. **Poblar**, meaning 'to settle' (literally, 'to people'), carries the central meaning of the English term, 'to send people to establish a settlement', by implication where there was no establishment of the nation in question previously. **Mo(n)ción** in this context refers to the motion of the sea, that is, to aspects of the sea that move ships, both the prevailing winds and the currents (or, in some places, tides) - for simplicity it is usually translated 'winds'. Finally, **Luteranos** was the term applied by the Spaniards to all Protestants. But since neither the English Anglicans nor the French Calvinists were, theologically speaking, 'Lutherans', it has seemed better to translate the term as 'Lutherites'. This has the advantage that the shape of the English term carries the derogatory implication of the Spanish term.

Andrada's text is replete with names - toponyms, ethnonyms and personal names - not always consistently spelled. In the translation, names are generally reproduced as in the text, even where Andrada gives Spanish versions of Portuguese personal names and toponyms (e.g. Pablo for Paulo, Isleos for Ilhéus). But the following exceptions have been made.

(1) Toponyms of parts of Europe outside Iberia are normally given in the form in which they are commonly pesented to the modern English reader (e.g., Holland, Lisbon, Seville, La Rochelle, Bordeaux).

(2) Names of extra-European countries, seas and towns well-known to the modern English reader, and also all well-known personal names, are given in a recognisable form, either in a standard form (e.g., Brazil, Rio de Janeiro, Vera Cruz, Havana, Red Sea, Sumatra, Siam, Solomon, Ptolemy, Francis Drake), or in a form close to the standard form but also close to the Spanish (e.g., Magellan Strait for **estrecho de Magallanes**).

(3) The cities named **ciudad Sebastiana/Filipina** are referred to in translation as 'the City of Sebastian/Philip'. Obscure islands and capes are left in their precise textual form (e.g., Isla de la Sal, Cabo de Sabão). But better-known islands and capes are given more recognisable if not wholly consistent forms (e.g., Island of St Helena, Cape Verde, Cape Verde Islands, Cape of Good Hope, Island of Madeira, Island of Santa Catalina); but the Portuguese islands in the Gulf of Guinea are given their Portuguese names, Príncipe and São Tomé.

(4) In toponyms the letter v is generally preferred to the letter b, hence San Vicente, not San Bicente; and in personal names initial j to i, hence Jaime, not Iaime.

(5) 'Sierra Leona', the Spanish version of the sixteenth-century Portuguese form, 'Serra Leõa', has been retained, to distinguish the territory connoted, mainly the Sierra Leone estuary, from the much larger territory of the modern state of Sierra Leone.

(6) The more correct form of the less common names is given in the Indexes of Toponyms and Personal Names; alternatively, where the translation has employed a standard English form, the textual version of the less common names is given.

In the chapter and section headings, and in the annotation, the modern and/or correct forms are employed.

APPENDIX C : A seventeenth-century collection of Spanish books, including Andrada's Instrucion, in Dr Williams's Library, London

Andrada's **Instrucion** is one of a number of Spanish works in Dr William's Library, London, that seem to have been largely unnoticed by Hispanists. I became aware of the existence of the **Instrucion** when I began to make bibliographical notes on each item in the collection for the eventual publication of a descriptive catalogue. I then brought this particular work to the attention of some historians and on the basis of their knowledge of Hispanic historiography, coupled with the negative results yielded by my own searches in other British and Spanish libraries, I came to the conclusion that it had never been recorded and that Dr Williams's Library held the only known copy. At that time I also entertained the idea of publishing the Spanish text in an annotated edition, but later realised that given its content the task was better left to an historian. The present edition, containing a facsimile of the original text, an English translation, and detailed scholarly apparatus, fulfils my hopes; and when I was invited to contribute to it by setting the work within the wider frame of the collection of which it is a part, I was happy to accept.

Dr Williams's Library is a Dissenting institution that first opened its doors to the public in 1729 and now houses a very rich library of Nonconformist material. It came into being thanks to the benefaction of Dr Daniel Williams (c.1643-1716), a Presbyterian divine, who in his will of 1711 bequeathed a collection of books comprising his own books and those of Dr William Bates (1625-1699), another distinguished Presbyterian minister whose valuable library Dr Williams had purchased in 1699.

The bequest was first described in a catalogue published in 1727 in which some 6,000 volumes in Greek, Latin, English, French, Italiam and Spanish are listed, but which unfortunately offers little help in determining which books were Williams' own and which came from Bates' library. As expected, the bulk of the collection is made up of religious and theological matters but other disciplines, such as literature and history, are also represented. Stephen K. Jones, when writing on the history of Dr Williams's Library, felt justified in surmising that "we owe to Williams and Bates equally the more solid theology; and to the silver-tongued Bates the belle-lettres, in special the numerous Italian and

Spanish books".[1] For my part, I think it likely that all or nearly all of the
Spanish books in the 1727 catalogue, irrespective of subject matter, were
acquired by Bates; and that the collection is best understood as a selection of
books assembled by a discerning reader with an interest in things Spanish. In
spite of his learning, nothing in Williams' life suggests that he himself ever
developed such an interest. Bates, on the other hand, was known as a "devourer
of books" who delighted in "whatsoever belonged to the finer and more polite sort
of literature".[2] Moreover, the highest percentage of books in the Spanish
collection published within any specific decade between 1550-1700 corresponds to
volumes printed in the 1640s, at a time when Bates, who was born in 1625, would
have been old enough to start a library. The corresponding period for Williams,
who was born c. 1643, would have been the 1660s, but dates from this and
subsequent decades appear in a drastically diminishing number of items. The
argument is not conclusive but further evidence may be found in the fact that the
Spanish collection does not incorporate a single volume printed after the death
of Bates in 1699. Had Williams shared with Bates the same interest in the
acquisition of Spanish books he would surely have purchased at least some volumes
printed during the seventeen years by which he outlived his fellow divine.

The 1727 catalogue lists some 125 Spanish books, including a few translations of
foreign books into Spanish and of Spanish books into French or English.
Literature is represented by some 52 volumes, followed in numbers by history,
religious matters, and a medley of books on miscellaneous topics. In some
instances it is difficult, if not impossible, to determine whether a book was
acquired for its literary value or for its religious or political content.

The earliest Spanish writers represented in the literary section are Juan de Mena
with a volume that includes **Laberinto de Fortuna, La coronación**, and **'coplas'**
[Antwerp, 1552], and Fernando de Rojas with a **Celestina. Tragicomedia de Calisto
y Melibea** [Amsterdam, 1599].[3] Prose narrative includes a **Vida de Lazarillo de
Tormes** [Paris, 1660] with Spanish text and French translation printed side by
side; Montemayor's **Diana** [Paris, 1611]; Alemán's **Guzmán de Alfarache** [Part I:
Madrid, 1600; Part II: Burgos, 1619]; Cervantes' **Don Quijote** [Parts I and II:

---

[1] Stephen Kay Jones, **Dr Williams and his Library** (Friends of Dr. Williams's
Library, Inaugural Lecture 1947), Cambridge, 1948, p.14

[2] ibid., p.4

[3] In all cases I give the place and date of publication of the copies in
Dr. Williams's Library.

Madrid, 1647]; Pérez de Montalbán's **Ocho novelas ejemplares** [Madrid, 1628]; and Gracián's **El criticón** in the English translation of Paul Ricaut. Poetry is represented by Juan de Mena, Boscán, Garcilaso, Lope de Vega, Góngora, Quevedo, Bocángel, Villamediana, and other lesser figures. There is a copy of **Doce comedias de Lope de Vega** [Barcelona, 1618] and two volumes of miscellaneous plays by Lope, Góngora, Calderón, Moreto, Zárate, and others. Some special attention is awarded to A. Hurtado de Mendoza whose **Fiesta de Aranjuez** and its companion piece **Querer por sólo querer** [Madrid, 1623] are catalogued together with translations into English by Sir Richard Fanshawe. In addition to **El criticón**, other works by Gracián include **El héroe**, [Madrid, 1639], **El político** [Milan, 1646], the early version of his treatise on wit and conceit **Arte de ingenio** [Madrid, 1642], and an anonymous translation of **El oráculo manual** published in London, 1685. The copy of **El político** is of great bibliographical value, being the only known copy of a hitherto unrecorded edition of this treatise. Huarte de San Juan's **Examen de ingenios** [Leiden, 1591] is also worthy of mention, as are copies of collectanea by Hernán Nuñez, M. de Santa Cruz and A. Sánchez de la Ballesta which together with Mal Lara's **Filosofía vulgar** [Madrid, 1618] evince an interest in apothegms and proverbs further confirmed by a French translation of Spanish proverbs made by the lexicologist C. Oudin.

Five authors seem to have attracted the collector's attention in a particular way: Lope de Vega, Pérez de Montalbán, Góngora, Quevedo and Gracián. The choice does not appear fortuitous and the content of the collection affords some evidence that Bates may have been aware of the characteristics of style and literary approach that divided some of those writers into opposing camps. It is revealing that both Montalbán's well known **Para todos** [Madrid, 1640] and M. de los Reyes's **Para algunos** [Madrid, 1640] should figure in the catalogue. A contemporary testifies to Bates' personal wit which he describes as "never vain or light but most facetious and pleasant".[4] This trait in his personality could possibly explain why he acquired copies not only of Gracián's **Arte de ingenio** but also of Mateo Pelligrini's Italian counterpart **Fonti dell' ingegno** [Bologna, 1650]. A similar interest may have induced him to add to his collection **Agudezas** [Madrid, 1674], a Spanish rendering of John Owen's **Epigrammatum libri tres**.

Doubtless sixteenth and seventeenth century Spanish literature is not comprehensively represented but it is possible to argue that the bulk of the books was selectively chosen and that the collection grew in part round generic cores of interest with the purchase and perusal of a given volume seemingly

---

[4]   Jones, op.cit., p.4.

leading to the acquisition of other related volumes. A striking illustration is provided by **The Critick** [London, 1681], the English translation of Gracián's narrative masterpiece **El criticón**. In the prologue the translator, Paul Ricaut, suggests that a connection possibly exists between this work and the history of Hai Ebn Yokdhan written "in Arabick by Eben Tophail and translated into Latin by Dr Pocock". One is pleasantly surprised to discover that the 1727 catalogue lists a copy of Abentofail's **Philosophus autodidactus** [Oxford, 1621] in the Latin rendering of Pocock.

A second large segment in the collection is made up of books on Spanish history, including biography, letters, genealogies and other related material. Volumes in this category fall within fairly well-defined groups reflecting specific areas of interest in the mind of the collector. Spanish history, in its widest context, is represented by Mariana's **Historia General de España** [Madrid, 1650]; and by V. Malvezzi's **Sucesos principales de la monarquía de España** [Madrid, 1640] on a more limited time-scale. Mariana's volume is supplemented by P. Mantuano's **Advertencias a la Historia de Juan de Mariana** [Milan, 1611] which contains a negative critique of the work, and by T. Tamayo de Vargas's **Historia General de España defendida** [Toledo, 1616] in answer to Matuano's criticism. Curiosity for the New World is satisfied by the inclusion of Acosta's **De natura Novi Orbis** [Cologne, 1596] and its companion piece **Historia natural y moral de las Indias** [Madrid, 1608] of which there is also a copy of the English translation by Edward Grimstone [London, 1604].

A series of books on the Netherlands, Portugal and Catalonia clearly relates to areas of political and military conflict within the domains of the Spanish Monarchy. The war in the Low Countries is the subject of B. de Mendoza's **Comentarios** [Madrid, 1592] and C. Coloma's **Las guerras de los Estados Bajos** [Antwerp, 1625], which together chronicle the conflict from 1567 to 1599. They are supplemented by **Relaciones del Cardenal Bentivollo** [Madrid, 1638], a Spanish translation of the Italian original which informs on the truce of 1609 and also touches upon matters of religion in Flanders, France, England, Scotland, Ireland and Denmark. The conflict in Catalonia is the concern of a volume of some rarity, F. de Rioja's **Aristarco** [n.p.,n.d., but probably Barcelona, 1640], which attacks Catalan secessionist pretentions. Material on the mid seventeenth-century Portuguese movement of independence includes A. M. Vasconcelo's **Sucesión de Felipe II en la Corona de Portugal** [Madrid, 1639], favourable to the Spanish king; **Apologético** [Zaragoza, 1642], directed against the Duke of Braganza and other **'conjurados'**, published anonymously but attributed to J. A. de la Parra; and J. Caramuel's **Respuesta al Manifiesto del Reino de Portugal** [Antwerp, 1642], where the text of the manifesto is followed by Caramuel's own critique of its claims. The obvious concern with war and rebellion that runs as a unifying motif throughout these volumes is further highlighted by the inclusion of L. Valle de la Cerda's **Avisos en materia de estado y guerra** [Madrid, 1599], where the author addresses questions of war and peace, rebellious subjects, and the suppression of revolts.

Two Spanish monarchs attract special attention: Charles V in J. A. Vera y Zuñiga's **Epítome de la vida y hechos del Emperador Carlos V** [Madrid, 1622]; and Philip II in a number of volumes, including L. Cabrera de Córdoba's **Felipe Segundo de España** [Madrid, 1619] and two editions of B. Porreño's **Dichos y hechos de Felipe II** [Madrid, 1639; Brussels, 1666]. There is also a copy of D. Hurtado de Mendoza's **Guerra de Granada hecha por el Rey Felipe II** [Lisbon, 1627]. Material critical of the Spanish king is available in a number of items penned by his erstwhile secretary and confidant, Antonio Pérez: his **Relaciones** [Paris, 1598] printed together with some of Pérez's letters and aphorisms, and two volumes of his **Cartas** [Paris n.d; Paris, 1603]. Mention should be made of a copy of F. Losa's **Vida de Gregorio López** (Mexico, 1613) whose life aroused much interest when it was suggested that the saintly and learned hermit had been no other than Prince Charles, Philip II's ill-fated son. Interest in this fanciful rumour is attested by the existence of an anonymous English translation of Losa's biography, **The holy life of Gregory Lopez** (n.p., 1675), of which there is also a copy in the collection.

There can be little doubt that the figure of Philip II had engaged the attention of the collector in a particular way. This interest may be sufficient to explain the acquisition of Andrada's **Instrucion**, where the author addresses himself directly to the Spanish king. Access to a book dealing with a global strategy of defence and fortifications against the maritime incursions of the French and the English would have been of potential value to an enemy had it been acquired after it began to circulate. But by the time Bates purchased it in the mid seventeenth century any useful information provided by Andrada's confidential plans would have become obsolete. The book has no title-page, a fact recorded in the 1727 catalogue in a note that reads **"caret titulo"**. As the well preserved copy also lacks a colophon and has the name of a previous owner signed on the first page it is possible to surmise that the book was printed without a separate title-page. The absence of preliminary pages, which would normally have contained the **'aprobación'**, **'censura'**, and **'tasa'**, strongly suggests that the book was never intended for publication, but was in fact a confidential printed document sent to the king for limited circulation among his ministers and advisers.

As one would expect, this collection of Spanish books is not without its fair
share of religious books, including liturgies, sermons, lives of saints,
devotional and ascetic treatises, and other material. There is a copy of an
anonymously translated **Liturgia inglesa** [London, 1623] which appears to keep
company with Fray J. de Alcocer's **Ceremonial de la Misa** [Madrid, 1614]. Jesuit
writers contribute the widely disseminated **Catecismo** [Cuenca, 1628] of J. de
Ripalda, and two volumes by L. de la Puente, including the famous treatise on
prayer and meditation, **Guía espiritual** [Madrid, 1614]. But it is the Jesuit E.
de Nieremberg that makes the largest contribution with six volumes in Spanish and
four in Latin, including **Diferencia entre lo temporal y lo eterno** [Madrid, 1646],
of which there is also a copy of the Latin edition [Cologne, 1654]; **Corona
virtuosa** [Madrid, 1643] and **Obras y días** [Madrid, 1641], two treatises on
Christian virtue aimed at kings and magnates; and **Partida a la eternidad y
preparación para la muerte** [Madrid, 1645]. The latter volume is bound together
with **Curiosa y oculta filosofía** [Madrid, 1643], but this and **De arte voluntatis**
[Paris, 1639] are philosophical and speculative works rather than strictly
religious ones.

A number of miscellaneous items reveal a practical bent of mind in the collector.
Royal and ecclesiastical secretaries are the subject of two volumes, and there
are also publications on mnemonics, metallurgy, speech-therapy, and hunting: J.
Velázquez de Acebedo's **Arte de memoria** [Madrid, 1626]; A. A. Barba's **Arte de los
metales** [Madrid, 1640]; J. P. Bonet's **Arte para enseñar a hablar a los mudos**
[Madrid, 1620]; and J. Mateo's **Origen y dignidad de la caza** [Madrid, 1634].
Concern with political theory is evinced by the inclusion of Saavedra Fajardo's
Idea de un príncipe político cristiano [Antwerp, 1659], and Fray J. Márquez's **El
gobernador cristiano** [Madrid, 1640], two anti-Machiavelli treatises which enjoyed
a large readership in the seventeenth century.

In a sermon preached at Bates' funeral, John Howe declared that the deceased
"knew how to chuse and was curious in his choice [of books] ... Nothing mean was
welcome in his Library, or detained there".[5] Concerning Bates' selection of
Spanish books these encomiastic remarks are largely justified. In his choice
Bates displayed good literary taste, a wide ranging interest, a curiosity that
seems to have led him from book to book in quest of complementary knowledge, and
a fairness of mind that appears to have impelled him to look to both sides of an
argument. There are, of course, instances where his judgement seems to have

---

[5]   ibid.; also Ernest A.Payne, **A Venerable Dissenting Institution: Dr
Williams's Library 1729-1979** (Friends of Dr. Williams's Library, Thirty-third
Lecture 1979), London, 1979, p.9.

failed him. In purchasing J. de Huerta's **Problemas filosóficos** [Madrid, 1628], an insubstantial little book, Bates was probably deceived by the false appeal of its title. And one can only be puzzled at the presence in the collection of a book on breast-feeding and mother's milk.

In his will of 1711 Dr Daniel Williams requested that "duplicates and useless books, and unfit to be set in a public library, be given away to such as they may be useful".[6] We know that the Trustees dutifully complied with this and other clauses in the will but not before the first meeting of the Trust held in December 1729.[7] By then, the 1727 catalogue had been printed, and I can confirm that all the Spanish books listed in this first catalogue are still available in Dr Williams's Library today. It would therefore appear that none of Bates' Spanish books was ever sold as 'useless' or 'unfit', and we are fortunate that his collection has been preserved intact - with the possible exception of those volumes that may have perished in the Fire of London when it is said that Bates lost £200 worth of books. At a later stage in the development of Dr Williams's Library the Spanish collection was slightly enlarged by the acquisition of, among other books, two volumes of Calderon's plays from the library of George Henry Lewes and George Eliot. But that is another story.

Angel M.García-Gómez,
University College, London

---

[6] Jones, op.cit., p.10.

[7] Payne, op.cit., p.23, n.8.

ABREU DE BRITO 1931 = Domingos de Abreu e [sic] Brito, **Un inquérito á vida administrativa e económica de Angola de do Brasil,** ed. Alfredo de Albuquerque Felner, Coimbra, 1931

[The text here published was actually entitled 'Sumario e descripção do reino de Angola e do descobrimento da Ilha de Loanda: e da grãdeza das capitanias do estado do Brasil feito por Domingos Dabreu de Brito Portugues: dirigido ao Mui Alto e Poderoso Rey Dom Philippe Pro. deste nome, pera augmentação do estado e renda de sua coroa, anno de M.D.LXXXXII'.]

AIRES DE CASAL 1817 = Manuel Aires de Casal, **Corografia Brazilica,** Rio de Janeiro, 1817, reprinted São Paulo, 1943

ALBUQUERQUE 1985 = Luís de Albuquerque, 'Portuguese books on nautical science: Pedro Nunes to 1650', Série separatas 168, Centro de Estudos de História e Cartografia Antiga, Lisbon, 1985 (also in **Revista da Universidade de Coimbra,** 33, 1985, 259-278)

ALBUQUERQUE/MADEIRA SANTOS 1988 = Luís de Albuquerque and Maria Emília Madeira Santos, **História Geral de Cabo Verde: corpo documental,** 1, Lisbon, 1988

ALMADA 1984 = André Álvares de Almada, **Brief treatise on the Rivers of Guinea,** annotated English translation and interim edition of **Tratado breve dos Rios de Guiné (c.1594),** notes by J. Boulègue and P.E.H.Hair, 2 vols., Liverpool, 1984

[Chapter and paragraph numbers are given, the former matching the 1946 Lisbon edition of **Tratado breve dos Rios de Guiné.**]

ALMEIDA 1930 = Fortunato de Almeida, **História da Igreja em Portugal,** 2nd. ed., revised by D. Peres, Lisbon, 1930

ÁLVARES 1948 = Manuel Álvares, **Naufrágio da Nau 'S.Paulo',** ed. Frazão de Vasconcelos, Lisbon, 1948

ANDREWS 1959 = K.R.Andrews, **English privateering voyages to the West Indies 1588-1595,** Hakluyt Society, London, 1959

ANDREWS 1978 = K.R.Andrews, **The Spanish Caribbean: trade and plunder 1530-1630,** New Haven, 1978

ANDREWS 1981 = K.R.Andrews, 'Beyond the Equinoctial: England and South America in the sixteenth century', **Journal of Imperial and Commonwealth History,** 10, 1981, 4-24

ANDREWS 1982 = K.R.Andrews, 'In the way to Peru: English ambitions in America South of Capricorn', **Terrae Incognitae,** 14, 1982, 61-75

ANDREWS 1984 = K.R.Andrews, **Trade, plunder and settlement: maritime enterprise and the genesis of the British Empire 1480-1630**, Cambridge, 1984

ARCHIVO COLONIAL = **Archivo Colonial**, t.3, Museo Mitre, Buenos Aires, 1916

AXELSON 1973 = E.Axelson, **Portuguese in South-East Africa 1488-1600**, Cape Town, 1973

BAIÃO 1914 = António Baião, **Affonso d'Albuquerque**, Lisbon, 1914

BAGROW 1966 = Leo Bagrow, **History of cartography**, 2nd ed., revised by R.A. Skelton, Cambridge: Mass., 1966

BARCO CENTENERA, see GUTIÉRREZ 1912

BARLOW 1932 = Roger Barlow, **A brief summe of geographie**, ed. E.G.R.Taylor, Hakluyt Society, London, 1932

BLAKE 1937 = J.W.Blake, **European beginnings in West Africa 1454-1578**, 1937, reprinted, with an appendix, as **West Africa: quest for God and gold 1454-1578**, London, 1977

BOULÈGUE 1987 = Jean Boulègue, **Le Grand Jolof (XIIIe-XVIe siècle)**, Blois/ Paris, 1987

BOULÈGUE 1989 = Jean Boulègue, **Les Luso-Africains de Sénégambie**, Lisbon, 1989

BOURDON 1954 = Léon Bourdon, 'Deux aventuriers portugais: Gaspar Caldeira et Antão Luís (1564-1568)', **Bulletin des Etudes Portugaises**, 18, 1954, 5-56

BOURDON/ALBUQUERQUE 1977 = Léon Bourdon and Luís de Albuquerque, **Le "livro de marinharia" de Gaspar Moreira**, Lisbon, 1977

BOXER 1959 = C.R.Boxer, ed., **The Tragic History of the Sea 1589-1622**, Hakluyt Society, Cambridge, 1959

BOXER 1968 = C.R.Boxer, ed., **Further selections from the Tragic History of the Sea 1559-1565**, Hakluyt Society, Cambridge, 1968

BOXER 1969a = C.R.Boxer, 'A note on Portuguese reactions to the revival of the Red Sea spice trade and the rise of Atjeh, 1540-1600', **Journal of South Asian History**, 10, 1968, 415-428

BOXER 1969b = C.R.Boxer, 'Portuguese and Spanish projects for the conquest of Southeast Asia, 1580-1600', **Journal of Asian History**, 3, 1969, 118-136

BOXER 1972 = C.R.Boxer, 'The principal ports of call of the "Carreira da Índia" (16th to 18th centuries)', **Receuils de la Société Jean Bodin**, 33, 1972, 29-65

BOXER 1984 = C.R.Boxer, **From Lisbon to Goa 1500-1700**, Lisbon, 1984

BOXER 1985 = C.R.Boxer, **Portuguese conquest and commerce in Southeast Asia, 1500-1750**, London, 1985

BRÁSIO 1963,1964 = António Brásio, **Monumenta missionaria africana**, 2nd ser., 2, Lisbon, 1963; 3, Lisbon, 1964

BRODRICK 1947 = James Brodrick, **The progress of the Jesuits (1556-79)**, London, 1947

CADAMOSTO 1966 = Tulia Gasparrini Leporace, ed., **Le navigazioni atlantiche del Veneziano Alvise da Mosto**, Venice, 1966

CAETANO DE SOUSA **1948** = António Caetano de Sousa, **História genealógica da casa real portuguesa**, revised ed., Lisbon, 1948

CARDIM 1978 = Fernão Cardim, **Tratados da Terre e Gente do Brasil**, ed. B. Caetano et al., São Paulo, 1978

CHA 1977 = R.Oliver, ed., **Cambridge History of Africa, vol.3**, London, 1977

CHAUNU 1955 = Huguette and Pierre Chaunu, **Séville et l'Atlantique (1504-1650)**, 8 vols., Paris, 1955-1959

CHURCH 1980 = R.J.Harrison Church, **West Africa**, 8th ed., London, 1980

COUTO 1778 = Diogo do Couto, **Décadas da Asia**, 14 vols., Lisbon, 1778-1788

COUTO 1903 = Diogo de Couto, **Vida de D.Paulo de Lima Pereira**, Lisbon, 1903

CSP Foreign 1583 = **Calendar of State Papers, Foreign, 1583**, ed. A.J.Butler and Sophie C. Lomas, London, 1913

CSP Spanish = **Calendar of State papers, Spanish, 1587-1603**, ed. M.A.S.Hume, London, 1899

DE MAREES 1987 = Pieter de Marees, **Description and historical account of the Gold Kingdom of Guinea (1602)**, trans. and ed. A.van Dantzig and A.Jones, Oxford, 1987

DE MATOS 1988 = Artur Teodoro de Matos, 'As escalas do Atlântico no século XVI', **Revista de Universidade de Coimbra**, 34, 1988, 157-183, also in Série separatas 197, Centro de Estudos de História e Cartografia Antiga, Lisbon, 1988

DÍAZ DE GUZMÁN 1890 = Ruy Díaz de Guzmán, **Anales del descubrimiento, poblacíon y conquista del Río de la Plata**, Asunción, 1980

DOMINGUEZ 1891 = L.L.Dominguez, ed., **The conquest of the River Plate (1535-1555)**, Hakluyt Society, London, 1891

DONELHA 1977 = André Donelha, **Descrição da Serra Leoa e dos Rios de Guiné do Cabo Verde (1625)/ An account of Sierra Leone and the Rivers of Guinea of Cape Verde (1625)**, ed. A Teixeira da Mota and P.E.H.Hair, Mémorias 19, Centro de Estudos de Catografia Antiga, Lisbon, 1977

DUFFY 1955 = James Duffy, **Shipwreck and empire**, Cambridge, Mass., 1955

FERNANDES 1951 = Valentim Fernandes, **Description de la Côte Occidentale d'Afrique (Sénégal au Cap de Monte, Archipels)**, ed. T. Monod, A. Teixeira da Mota and R.Mauny, Bissau, 1951

FERNÁNDEZ ASIS 1943 = V.Fernández Asis, ed., **Epistolario de Felipe II sobre asuntos de mar**, Madrid, 1943

FERNÁNDEZ DURO 1896 = Cesáreo Fernández Duro, **Armada Española**, vol.2, Madrid, 1896

FIGUEIREDO FALCÃO 1859 = Luiz de Figueiredo Falcão, **Livro em que se contém a fazenda e real patrimonio dos reinos de Portugal**, Lisbon, 1859

FONSECA 1926 = Quirino da Fonseca, **Os Portugueses no mar, vol. 1, Ementa histórica das naus portuguesas**, [Lisbon, 1926]

FRAZÃO DE VASCONCELOS 1948 = J.A.A.Frazão de Vasconcelos, **Naufrágio da Nau 'São Paulo'**, Lisbon, 1948

FREYRE 1946 = Gilberto Freyre, **The Masters and the Slaves**, New York, 1946

FRIAS 1955 = Pedro de Frias, **Cronica del-Rei D.António**, Coimbra, 1955

GAMBLE 1957 = David P.Gamble, **The Wolof of Senegambia**, London, 1957

GANDIA 1934 = Enrique de Gandia, 'Jaime Rasquin y su expedición del año 1559', **Boletin de Instituto de Investigaciones Historicas** [Buenos Aires], 13, 1934-1935, 241-322

GARAY 1899 = Blas Garay, ed., **Colección de documentos relativos à la historia de América particularmente à la historia del Paraguay, tomo 1**, Asuncíon, 1899

GOMES DE BRITO 1955 = Bernardo Gomes de Brito, **História Trágico-Marítima**, ed. António Sergio, Lisbon, 1955

GOODMAN 1988 = D.C.Goodman, **Power and penury: government, technology and science in Philip II's Spain**, Cambridge, 1988

GRAY 1965 = Richard Gray and David Chambers, **Materials for West African history in Italian archives**, London, 1965

GUTIÉRREZ 1912 = Martín del Barco Centenera, **La Argentina**, eds. Juan Maria Gutiérrez and Enrique Peña, Buenos Aires, 1912

HAIR 1966 = P.E.H.Hair, 'The spelling and connotation of the toponym "Sierra Leone" ', **Sierra Leone Studies**, n.s.18, 1966, 43-58

HAIR 1969 = P.E.H.Hair, 'Some French sources on Upper Guinea, 1540-1575', **Bulletin de l'Institut Français d'Afrique Noire**, sér. B, 31, 1969, 1030-1034

HAIR 1970 = P.E.H.Hair, 'Sierra Leone in the Portuguese Books of Complaint, 1567-1568', **Sierra Leone Studies**, n.s.26, 1970, 2-10

HAIR 1970b = P.E.H.Hair, 'Protestants as pirates, slavers and proto-missionaries: Sierra Leone 1568 and 1582', **Journal of Ecclesiastical History**, 21, 1970, 203-224

HAIR 1976 = P.E.H.Hair, 'Some minor sources for Guinea, 1519-1559: Enciso and Alfonce/Fonteneau', **History in Africa**, 3, 1976, 19-46

HAIR 1978 = P.E.H.Hair, 'Sources on early Sierra Leone: (14) English accounts of 1582', **Africana Research Bulletin**, 9, 1978, 64-99

HAIR 1984 = P.E.H.Hair, 'Sources on early Sierra Leone: (21) English voyages of the 1580s - Drake, Cavendish, and Cumberland', **Africana Research Bulletin**, 13, 1984, 62-88

HAIR 1987 = P.E.H.Hair, 'The abortive Portuguese settlement of Sierra Leone 1570-1625', in **Vice-Almirante A.Teixeira da Mota: in memoriam, 1**, Lisbon, 1987, 171-208

HAIR 1988 = A.Teixeira da Mota and P.E.H.Hair, **East of Mina: Afro-European relations on the Gold Coast in the 1550s and 1560s**, African Studies Program, University of Wisconsin-Madison, 1988

HAKLUYT 1589 = Richard Hakluyt, **The Principall Navigations, Voiages and Discoveries of the English Nation**, London, 1589, facsimile reprint, ed., D.B. Quinn and R.A. Skelton, Cambridge, 1965

HAKLUYT 1598 = Richard Hakluyt, **The Principal Navigations ...**, 3 vols., London, 1598-1600, reprinted 12 vols., Glasgow, 1904

    [Citation is of the 1598 vol./pt./page, this being supplied in the modern edition.]

HARING 1947 = C.H.Haring, **The Spanish empire in America**, New York, 1947

HEULHARD 1897 = Arthur Heulhard, **Villegagnon**, Paris, 1897

HOFFMAN 1980 = Paul E.Hoffman, **The Spanish crown and the defense of the Caribbean, 1535-1585**, Baton Rouge, 1980

JONES 1983 = Adam Jones, **German sources for West African History 1599-1699**, Wiesbaden, 1983

JONES 1983b = Adam Jones, **From slaves to palm kernels: a history of the Galinhas country (West Africa)**, Wiesbaden, 1983

JULIEN 1948 = Ch.-André Julien, **Les voyages de découverte et les premiers établissements (XVe-XVIe siècles)**, Paris, 1948

KAGAN 1974 = R.L.Kagan, **Students and society in early modern Spain**, Baltimore, 1974

KAMEN 1985 = H.Kamen, **Inquisition and society in Spain in the sixteenth and seventeenth centuries**, London, 1985

LAGUARDA TRÍAS 1972 = Rolando A.Laguarda Trías, 'Las latitudes del Diário de Pero Lopes de Sousa y la localización del Puerto de los Patos', Série separatas 69, Agrupamento de Estudos de Cartografia Antiga, Lisbon, 1972 (also in **Revista de Ciências do Homem**, 4, série A, 1971)

LEITE 1955 = Serafim Leite, ed., **Cartas do Brasil do P.Manuel da Nóbrega**, Coimbra, 1955

LEVILLIER 1915 = R.Levillier, **Correspondencia de los Oficiales Reales de Hacienda del Río de la Plata con los Reyes de España**, t.1, Madrid, 1915

LOPES/PIGAFETTA 1965 = Filippo Pigafetta and Duarte Lopes, **Description du Royaume de Congo et des contrées environnantes**, [transl. of **Relatione del Reame di Congo ...**, Rome, 1591], ed. Willy Bal, Louvain/Paris, 1965

LÓPEZ DE VELASCO 1971 = Juan López de Velasco, **Geografía y descripción universal de las Indias**, ed. M.J.de la Espada, Madrid, 1971

LORIMER 1989 = Joyce Lorimer, **English and Irish settlement on the River Amazon 1550-1646**, Hakluyt Society, London, 1989

LUSSAGNET 1953 = Suzanne Lussagnet, ed., **Les français en Amérique pendant le deuxième moitié du XVIe siècle: Le Brésil et les Brésiliens par André Thevet**, Paris, 1953

MACGREGOR 1955 = I.A.Macgregor, 'Johore Lama in the sixteenth century', **Journal of the Malayan Branch of the Royal Asiatic Society**, 28/2, 1955, 48-125

MADEIRA SANTOS 1988 = Maria Emília Madeira Santos, 'As estratégicas ilhas de
    Cabo Verde ou a "fresca Serra Leoa": uma escolha para a política de
    expansão portuguesa no Atlântico', Série separatas 212, Centro de Estudos
    de História e Cartografia Antiga, Lisbon, 1988 (also in **Revista da
    Universade de Coimbra**, 34, 1988, 485-491)

MADOX 1976 = E.S.Donno, ed., **An Elizabethan in 1582: the diary of Richard
    Madox**, Hakluyt Society, London, 1976

MAGALHÃES 1922 = Pero de Magalhães, **The Histories of Brazil**, trans. J.B.
    Stetson, New York, 1922

MALHEIRO DIAS 1924 = Carlos Malheiro Dias et al., **História da colonização
    portuguesa do Brasil**, 3 vols., Porto, 1924

MONOD 1983 = Théodore Monod, **L'Ile d'Arguin (Mauritanie): essai historique**,
    Memórias 23, Centro de Estudos de Cartografia Antiga, Lisbon, 1983

MORAES 1972 = Nize Izabel de Moraes, 'Le commerce des peaux à la Petite Côte
    au XVIIe siècle ('Sénégal)', **Notes Africaines**, 134, 1972, 37-45,111-116

NUNES COSTA 1953 = M.A.de Nunes Costa, 'D.António e o trato inglês da Guiné
    1587-93', **Boletim Cultural da Guiné Portuguesa**, 8, 1953, 693-797

OLIVEIRA FREITAS 1975 = Amadeu Fagundes de Oliveira Freitas, **Geopolitica
    bandeirante**,Porto Alegre, 1975

PACHECO PEREIRA = Duarte Pacheco Pereira, **Esmeraldo de Situ Orbis: Côte
    occidentale d'Afrique du Sud Marocain au Gabon**, ed. R. Mauny, Bissau,
    1956

PAEZ 1937 = Simão Ferreira Paez, **As famozas armadas portuguesas 1496-1650**, Rio
    de Janeiro, 1937

PARRY/KEITH 1984 = J.H.Parry and R.G.Keith, **New Iberian World**, 5 vols., vol.
    5, New York, 1984

PEREIRA DA COSTA 1973 = José Pereira da Costa, 'Socotorá e o domínio portoguês
    no Oriente', Série separatas 82, Agrupamento de Estudos da Cartografia
    Antiga, Lisbon, 1973 (also in **Revista da Universidade de Coimbra**, 23)

PIRES 1944 = **The Suma Oriental of Tomé Pires**, ed. A.Cortesão, 2 vols. single
    pag., Hakluyt Society, London, 1944

PMC 1960 = A.Cortesão and A.Teixeira da Mota, **Portugaliae Monumenta Carto-
    graphica**, 6 vols., Lisbon, 1960

PURCHAS 1625 = Samuel Purchas, **Purchas his Pilgrimes**, 4 vols., London, 1625, reprinted, 20 vols., Glasgow, 1905-7

[Citation is of the 1625 vol./pt./page, this being supplied in the modern edition.]

QUINN 1977 = David B.Quinn, **North America from earliest discovery to first settlements**, New York, 1977

QUINN 1979 = David B.Quinn, **New American World**, 5 vols., London, 1979

RAU 1972 = Virginia Rau et al., 'Les escales de la "Carreira da Índia" (XVIe-XVIIIe siècles)', in **Les grandes escales, deuxième partie, Les temps modernes**, Recueils de la Société Jean Bodin, Bruxelles, 1972, 7-28

RODNEY 1970 = W.Rodney, **A history of the Upper Guinea coast 1545 to 1800**, London, 1970

RODRIGUES 1931,1938 = Francisco Rodrigues, **História da Companhia de Jesus na Assistência de Portugal**, Porto, vol.1, 1931; vol.2, 1938

RONCIÈRE 1923 = C.de la Roncière , **Histoire de la marine française**, 2nd ed., Paris, 1923

RUBIO 1942 = Julian Maria Rubio, **Exploración y conquista del Río de la Plata siglos XVI y XVII**, Barcelona, 1942

RUMEU DE ARMAS 1945 = Antonio Rumeu de Armas, **Piraterias y ataques navales contra las Islas Canarias**, 4 vols., Madrid, [1945]

RUSSELL-WOOD 1968 = A.J.R.Russell-Wood, **Fidalgos and philanthropists: the Santa Casa da Misericórdia of Bahia, 1550-1755**, London, 1968

RYDER 1965 = A.F.C.Ryder, **Materials for West African history in Portuguese archives**, London, 1965

SAAD 1983 = Elias N.Saad, **Social history of Timbuktu**, London, 1983

SALVADOR 1965 = Frei Vicente de Salvador, **História do Brasil 1500-1627**, 4th ed., São Paulo, 1965

SANTARÉM 1843 = Visconde de Santarém, **Quadro elementar das relações políticas e diplomáticas de Portugal, t.3**, Paris, 1843

SARMIENTO 1895 = C.R.Markham, ed., **Narrative of the voyages of Pedro Sarmiento de Gamboa to the Straits of Magellan**, Hakluyt Society, London, 1895

SARMIENTO 1944 = Pedro Sarmiento de Gamboa, 'Relación y derrotero del viaje y
    descubrimiento del Estrecho de la Madre-de-Dios antes llamado de
    Magellanes', in **Colección de Diarios y Relaciones para la Historia de los
    Viajes y Descubrimientos**, 3, Madrid, 1944

SERGIO 1955, see GOMES DE BRITO

SERRÃO 1956 = Joaquim Veríssimo Serrão, **O reinado de D.António Prior de Crato,
    vol.1**, Coimbra, 1956

SERRÃO 1980,1979 = Joaquim Veríssimo Serr~o, **História de Portugal**, vol.3
    [1495-1580], 2nd.ed., Lisbon, 1980; vol.4 [1580-1640], Lisbon, 1979

SOARES DE SOUZA 1851 = Gabriel Soares de Souza, **Tratado descriptivo do Brazil
    em 1587**, ed. F.A. de Varnhagen, Rio de Janeiro

    [As well as pagination, chapter numbers are given, to enable consultation
    of any of the later editions of this work by Gabriel Soares de Sousa. Up
    to p.110, the edition contains the 'Roteiro do Brazil', thereafter
    'Grandezas da Bahia', each with separate chapter numbers. The date of
    1587 has been retained in the text although the work is now thought to
    date probably from 1584.]

SOUSA VITERBO 1900 = Sousa Viterbo, **Trabalhos nauticos dos portugueses nos
    séculos XVI e XVII**, 2 vols., Lisbon, 1898,1900

SOUTHEY 1922 = Robert Southey, **History of Brazil**, London, 1822, reprinted New
    York, 1970

STADEN 1874 = R.F.Burton, ed., **The captivity of Hans Staden**, Hakluyt Society,
    London, 1874

STADEN 1928 = **Hans Staden, The true history of his captivity 1557**, trans. M.
    Letts, London, 1928

TAYLOR 1935 = E.G.R.Taylor, ed., **The original writings and correspondence of
    the two Richard Hakluyts**, 2 vols., single pag., Hakluyt Society, London,
    1935

TAYLOR 1959 = E.G.R.Taylor, ed., **The troublesome voyage of Captain Edward
    Fenton**, Hakluyt Society, London, 1959

TEIXEIRA DA MOTA 1968 = Avelino Teixeira da Mota and Jorge Morais-Barbosa,
    eds., **Diário da Navegação de Pero Lopes de Sousa (1530-1532)**, Lisbon,
    1968

TEIXEIRA DA MOTA 1968b = A. Teixeira da Mota, 'Ilha de Santiago e Angra de
    Bezeguiche, escalas da Carreira da Índia', **Do Tempo e da História**, 2,
    1968, 141-9

TEIXEIRA DA MOTA 1969 = A.Teixeira da Mota, 'Os regimentos do Cosmógrafo-mor de 1559 e 1592 e as origens do ensino náutico em Portugal', Série separatas 51, Centro de Estudos de Cartografia Antiga, Lisbon, 1969, (also in **Memorias da Academia das Ciências de Lisboa**, Classe de Ciências, 13)

TEIXEIRA DA MOTA 1970 = A.Teixeira da Mota, 'A malograda viagem de Diogo Carreiro à Tombuctu em 1565', Série separatas 57, Agrupamento de Estudos de Cartografia Antiga, Lisbon, 1970 (also in **Boletim Cultural da Guiné Portuguesa**, 25, 1970)

TEIXEIRA DA MOTA 1973 = A.Teixeira da Mota, 'Reflexos do tratado de Tordesilhas na cartografia náutica do século XVI', Série separatas 80, Centro de Estudos de Cartografia Antiga, Lisbon, 1973 (also in **Revista da Universidade de Coimbra**, 23, 1973)

TEIXEIRA DA MOTA 1980 = A.Teixeira da Mota, 'Viagens espanholas das Canárias à Guiné no século XVI segundo documentos dos arquivos portugueses', **III Coloquio de Historia Canario-Americana (1978)**, Las Palmas, 1980, 2:219-50

TROCMÉ 1952 = E.Trocmé and M.Delafosse, **Le commerce Rochelais de la fin du XVe siècle au début du XVIIe**, Paris, 1952

VARNHAGEN 1959 = Francisco Adolfo de Varnhagen, **História Geral do Brasil**, 6th ed., São Paulo, 1959

VAZ MONTEIRO 1974 = J.R.Vaz Monteiro, 'A viagem de regresso da Índia da nau "São Pantaleão" no ano de 1596', Série separatas 91, Agrupamento de Estudos de Cartografia Antiga, Coimbra, 1974

VELLERINO 1575 = Baltasar Vellerino de Villalobos, 'Luz de navegantes', MS in Museo Naval, Madrid (photocopy of a few pages on the southern Caribbean coast kindly shown me by Professor Ursula Lamb)

VOGT 1979 = John Vogt, **Portuguese rule on the Gold Coast 1469-1682**, Athens, 1979

WALLIS 1984 = Helen Wallis, 'The cartography of Drake's voyage', in Norman J. W.Thrower, ed., **Sir Francis Drake and the Famous Voyage**, Berkeley, 1984, 121-163

WATERS 1958 = David Waters, **The art of navigation in England in Elizabethan and early Stuart times**, London, 1958

WILLIAMSON 1927 = J.A. Williamson, **Sir John Hawkins**, Oxford, 1927

INDEXES

Names are listed in the form in which they appear in the translation, which in many cases represents the form in the Spanish text. The correct form in Portuguese and other languages, when given in the notes, appears in square brackets. The numbers represent, first, the foliation of the text as shown in the translation; secondly, after a colon and *, a chapter/note of the annotation to the text; and finally, after a colon and **, a note to the Introduction (which is not itself indexed).

ADDITIONAL NAMES IN THE NOTES
(other than in references)

Names are listed in the form in which they appear in the translation, a subsequent name in square brackets being the form in the Spanish text. Only those notes are listed which contain major references to the toponym or ethnonym. The numbers represent, first, the foliation of the text and translation; secondly, after a colon and *, a chapter/note of the annotation to the text; and finally, after a colon and **, a note to the Introduction (which is not itself indexed).

LIST OF ILLUSTRATIONS

(for short titles of sources, see Bibliography)

298